I0130365

GLOBAL THINK TANKS

This completely revised edition of *Global Think Tanks: Policy Networks and Governance* provides a clear description of, and context for, the global proliferation of think tanks. It explores the origins, development, and diversity of think tanks and policy networks, discusses past and current issues facing transnational think tanks, and considers the possible future challenges and developments. The updated content reflects recent trends such as globalization, digitalization, diversity, populism, and disinformation; and it also includes a new chapter on the impact of emerging technologies on global think tanks and governance.

The book:

- identifies, maps, and analyzes these phenomena of proliferation, expansion, and networking;
- provides a primer and a roadmap for global public policy practitioners, participants, and the interested public;
- illustrates the global growth of think tanks that the world has experienced over the past eight years;
- analyzes the impact and emerging potential of new technologies and increasing diversity; and
- considers how global think tanks and policy networks can continue to improve their impact and overall reach.

This volume will be of great interest to all students of international relations and international organizations, alongside policy professionals working at think tanks around the world.

James G. McGann, PhD, is a senior lecturer at the Lauder Institute of the Wharton School and the School of Arts and Sciences at the University of Pennsylvania, and the director of the Think Tanks and Civil Societies Program (TTCSP) at the University of Pennsylvania.

Laura C. Whelan is a Benjamin Franklin Scholar at the University of Pennsylvania, and a research assistant and summit coordinator intern at the Think Tanks and Civil Societies Program (TTCSP).

GLOBAL INSTITUTIONS

Edited by Thomas G. Weiss
The CUNY Graduate Center, New York, USA
and Rorden Wilkinson
University of Sussex, Brighton, UK

About the series

The 'Global Institutions Series' provides cutting-edge books about many aspects of what we know as 'global governance.' It emerges from our shared frustrations with the state of available knowledge—electronic and print-wise—for research and teaching. The series is designed as a resource for those interested in exploring issues of international organization and global governance. And since the first volumes appeared in 2005, we have taken significant strides toward filling many conceptual gaps.

The series consists of two related "streams" distinguished by their blue and red covers. The blue volumes, comprising the majority of the books in the series, provide user-friendly and short (usually no more than 50,000 words) but authoritative guides to major global and regional organizations, as well as key issues in the global governance of security, the environment, human rights, poverty, and humanitarian action among others. The books with red covers are designed to present original research and serve as extended and more specialized treatments of issues pertinent for advancing understanding about global governance.

The books in each of the streams are written by experts in the field, ranging from the most senior and respected authors to first-rate scholars at the beginning of their careers. In combination, the components of the series serve as key resources for faculty, students, and practitioners alike. The works in the blue stream have value as core and complementary readings in courses on, among other things, international organization, global governance, international law, international relations, and international political economy; the red volumes allow further reflection and investigation in these and related areas.

The books in the series also provide a segue to the foundation volume that offers the most comprehensive textbook treatment available dealing with all the major issues, approaches, institutions, and actors in contemporary global governance. The second edition of our edited *work International Organization and Global Governance* (2018) contains essays by many of the authors in the series.

Understanding global governance—past, present, and future—is far from a finished journey. The books in this series nonetheless represent significant steps toward a better way of conceiving contemporary problems and issues as well as, hopefully, doing something to improve world order. We value the feedback from our readers and their role in helping shape the on-going development of the series.

Protecting the Internally Displaced (2019)
Rhetoric and Reality
Phil Orchard

Accessing and Implementing Human Rights and Justice (2019)
Kurt Mills and Melissa Labonte

The IMF, the WTO & the Politics of Economic Surveillance (2019)
Martin Edwards

Multinational Rapid Response Mechanisms (2019)
John Karlsrud and Yf Rykers

Towards a Global Consensus Against Corruption (2019)
International Agreements as Products of Diffusion and Signals of Commitment
Mathis Lohaus

Negotiating Trade in Uncertain Worlds (2019)
Misperception and Contestation in EU-West Africa Relations
Clara Weinhardt

Negotiations in the World Trade Organization (2019)
Design and Performance
Michal Parizek

The International Organization for Migration (2020)
Challenges, Commitments, Complexities
Megan Bradley

Humanitarian Negotiations with Armed Groups (2020)
The Frontlines of Diplomacy
Jonathan Ashley Clements

Diaspora Organizations in International Affairs
Edited by Dennis Dijkzeul and Margit Fauser

Global Think Tanks
Policy Networks and Governance
2nd edition
James G. McGann with Laura C. Whelan

A complete list of titles can be viewed online here: https://www.routledge.com/
Global-Institutions/book-series/GI .

GLOBAL THINK TANKS

Policy Networks and Governance

Second Edition

James G. McGann
with Laura C. Whelan

R Routledge
Taylor & Francis Group

LONDON AND NEW YORK

Second edition published 2020
by Routledge
2 Park Square, Milton Park, Abingdon, Oxon OX14 4RN

and by Routledge
52 Vanderbilt Avenue, New York, NY 10017

Routledge is an imprint of the Taylor & Francis Group, an informa business

© 2020 James G. McGann

The right of James G. McGann to be identified as author of this work has been asserted by him in accordance with sections 77 and 78 of the Copyright, Designs and Patents Act 1988.

All rights reserved. No part of this book may be reprinted or reproduced or utilized in any form or by any electronic, mechanical, or other means, now known or hereafter invented, including photocopying and recording, or in any information storage or retrieval system, without permission in writing from the publishers.

Trademark notice: Product or corporate names may be trademarks or registered trademarks, and are used only for identification and explanation without intent to infringe.

First edition published by Routledge 2011

British Library Cataloguing in Publication Data
A catalogue record for this book is available from the British Library

Library of Congress Cataloging-in-Publication Data
Names: McGann, James G., author. | Whelan, Laura C., author.
Title: Global think tanks : policy networks and governance / James G. McGann with Laura C. Whelan.
Description: [Second edition]. | Abingdon, Oxon ; New York, NY : Routledge, 2020. |
Series: Global institutions | Includes bibliographical references and index.
Identifiers: LCCN 2019045584 (print) | LCCN 2019045585 (ebook) | ISBN 9780367278540 (hardback) | ISBN 9780367278557 (paperback) | ISBN 9780429298318 (ebook)
Subjects: LCSH: Policy networks. | Policy sciences. | Research institutes. | Comparative government.
Classification: LCC H97.7 .M34 2020 (print) | LCC H97.7 (ebook) | DDC 320.6--dc23
LC record available at https://lccn.loc.gov/2019045584
LC ebook record available at https://lccn.loc.gov/2019045585

ISBN: 978-0-367-27854-0 (hbk)
ISBN: 978-0-367-27855-7 (pbk)
ISBN: 978-0-429-29831-8 (ebk)

Typeset in Bembo
by Taylor & Francis Books

CONTENTS

TABLES

ABOUT THE AUTHORS

James G. McGann, PhD, is a senior lecturer at the Lauder Institute of the Wharton School and the School of Arts and Sciences at the University of Pennsylvania, and the director of the Think Tanks and Civil Societies Program (TTCSP) at the University of Pennsylvania. He is also a senior fellow at the Foreign Policy Research Institute, a think tank based in Philadelphia. Prior to coming to the University of Pennsylvania, Dr McGann was an assistant professor of Political Science at Villanova University where he taught international relations, international organizations and international law.

Dr McGann has served as a consultant and advisor to the World Bank; the United Nations; the United States Agency for International Development; the Soros, Rockefeller, MacArthur, Hewlett, and Gates foundations; the Carnegie Corporation; and foreign governments on the role of nongovernmental, public policy, and public engagement organizations in the United States and developing and transitional countries. He has served as the Senior Vice President for the Executive Council on Foreign Diplomats, the public policy program officer for the Pew Charitable Trusts, and the assistant director of the Institute of Politics, John F. Kennedy School of Government at Harvard University. He also served as a senior advisor to the Citizens' Network for Foreign Affairs and the Society for International Development.

Dr McGann earned his MA and PhD from the University of Pennsylvania. He was a National Fellow at Stanford University while writing his doctoral thesis, which examined the nature and evolution of public-policy research organizations in the United States, such as Brookings Institution, Heritage Foundation, RAND Corporation, Urban Institute, and others. He compared the mission, structure, and operating principles of these leading think tanks to determine how those factors influenced the institutions' role in policymaking. His research and consulting have enabled him to work with governments and civil society organizations in over 110 countries. He has authored over 16 books on think tanks and is the creator and editor of the annual *Global Go To Think Tank Index*.

Laura C. Whelan is a Benjamin Franklin Scholar at the University of Pennsylvania, and a research assistant and summit coordinator intern at the Think Tanks and Civil Societies Program (TTCSP). She has previously interned for Chatham House (The Royal Institute of International Affairs), conducting archival research for its centenary, and the Urban Institute, conducting research for the use of emerging technologies and data science in policy research. Laura is also the co-Editor-in-Chief of the *Penn Bioethics Journal*.

ACKNOWLEDGMENTS

James G. McGann would like to thank his very dedicated and able research interns from the University of Pennsylvania for their assistance with collecting data and conducting background research for this book, namely George Costidis and Christopher Chau, who were invaluable in their data collection and background research, Miriam Himelstein, for her copy-editing, and Daniel Jarrad, for his initial research. A special thanks to Laura Whelan, an exceptional and very gifted research intern, whose assistance in updating and editing the book helped to make this second edition possible.

I would also like to thank all the think tank scholars and executives who provided background information on their organizations and programs for this book. I am indebted to the Lauder Institute for its continuing support for the Think Tanks and Civil Societies Program.

Lastly, I would like to thank Maya, my daughter, and Emily, my wife, for their support and encouragement.

Laura C. Whelan would like to thank her parents, Julie and Roger, and siblings, John and Maggie, for their never-ending support and kindness. She would also like to thank Dr McGann for his mentorship, support, and friendship.

LIST OF ABBREVIATIONS

ACBF	African Capacity Building Foundation
AI	Artificial Intelligence
AIPAC	American Israel Public Affairs Committee
ALREF	Army Long-Range Environmental Forecasting
ASEAN	Association of Southeast Asian Nations
ASEAN-ISIS	Association of Southeast Asian Nations—Institute of Strategic and International Studies
CARI	Argentine Council for International Relations
CEBRI	Brazilian Center for International Relations
CEIP	Carnegie Endowment for International Peace
Centcom	Central Command
CEPA	Center for Education Policy Analysis, Stanford University
CER	Centre for European Reform
CFR	Council on Foreign Relations
CIA	Central Intelligence Agency
CPRS	Central Policy Review Staff
CPS	Centre for Policy Studies
CRF	China Reform Forum
CSR	Corporate Social Responsibility
DARPA	Defense Advanced Research Projects Agency
DIA	Defense Intelligence Agency
ECFR	European Council on Foreign Relations
EDRI	Ethiopian Development Research Institute
FBI	Federal Bureau of Investigation
FIDH	Fédération Internationale des droits de l'Homme (International Federation of Human Rights)
FPRI	Foreign Policy Research Institute

GAIN	Global Alliance for Improved Nutrition
GAVI	Global Alliance for Vaccines and Immunisation
GCAP	Global Call to Action Against Poverty
GDN	Global Development Network
GEF	Global Environment Facility
GMF	German Marshall Fund
GPG	Global Public Good
GSS	General Social Survey
IAEA	International Atomic Energy Agency
ICG	International Crisis Group
IDRC	International Development Research Centre
IISS	International Institute for Strategic Studies
IMF	International Monetary Fund
IPI	International Peace Institute
KAS	Konrad-Adenauer-Stiftung
KNET	Knowledge Network
MGI	McKinsey Global Institute
MMV	Medicines for Malaria Venture
NASA	National Aeronautics and Space Administration
NATO	North Atlantic Treaty Organization
NDRC	China's Planning Commission
NGO	Non-governmental organization
NPEC	NonProliferation Education Center
NSC	National Security Council
OECD	Organisation for Economic Co-operation and Development
PIIE	Peterson Institute for International Economics
PLO	Palestine Liberation Organization
SAIC	Science Applications International Corporation
SPUP	School of Public and Urban Policy, University of Pennsylvania
STOP	Sex Trafficking Operations Portal, NORC, University of Chicago
TTCSP	Think Tanks and Civil Societies Program, University of Pennsylvania
TTI	Think Tank Initiative
TTN	Transitional Think Nets
TTT	Traditional Think Tanks
UN	United Nations
UNSCOM	United Nations Special Commission
USAID	US Agency for International Development
WCD	World Commission on Dams
WEFA	Wharton Economic Forecasting Associates

INTRODUCTION

Ideas are powerful, but in a world of increasingly diverse, globalized, and forged sources of information, the good ideas can be lost. Often, policymakers suffer not from a lack of information but from an avalanche of information. Policymakers need better ways of organizing and filtering policy ideas in order to respond more effectively to an ever changing policymaking environment. Public policy research institutions, or think tanks, as they are more commonly referred to, have extended their capacity to address policy issues that stretch across borders in the face of an ever connected world. The great innovations for global public policy are the proliferation, physical expansion, and networking of public policy research institutions. These three distinct trends have magnified the potential for think tanks to contribute to the resolution of the problems facing global public policy. With the help of think tanks, global public policy—the financing and delivery of global public goods—is becoming a reality.

In this second edition, our goal is to identify, map, and analyze these phenomena of proliferation, expansion, and networking in order to provide a primer and a roadmap for global public policy practitioners, participants, and the interested public. In particular, this second edition will illustrate the global growth of think tanks that the world has experienced over the past eight years, as well as analyzing the impact and emerging potential of new technologies and increasing diversity. We begin by identifying the forces driving these phenomena and by addressing some of the historical and current factors that have dominated policy debates around the world. Next, we follow with our "mapping" study, in which we attempt to identify the range of existing global think tanks and a representative group of global public policy networks, and then to conduct detailed profiling of these organizations. From this mapping study, we extrapolate trends in current think tank research that provide a basis for understanding the impact that think tanks have on policymakers. With our mapping analysis and a literature review as a foundation, we identify and critique the role of global think tanks and global public policy networks in civil society, and analyze the challenges and opportunities facing global think tanks and policy networks. We seek to recommend improvements to think tanks and global public policy networks so that they can continue to contribute to global public policy and serve as a catalyst for civic engagement around the world. Lastly, we analyze the potential opportunities for big data, predictive modelling with machine learning and natural language processing to revolutionize the capabilities and speed of think tank's research, as well as its potential to depoliticize global issues.

As a brief introduction to the following analysis, the challenges facing global think tanks and policy networks include traditional challenges, common to many local and regional think tanks, and incorporate an addition subset of tests. As with most think tanks, they work to maintain their funding and independence, and, for the think tanks and networks that originate in developing countries, manage Western influence. When think tanks and networks extend to operate on a global scale, they face further challenges of defining an issue niche and maintaining a multidisciplinary approach. Think tanks must choose a global expansion strategy, learn new civil society norms in international locales, and execute and maintain effective partnerships. Policy networks face many of these same challenges in addition to the particular difficulties of shaping their organizational structure, managing members, and maintaining a relevance that is greater than the sum of its affiliated parts.

During the process of global expansion, think tanks and policy networks enjoy access to new opportunities that provide a reward for undergoing new management and strategy challenges. Global expansion inevitably means greater funding requirements, but also greater access to new funding possibilities, such as local governments and corporations in new international locales. Global expansion can also build the research capacity of developing countries, most notably when Western influence is well-managed and the local civil society norms are respected. The flexibility that comes with being a member of a policy network invites multi-sectoral solutions to traditional policy problems. These solutions are often more complete and innovative than those derived from a single sector.

For policymakers, the expansion of think tanks and policy networks across the globe is a boon to the need for precise, time-sensitive information and multidisciplinary problem-solving approaches. Global policy has been, and continues to be, revolutionized by the budding ability of global think tanks and policy networks to establish locations in politically-closed areas, to connect grassroots civil society forces and field researchers with policymakers, and to take on global policy tasks in areas such as the environment, international finance, and international security that cannot be effectively addressed by domestically-oriented governments or policy research institutions.

The term "think tank" itself was introduced in the United States during World War II to characterize the secure environment in which military and civilian experts were situated so that they could develop invasion plans and other military strategies. After the war, the term was applied to contract researchers such as the RAND Corporation that operated a mixture of deep thinking and program evaluation for the military. The use of the term was expanded in the 1960s to describe other groups of experts who formulated various policy recommendations, including some research institutes concerned with the study of international relations and strategic questions. By the 1970s, the term think tank was applied to those institutions focusing not only on foreign policy and defense strategy, but also on current political, economic, and social issues.

The growth in numbers and influence of independent public policy research organizations has been noted by a growing number of scholars, donors, and practitioners in the United States and abroad.[1] Regional and global intergovernmental organizations such as the United Nations (UN), World Bank, Asian Development Bank, and North Atlantic Treaty Organization (NATO) have come to recognize the significant role these institutions play in the policymaking process. Subsequently, think tanks have organized nascent think tank networks to help develop and assess policies and programs and serve as a link to civil society groups at the national, regional, and global levels.

Think tanks, which function as public policy research, analysis, and engagement institutions, generate policy-oriented research, analysis, and advice on domestic and international issues, enabling policymakers and the public to make informed decisions about public policy issues. Think tanks may be affiliated with a political party, a university, a government, or independent institutions that are structured as permanent bodies, not ad hoc commissions. These institutions often act as a bridge between the academic and policymaking communities, serving the public interest as independent voices that translate applied and basic research into a language and form that is understandable, reliable, and accessible for policymakers and the public. However:

> the idea of think tanks as a research communication "bridge" presupposes that there are discernible boundaries between (social) science and policy. Moreover, the social interactions and exchanges involved in "bridging," themselves muddy the conception of "boundary allowing for analysis to go beyond the dualism imposed in seeing science on one side of the bridge, and the state on the other," to address the complex relation between experts and public policy.[2]

This being said, there is no doubt that there is a gap between the world of ideas and the world of policy where academics and policymakers are defined by different organizational cultures, time constraints, and incentive systems. Public policy research organizations help to bridge this divide by performing a variety of critical roles in the policymaking process: offering original research and analysis as well as generating new information; providing policy advice; evaluating public policies and programs; conducting large scale surveys; identifying, training and developing talent; providing a home for public figures who are out of office or planning to assume key positions in future administrations; providing a neutral territory in which informal diplomacy can be conducted, or floating trail policy balloons; convening experts in and outside government to float policy proposals and build consensus; and educating and engaging policymakers, the media, and the public.[3]

Think tanks now operate in a variety of political systems, engage in a range of policy-related activities, and comprise a diverse set of institutions that have varied organizational forms. As of December 2018, 8,248 academically-oriented research institutions (similar in nature to universities, but without students), contract research organizations, policy advocates and political party affiliated think tanks can now be found in 188 countries.

While their organizational structure, modes of operation, targeted audience or market, and means of support may vary from institution to institution and from country to country, most think tanks share a common goal of producing high quality research and analysis that is married with some form of public engagement.

Think tanks have a range of functions including one or more of the following: mediating function between government and public; identifying, articulating, and evaluating current or emerging issues, problems, or proposals; transforming ideas and problems into policy issues; serving as an informed and independent voice in policy debates; and providing a constructive forum for the exchange of ideas and information between key stakeholders in the policy formulation process.[4] These functions have, and possibly increase in, importance at the global level. The actual realization of these opportunities and the availability of these opportunities across the entire span of global think tanks and policy networks is not clearly known and difficult to calculate exactly without a standardized and widespread form of measurement.

That being said, all think tanks face the same challenge: how to achieve and sustain their independence so that they can speak "truth to power" or simply bring knowledge, evidence, and expertise to bear on the policymaking process. Unfortunately, not all think tanks have the financial, intellectual, and legal independence that enables them to inform or influence public decision making. This problem is most acute in developing and transitional countries where the means of support for think tanks as well as for civil society at large are underdeveloped and the legal space in which these organizations operate is poorly defined. It is these characteristics that distinguish think tanks in the northern and western hemispheres from their counterparts in developing and transitional countries.

Policy research organizations have been growing both in numbers and in impact in recent years. A survey of think tanks conducted in 1999 found that two-thirds of all public policy research and analysis organizations in the world were established after 1970 and half since 1980 (see Figure I.1). In the first edition of this book, figures from the *2006–2007 Global Go To Think Tank Index* indicated that the number of think tanks declined for the first time in 20 years. However, between 2011 and 2018, the number of new think tanks worldwide saw the largest increase to date (see Figure I.2). It is unclear whether such growth will be sustainable; at the first Africa Think Tank Summit in 2014, Dr Frannie Leautier, the then Executive Secretary of the African Capacity Building Foundation, reported that 30 percent of Africa's think tanks may close or be in serious crisis. Such predictions are serious cause for worry. Analogous to a "canary in the coal mine," the indigenous think tank sector can also function as a key indicator for the state of the civil society in that country. If analysts and critics associated with think tanks are allowed to operate freely, so too can the rest of civil society.

Between 2011 and 2018, policy research centers have been growing rapidly particularly in regions where they were formerly underrepresented, such as in developing and transitional countries in Sub-Saharan Africa; Eastern and Central Europe; East, South and Southeast Asia. Similar centers have also appeared throughout Latin America and the Caribbean, where they began their operations as early as the 1960s and 1970s.

The evolving meaning of a think tank need not concern us further, but the changing social and intellectual context must. Although the term was not yet invented, think tanks

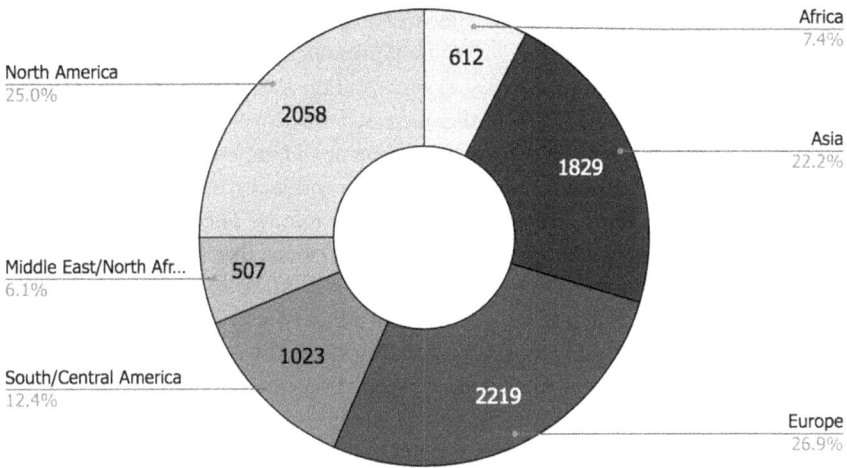

FIGURE I.1 Total think tanks globally by region

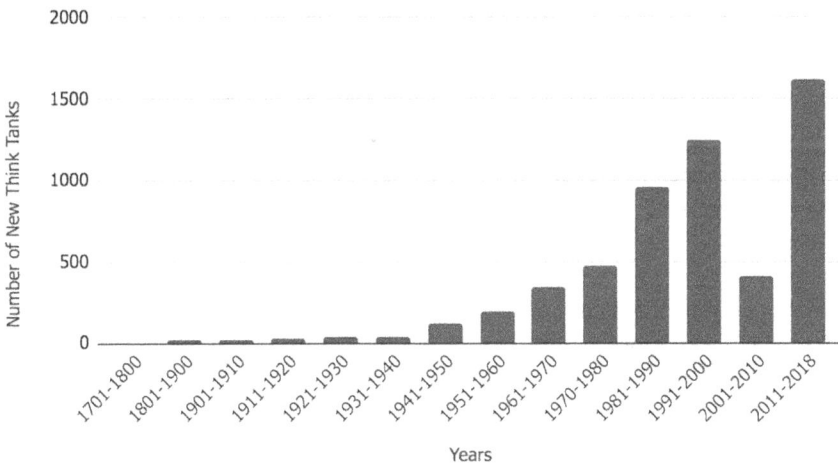

FIGURE I.2 Number of new think tanks established per year

began to appear around 1900 as a part of a larger effort to bring the expertise of scholars and scientists to bear on the burgeoning economic and social problems of that period. The growth of think tanks since that time is also tied to a series of major political, social, and economic events that shattered conventional wisdom and forced policymakers to seek innovative solutions to new and complex problems.

Thus, in the early part of the 20th century, the challenges of managing an advanced industrial economy and increased commitments abroad were behind the effort to tie science and reason to government. This was also the period in which Frederick Taylor published the enormously influential book, *Principles of Scientific Management*, which affected not only business, but also government planning.[5] The period following World War I saw the establishment of Chatham House and the Council on Foreign Relations; the period following World War II further increased the demand for defense experts and technocrats to help manage the defense establishment and its new security arrangements around the world. The social turmoil of the 1960s and its attendant political pressures provided the impetus for the creation of the Urban Institute, The Club of Rome, D66 Policy Research Bureau, and a host of other organizations that were the architects of social and environmental programs during this period. More recently, global populist movements have contributed to the expansion of a host of advocacy-oriented and triba-lized think tanks organized to advance a particular philosophy or issue.

As a result of this evolution, think tanks developed various methodologies to deal with different policy problems. Some subjects lend themselves to empirical research better than others. If, for example, a public policy institute concerns itself with questions regarding energy, pollution, and environment, it is possible to get meaningful quantitative data against which to answer such questions in addition to relevant non quantifiable factors. On the other hand, if a research institute concerns itself with an issue such as motivations for proliferation of weapons of mass destruction, different rules for evidence must be obtained. This corresponds to the famous distinction made by Karl Popper between "clouds and clocks," and it distinguishes a major fault line in the think tank universe. Similarly, think tanks can gather research to determine whether a policy transfer could be necessary or successful. A policy transfer refers to the "transnational policy process whereby knowledge about policies, administrative arrangements or institutions in one place is used in the development of policy elsewhere."[6] This can be tricky because the established and often intertwined socio-political and economic norms of one place may make an otherwise successful policy fail.

We begin by exploring the relationship between government and think tanks, espe-cially within the US public policy process. We then proceed to examine think tanks and policy networks, detailing the emergence and history of think tanks within the United States and compare it to the development of think tanks in other developed, developing, and transitional countries around the world. Particular attention is devoted to the various types of think tanks and policy networks that have emerged and are operating at the regional and global levels. With the general foundations fully established, we then inves-tigate the origins and emergence of both global think tanks and policy networks. We incorporate discussions on past and current challenges facing transnational think tanks and policy networks in addition to considering what the future holds for both. Illustrations of global or transnational think tanks are provided, particularly those that illuminate the various aspects and details discussed in the book. We follow with some suggestions as to how global think tanks and policy networks can continue to improve their impact and overall reach. Lastly, we conclude with a discussion of the impact of emerging technol-ogies and increasing diversity on the research capabilities and impact of think tanks.

Listed in Table I.1 and Table I.2 are the countries with the largest number of think tanks. Not included are the countries which do not have any think tanks currently in operation. Additional graphs for the countries with ten or more think tanks as well as the global distribution of think tanks by country are also included.

TABLE I.1 Countries with ten or more think tanks

Africa		Asia/Oceania		Eastern Europe		Latin America and Caribbean		Middle East and North Africa		North America		Western Europe	
Benin	17	Afghanistan	22	Albania	15	Argentina	225	Bahrain	13	Canada	100	Austria	74
Botswana	13	Armenia	30	Belarus	22	Barbados	10	Egypt	39	United States	1,893	Belgium	60
Burkina Faso	16	Azerbaijan	16	Bosnia and Herzegovina	13	Bolivia	66	Iran	64	Mexico	86	Denmark	51
Cameroon	22	Bangladesh	36	Bulgaria	44	Brazil	103	Iraq	32			Finland	29
Cote d'Ivoire	13	Cambodia	14	Croatia	11	Chile	60	Israel	70			France	203
Ethiopia	26	China	507	Czech Republic	27	Colombia	64	Jordan	28			Germany	218
Ghana	38	Georgia	35	Estonia	20	Costa Rica	41	Kuwait	16			Greece	46
Kenya	56	Hong Kong	42	Finland	18	Cuba	25	Lebanon	28			Ireland	16
Malawi	15	India	509	Hungary	46	Dominican Republic	40	Morocco	15			Italy	114
Mali	11	Indonesia	31	Latvia	11	Ecuador	29	Palestine	36			Netherlands	83
Mauritius	10	Japan	128	Lithuania	22	El Salvador	22	Qatar	15			Norway	22
Namibia	16	Kazakhstan	31	Macedonia, Former Yugoslav Republic of	21	Guatemala	21	Saudi Arabia	10			Portugal	25
Nigeria	51	Kyrgyzstan	28	Poland	60	Honduras	12	Syria	10			Spain	66
Senegal	17	Malaysia	23	Romania	54	Mexico	85	Tunisia	21			Sweden	90

(Continued)

TABLE I.1 (Cont.)

Africa		Asia/Oceania		Eastern Europe		Latin America and Caribbean		Middle East and North Africa		North America	Western Europe	
South Africa	92	Mongolia	10	Russia	215	Nicaragua	15	Turkey	48		Switzerland	78
Tanzania	18	Nepal	13	Serbia	14	Panama	14	UAE	15		United Kingdom	321
Uganda	32	Pakistan	25	Slovakia	27	Paraguay	33	Yemen	27			
Zambia	14	Philippines	21	Ukraine	39	Peru	43					
Zimbabwe	26	Singapore	18			Trinidad & Tobago	13					
		South Korea	60			Uruguay	25					
		Sri Lanka	32			Venezuela	22					
		Taiwan	61									
		Thailand	15									
		Uzbekistan	12									
		Vietnam	11									

TABLE I.2 Global distribution of think tanks by country

Africa		Asia		Eastern Europe		Central and South America		Middle East		North America		Western Europe	
Angola	4	Afghanistan	22	Albania	15	Antigua & Barbuda	6	Algeria	9	Canada	100	Andorra	2
Benin	17	Armenia	30	Belarus	22	Argentina	227	Bahrain	48	Mexico	86	Austria	74
Botswana	13	Australia	42	Bosnia and Herzegovina	13	Bahamas	3	Cyprus	3	United States	1,872	Belgium	60
Burkina Faso	16	Azerbaijan	16	Bulgaria	44	Barbados	10	Egypt	64			Denmark	51
Burundi	4	Bangladesh	36	Croatia	11	Belize	5	Iran	6			Finland	29
Cameroon	22	Bhutan	3	Czech Republic	27	Bolivia	66	Iraq	69			France	203
Cape Verde	2	Brunei	8	Estonia	20	Brazil	103	Israel	13			Germany	218
Central African Republic	2	Cambodia	14	Finland	18	Chile	64	Jordan	28			Greece	46
Chad	3	China	507	Hungary	46	Colombia	64	Kuwait	36			Iceland	8
Congo	3	Fiji	4	Kosovo	4	Costa Rica	42	Lebanon	16			Ireland	16
Congo, Democratic Republic of	8	Georgia	35	Latvia	11	Cuba	25	Libya	21			Italy	114
Cote d'Ivoire	13	Hong Kong	42	Lithuania	22	Dominica	3	Morocco	10			Liechtenstein	2
Eritrea	5	India	509	Macedonia, Former Yugoslav Republic of	21	Dominican Republic	40	Oman	15			Luxembourg	8
Ethiopia	26	Indonesia	31	Moldova	9	Ecuador	29	Palestine	32			Malta	4

(Continued)

TABLE 1.2 (Cont.)

Africa		Asia		Eastern Europe		Central and South America		Middle East		North America	Western Europe	
Gabon	2	Japan	128	Montenegro	4	El Salvador	14	Qatar	15		Monaco	2
Gambia	6	Kazakhstan	31	Poland	60	Grenada	1	Saudi Arabia	15		Netherlands	83
Ghana	38	Kyrgyzstan	28	Romania	54	Guadeloupe	5	Syria	27		Norway	22
Guinea	2	Laos	4	Russia	215	Guatemala	22	Tunisia	3		Portugal	25
Guinea-Bissau	1	Maldives	6	Serbia	14	Guyana	4	Turkey	39		Spain	66
Kenya	56	Mongolia	10	Slovakia	27	Haiti	3	UAE	10		Sweden	90
Lesotho	4	Nepal	13	Ukraine	39	Honduras	12	Yemen	28		Switzerland	78
Liberia	4	New Zealand	11			Jamaica	7				United Kingdom	321
Madagascar	4	North Korea	2			Martinique	2				Vatican City	1
Malawi	15	Pakistan	25			Monserrat	1					
Mali	11	Papua New Guinea	2			Nicaragua	15					
Mauritania	8	Philippines	21			Panama	14					
Mauritius	10	Samoa	1			Paraguay	33					
Mozambique	5	Singapore	18			Peru	43					
Namibia	16	South Korea	60			Puerto Rico	5					
Niger	4	Sri Lanka	32			St. Kitts-Nevis	1					
Nigeria	51	Taiwan	61			St. Lucia	3					

Country	No.	Country	No.	Country	No.
Rwanda	8	Tajikistan	7	St. Vincent and the Grenadines	2
Senegal	17	Thailand	15	Suriname	3
Seychelles	4	Uzbekistan	12	Trinidad & Tobago	13
Sierra Leone	2	Vanuatu	1	Uruguay	25
Somalia	6	Vietnam	11	Venezuela	22
South Africa	92				
Sudan	8				
Swaziland	5				
Tanzania	18				
Togo	5				
Uganda	32				
Zambia	14				
Zimbabwe	26				

Region totals: 612   1,798   696   937   507   2,058   1,523

World total: 8,131

Notes

1 See, James G. McGann, *Academics, Advisors and Advocates: Think Tanks and Policy Advice in the US* (Abingdon, Oxon: Routledge, 2007); James G. McGann and Erik C. Johnson, *Comparative Tanks, Politics and Public Policy* (Northampton, MA: Edward Elgar, 2005); Andrew Rich, *Think Tanks, Public Policy, and the Politics of Expertise* (Cambridge: Cambridge University Press, 2004); James A. Smith, *The Idea Brokers: Think Tanks and the Rise of the New Policy Elite* (New York: Free Press, 1991); James McGann and R. Kent Weaver, eds., *Think Tanks and Civil Societies: Catalysts for Ideas and Actions* (Lanham, MD: University Press of America, 2000); Diane Stone, Andrew Denham and Mark Garnett, eds., *Think Tanks Across Nations: A Comparative Approach* (Manchester: Manchester University Press, 1998); Donald E. Abelson, *Do Think Tanks Matter? Assessing the Impact of Public Policy Institutes* (Montreal: McGill-Queen's University Press, 2002); Donald E. Abelson, *A Capitol Idea Think Tanks and US Foreign Policy* (Montreal: McGill-Queen's University Press, 2006); James G. McGann, "Academics to Ideologues: A Brief History of Think Tanks in America," *PS: Political Science and Politics* (December 1992): 833–740; and R. Kent Weaver, "The Changing World of Think-Tanks," *PS: Political Science and Politics* 22, no.3 (September 1989): 563–578.
2 Diane Stone, *Non-Governmental Action Networks and Global Policy Processes Project* (September 2009).
3 Diane Stone, *Non-Governmental Action Networks and Global Policy Processes Project*. For an excellent discussion of the role of think tanks in DC, see Richard N. Haass, "Think Tanks and US Foreign Policy: A Policy-Maker's Perspective," *US Foreign Policy Agenda* (November 2002), an electronic journal of the US Department of State; and for an overview of the changing role of think tanks, see James G. McGann, "Think Tanks and the Transnationalization of Foreign Policy," *US Foreign Policy Agenda* (November 2002).
4 Peter Hayes, "The Role of Think Tanks in Defining Security Issues and Agendas," Global Collaborative Essay, *Northeast Asia Peace and Security Network* 21 (October 2004): 1–11.
5 Frederick Taylor, *The Principles of Scientific Management* (New York: Harper and Brothers, 1915).
6 Diane Stone, *Non-Governmental Action Networks and Global Policy Processes Project*.

1

NATIONAL, REGIONAL, AND GLOBAL THINK TANKS

Catalyst for ideas and action

- Think tanks in civil society
- Definition of a think tank
- Role of think tanks
- Current literature on think tanks
- Common structural forms of think tanks
- Think tank affiliations
- Global think tanks and think tank networks

This chapter is designed to introduce the concept of think tanks and the varying forms they take. The differing structures of think tanks provide unique advantages and disadvantages in their ability to meet the six specific sub-themes that we explore: future-orientation, policy agenda reconfiguration, collaboration, intellectual synthesis, data dissemination, and integrating the policy process.

Think tanks in civil society

Civil society comprises a range of associations that occupy the space between a government and its citizens. Think tanks are one type of civil society organization. As objective, independent policy analysts and producers representing neither the public nor the private sector, think tanks constitute an important part of a strong civil society. This is significant when one considers the generally accepted notion that a strong and vibrant civil society is an essential component of any healthy democracy. Civil society organizations can range from sports teams to labor unions to policy research organizations. Although, ideally, civil society constitutes itself as a force separate from the state, it rarely enjoys complete independence from the state.

Like so many others in the lexicon of political science, civil society is an idea that has no single, accepted definition. We contend that there is no single civil society but many civil societies that are defined by how the space between the government and the public is configured and is affected by the nature, type, and number of non-governmental organizations there are in a given country. In certain countries and political systems, the space between the government and the public is open and unfettered, while in other countries the space and degrees of movement within the civil society is quite limited.

Naturally, the extent to which states tend to interfere with the operation of civil society depends on the nature of the legal, political, social, and economic contexts and the type of civil society association concerned. It is no surprise that, given their proximity to government and the nature of policy advice, think tanks are often targets for government intervention in countries where there are authoritarian, corrupt, non-transparent governments. Moreover, it is vital to recognize that the conditions that enable think tanks to operate as an effective counterweight to the state and for-profit sector are not necessarily present in every civil society.

The objectivity and independence, as well as the knowledge and power, of think tanks make them critical balancing forces against state power and agency. Think tanks, therefore, contribute greatly to the strength of civil society. However, certain conditions are required if think tanks are to be afforded the independence and, consequently, permitted the objectivity they require. In the advanced industrialized democracies of Europe and North America, there exist legal, political, and financial frameworks that reserve a space in the political arena for the independent policy analysis think tanks provide. In contrast, the absence or restricted nature of such frameworks in much of the developing world severely limits the intellectual freedom of think tanks in these regions. This difference will constitute an important focus for the analysis of the role and effectiveness of these organizations in the context of developing and transitional countries.

Definition of a think tank

What exactly are think tanks, and how are they different from other organizations? Defining think tanks is not as easy as it may seem. At the broadest level, think tanks are institutions that provide public policy research, analysis, and advice. Such a definition casts a wide net. Many interest groups, university research centers, and other civil society organizations carry out policy research and advice as one of their activities, even if it is not the central one. On the other hand, many government agencies also carry out policy research and offer advice as a major function. In the US government there are many such offices, such as the independent agencies of the executive branch (e.g. the Interstate Commerce Commission, Food and Drug Administration, Federal Aviation Administration, Environmental Protection Agency, etc.)

In order to narrow the scope of inquiry, academic writing about think tanks has tended to limit the definition to include only policy research organizations that are independent of government and universities and that operate on a not-for-profit basis. This definition, however, is too narrow on two counts.

First, organizations that are almost totally dependent upon government contracts for their revenues—such as the RAND Corporation and many organizations to which the think tank label is routinely applied—cannot be considered
fully autonomous. Yet, they are clearly think tanks and have historically been
considered as such due to their role in conducting original research with the goal
of influencing and affecting public policy. Furthermore, while a high level of
government support does tend to shape the agenda of a think tank, it does not
necessarily distort the research function. Whether it does depends on the culture
and working relationships that have developed over time and on the nature of
the subjects being investigated.

Furthermore, in some continental European countries—notably Germany and
the Netherlands—think tanks frequently have close financial and personal ties to
political parties. Yet, despite their lack of full independence, they are certainly
think tanks, and despite the possible constraints on their research agendas, their
research function remains intellectually unlimited. In other parts of the world,
sponsorship by a government ministry is a legal necessity for a think tank to exist,
so excluding organizations with organizational links to government would convey
the misleading impression that those regions host no think tanks at all. Moreover,
in regions where resources for policy research are extremely scarce, for-profit linkages to university or contracting relationships with the private sector may be the
only way to cover a research institute's core personnel and facilities costs.

A middle course in defining think tanks therefore makes the most sense. Think
tanks are policy research organizations that have significant autonomy from government and, by inference, from the corporate world as well. But autonomy is a
relative rather than an absolute term. And while some think tanks may make a
profit, their main interest is not profit but influence, defined according to the
agenda of the particular institution. Adhering to this middle course, we can then
define think tanks as public policy research, analysis and engagement institutions
that generate policy-oriented research, analysis and advice on domestic and international issues which enable policymakers and the public to make informed decisions about public policy issues. Past names of think tanks that still seem relevant
include "brain boxes," "idea factories," and "thinking cells." Furthermore, think
tanks have many possible sources of funding—a factor which may often affect the
quality and area of research. While some that receive money from political parties
or the government may seem partial in their proposed solutions, others are more
independent, receiving money from a wide variety of sources that have no political
agenda (such as universities or the public). The source of think tanks' funding may
also affect what type of think tank they are (advocacy, educational, etc.), as will be
further discussed later in the chapter.

In summation, think tanks may be affiliated or independent institutions and are
structured as permanent bodies, not ad hoc commissions. These institutions often
act as a bridge between the academic and policymaking communities, serving in
the public interest as an independent voice that translates applied and basic research
into a language and form that is understandable, reliable, and accessible for

policymakers and the public. Policy research organizations perform a variety of roles: offering original research and analysis, generating new information, providing policy advice, evaluating public policies and programs, identifying, training and developing talent, providing a home for public figures who are out of office or planning to assume key positions in future administrations, convening experts in and outside government to float policy proposals and build consensus and educating and engaging policymakers, the media and the public.[1] Think tanks have one thing in common, however: "the individuals in them attempt to make academic theories and scientific paradigms policy relevant."[2]

Role of think tanks

Think tanks are also defined by their specific activities, six of which are salient. One role performed by many think tanks, especially those with staffs composed primarily of PhDs in the social sciences, is to carry out basic research on policy problems and policy solutions in a fashion similar to that done by university-based researchers. Research on policy problems may address questions such as: What are the challenges that two countries face in reunifying (such as East and West Germany) or splitting up (such as the Czech Republic and Slovakia)? How is the deregulation of financial markets or the privatization of transport likely to affect the range and price of services that are offered? How significant is the threat of nuclear proliferation among particular developing countries?

A second role performed by many think tanks is to provide advice on immediate policy concerns. Think tanks are often asked to analyze and provide advice on a range of policy issues or problems that are before Congress or the public. This can occur at several stages in the policymaking process and through a number of channels. Think tanks may organize briefings and hold seminars for policymakers and the media. They may publish policy briefs on pending legislation, and their staff may testify in legislative hearings. Advice-giving may also take the form of opinion pieces in newspapers or blogs. What distinguishes this second role from the first one is that think tanks draw on an existing stock of expertise rather than performing original research. The resulting policy advice is generally provided in a briefer, more accessible and less formal format, usually in response to time-sensitive demands.

A third role frequently performed by think tanks is the evaluation of government programs. This research answers questions such as: Which of two potential weapons systems being considered by the military is the most efficient expenditure of defense procurement dollars? Are local governments delivering services such as education and garbage collection in a relatively efficient manner compared to other municipalities of similar size? While these evaluations can take many forms, the most important is probably formal evaluation studies commissioned by government agencies themselves.

A fourth role frequently performed by think tank staff is the interpretation of policies and current events for the electronic and print media. This is not the same thing as disseminating think tank-produced research, but such an interpretive function can be and generally is based on ongoing research. Unlike opinion pieces, a think tank's interpretive role is usually performed on the news pages of newspapers and in sound bites for radio or television news broadcasts. Giving a perspective—or a spin—to news events helps to frame the way that they are viewed by both political elites and the broader public.

A fifth role that think tanks play is that of a facilitator of "issue networks" and the exchange of ideas. Rather than written products, the key elements here are verbal exchanges and personal relationships. Since most politicians are not specialists, they may not have either the inclination or the desire to absorb detailed technical studies of an issue, but through interaction with experts, they may come to share that group's general perspective on a policy problem. Think tanks often accomplish this by engaging policymakers and the public through briefings, seminars, and conferences—some of them broadcast by C-SPAN and through other remote media.

A sixth and final role for think tanks is to supply personnel to government and to serve as a place for politicians and policymakers who are out of power to recharge their batteries—or as a simple sinecure. Because think tanks serve as repositories for policy-oriented expertise, they play a very important human resource function for new governments when they are trying to fill policymaking positions from outside the bureaucracy. Think tanks also help to train the next generation of policymakers through their intern and fellowship programs.

Current literature on think tanks

Think tanks now operate in a variety of political systems, engage in a range of policy-related activities, and comprise a diverse set of institutions that have varied organizational forms. As noted in the *2018 Global Go To Think Tank Index*, over 8,000 academically-oriented research institutions (similar in nature to universities but without students), contract research organizations, policy advocates, and political party affiliated think tanks can now be found in 188 countries. While their organizational structure, modes of operation, audience or market and means of support may vary from institution to institution and from country to country, most think tanks share a common goal of producing high quality research and analysis that is combined with some form of public engagement.

Since the first edition of this book, think tanks have experienced a series of anniversaries, with centenary celebrations for those formed in the aftermath of World War I, and 75th anniversary celebrations for those formed in reaction to World War II. These anniversaries have sparked a period of self-reflection. Think tanks have dug back to find their own impact, producing visual representations, such as timelines and publications.[3] Chatham House, for example, has dived into its archives to plan a visual timeline that will wrap around its office as an immersive mural depicting their impact over the past century. In a corresponding piece written on think tanks for its peer-reviewed, academic journal *International Affairs*, Dr

Robin Niblett, President of Chatham House, joins a growing chorus of think tank presidents and scholars advocating for the rallying of think tanks around their converging principles in the face of increasing global turbulence and challenges to their relevance and credibility.[4]

Scholars outside think tanks have similarly turned to examining the role of civil society organizations in a time of global turbulence. Emerging after the first edition of this book have been studies on: the historical relationships and global effects of think tanks;[5] the concept of think tanks;[6] large-scale data collection and analyses on the diversity of information sources of global think tank's reports; the creation of new evaluation systems for global think tanks;[7] and the increasingly central role think tanks play in societies worldwide.[8]

Through the wealth of new literature that has arisen, it is clear that think tanks currently face the same challenge: how to achieve and sustain their independence so they can speak "truth to power" or simply bring knowledge, evidence, and expertise to bear on the policymaking process. Not all think tanks have the financial, intellectual, and legal independence that enables them to inform public decision-making. This problem is still the most acute in developing and transitional countries where the means of support for think tanks, as well as for civil society at large, is underdeveloped, and the legal space in which these organizations operate is poorly defined. It is these characteristics that distinguish think tanks in the northern and western hemispheres from their counterparts in developing and transitional countries.

The numbers and overall impact of policy research organizations have been growing and spreading. A survey of think tanks conducted in 1999 found that two-thirds of all the public policy research and analysis organizations in the world today were established after 1970, half since 1980. In the first edition of this book, figures from the *2006–2007 Global Go To Think Tank Index* indicated that the number of think tanks declined for the first time in 20 years. Then, we suspected that the trend may have been the result of a combination of complex factors, such as: shifts in funding, underdeveloped institutional capacity, and unfavorable government regulations that attempted to limit the number and influence of think tanks. However, between 2011 and 2018, the number of new think tanks worldwide saw the largest increase to date (see Figure I.2). It is unclear whether such growth will be sustainable; at the first Africa Think Tank Summit in 2014, Dr Frannie Leautier, the then Executive Secretary of the ACBF, reported that 30 percent of Africa's think tanks may close or be in serious crisis. Such predictions are serious cause for worry. Analogous to a "canary in the coal mine," the indigenous think tank sector can also function as a key indicator for the state of the civil society in that country. If analysts and critics associated with think tanks are allowed to operate freely, so too can the rest of civil society.

Common structural forms of think tanks

While think tanks may perform a number of roles in their host societies, not all think tanks are identical in their forms and functions. Over the last several decades, several distinctive organizational forms of think tanks have come into being that differ substantially in terms of their operating styles, patterns of recruitment, and aspirations to academic standards of objectivity and completeness in research. In the first edition of this book, we noted that most think tanks can be understood as variations on one or more of four basic ideal types: academic (or universities without students), contract researchers, advocacy tanks, and party think tanks. In this edition, we will also include a type that has emerged quickly and with the might of money behind them: the for-profit think tank.

The first two types—academic and contract research think tanks—have many similarities: both tend to recruit staff with strong academic credentials (e.g. PhDs from prestigious universities), and both tend to emphasize the use of rigorous social science methods and strive to have their research perceived as objective and credible by a broad audience. They differ largely in their funding sources, agenda-setting, and outputs.

Academic think tanks and contract researchers

Academic think tanks are typically funded by a mixture of foundations, corporations, and individuals. Their agenda is usually set internally and at least in part through a bottom-up process in which the researchers themselves play an important role. However, funders are increasingly active in agenda-setting at academic think tanks. Reflecting the academic training and orientation of their staff, the research outputs of academic think tanks most often take the form of academic monographs and journal articles. In contrast, contract researchers are usually funded in large part by contracts with government agencies. The funding agencies typically play a large role in setting the agenda, and outputs generally take the form of reports to those agencies rather than publicly circulated books and articles.

Contract researchers have an advantage on academic think tanks in terms of policy relevance, since policymakers often outline, in fairly specific terms, what questions they want answered. Their tension is primarily between the objectives of scholarly objectivity and the policy preferences of their clients, especially if they are heavily dependent on a particular client. When the funder/client of research has clear preferences, there is a risk that the funder may try to influence the results of research or refuse to release research that does not match those preferences. At a minimum, this tension may pose a threat to the perceived objectivity of that research. Sometimes the threat is quite literal: in 1995, the US Agency for International Development (USAID) sponsored a joint research project between a US and a South African think tank to assess the impact of USAID programs on South Africa post-apartheid civil society. One of the study's conclusions was that USAID programs deferred too much to the ruling African National Congress and were thus stunting the growth of civil society and pluralism in South Africa. USAID then refused to release the study until this conclusion was excised.

Advocacy tanks

Advocacy tanks and political party think tanks also have a family resemblance to one another. Advocacy tanks, while maintaining formal independence, are linked to particular ideological groupings or interests. They tend to view their role in the policymaking process as winning the war of ideas rather than a disinterested search for the best policies. In addition, their staff often includes more non-academics who are less interested in basic research. They frequently draw their resources disproportionately from sources linked to certain interests (e.g. corporations for conservative think tanks, labor unions for liberal ones). Staff typically are drawn more heavily from government, political parties, and interest groups than from university faculties and may be less credentialed in terms of social science expertise—but this is not always the case. Research products are likely to be closer to brief advocacy pieces than to academic tomes. The Heritage Foundation is one example of such an advocacy think tank. Since policymakers simply do not have the required time to sift through academic and often lengthy papers, think tanks like the Heritage Foundation issue analysis briefs that are concise and clearly illustrate various policy implications and options. In this sense, these organizations are able to better influence policy and disseminate information amongst policymakers than if they relied solely on academic papers, which are less likely to be read in the time-limited policy world.

"Advocacy tanks," which tend to have strong value positions and often take institutional positions on particular policy issues, face a tension between maintaining consistent value positions and perceptions of objectivity and completeness. To the extent that their messages are perceived to reflect inflexible values rather than "objective" analysis, they may simply be ignored by a large part of their potential audience. Similarly, the party affiliation of think tanks limits their objectivity, credibility and independence; when their party is not in power, their access to policymakers and influence on policymakers is much more limited.

In addition, some think tanks have an explicit policy specialization, with their own distinctive modes of agenda-setting, financing, and staffing. One is the NonProliferation Education Center (NPEC) in Washington, which deals only with public policy issues concerning nonproliferation policy. (That, however, includes a wider policy portfolio than one may think, including space launch capacity questions, economic sanctions, the operational policies of the National Institute of Health and the National Center for Disease Control, the functions of United Nations Special Commission (UNSCOM) and the International Atomic Energy Agency (IAEA) in Iraq, etc.).

Political party think tanks

Political party think tanks, similarly, are organized around the issues and platform of a political party and are often staffed by current or former party officials, politicians, and party members. The agenda is frequently heavily influenced by the needs of the party. This sort of think tank is most prevalent in Western Europe, particularly in Germany, where institutions such as Konrad-Adenauer-Stiftung (KAS) and Friedrich-Ebert-Stiftung dominate the think tank landscape. But the United States, while less frequently than its European counterparts, also sponsors quasi-public think tanks. One not affiliated or associated with any political party is the United States Institute of Peace. Another is the National Endowment for Democracy, which does have party affiliates: the National Democratic Institute and the International Republican Institute (as well as a business and a labor component).

Each of these ideal types of think tanks has its relative advantages and disadvantages. Academic think tanks, because they emphasize scholarly objectivity and the social science credentials of their staff, face a particularly strong tension between the goals of scholarly objectivity and completeness in research on the one hand, and policy relevance on the other hand. Academics generally favor the former, while policymakers prefer findings that are brief, clear, and free of the qualifications and fencesitting with which scholars frequently cover their conclusions.

For-profit think tanks

The past decade has seen a sharp rise in the number and influence of for-profit think tanks. As mentioned in the first edition of this book, a broad interpretation of the definition of think tanks would include as think tanks an array of American for-profit organizations in the Washington area known as "beltway bandits." These organizations (e.g. Science Applications International Corporation (SAIC) and dozens of others) are generally closely connected to particular Defense Department agencies and programs, and most concern themselves with highly technical engineering and budgetary analyses. One of their functions, especially on the budgetary side, is clearly policy research. Generally speaking, the public and political profiles of these organizations are very low. The definition would exclude, however, for-profit consultancy services, such as those high profile offices created by former senior officials such as Henry Kissinger, Joseph Sisco, Alexander Haig, Richard Armitage, and others. Such consultancy services thrive on business arbitrage, and knowledge of and access to government and prestige. However, despite not being defined as think tanks, some of these organizations do perform policy-oriented research. There are for-profit political risk companies that help businesses understand the international investment and political environments. Many large international businesses have their own political risk offices, but independent risk analysis is sometimes simultaneously purchased (from Wharton Economic Forecasting Associates (WEFA), for example). Sometimes very sophisticated social science analysis is done in such places, but since the aim is not to influence government and is primarily to make money, such organizations are excluded from this definition.

However, there is a growing sector of companies which are creating and investing in public sector arms that are focused on influencing government. Private consulting institutions have been expanding to create specialized think tanks at a rate which has steeply risen in the past decade. For example, the already-established consultancy McKinsey & Company launched and is now invested heavily in the

McKinsey Global Institute (MGI), whose mission is to "provide leaders in the commercial, public, and social sectors with the facts and insights on which to base management and policy decisions." This rise has been so steep that the *Global Go To Think Tank Index* expanded to include a ranking list of for-profit think tanks in 2012.[9] While some for-profit think tanks, such as MGI, arose out of already prosperous companies, in other parts of the world, where the governments of developing countries often limit NGOs through legislation in order to control civil society, emerging think tanks are choosing for-profit models in order to avoid such harmful constrictions.[10]

Think tank affiliations

Set out in Table 1.1 and Table 1.2 are the various types and characteristics of think tanks, and Table 1.3 sets out examples of each category, using some of the more well-known think tanks in the world.

These ideal types of think tanks have served as models for new organizations being established or points of departure for existing institutions that wanted to reinvent themselves. But most think tanks do not fit neatly into any one category, and the distinctions among them are becoming increasingly blurred. Hybrids between think tanks and organizational siblings that have some similarities to think tanks but stand outside the narrow definition of those organizations are also increasingly common. University research centers mirror academic think tanks; for-profit consulting agencies mirror government research organizations; temporary

TABLE 1.1 Categories of think tank affiliations

Category	*Definition*
Autonomous and independent	A public policy research organization that has significant independence from any one interest group or donor and autonomous in its operation and funding from government
Quasi-independent	A public policy research organization that is autonomous from government but controlled by an interest group, donor or contracting agency that provides a majority of the funding and has significant influence over operations of the think tank
University affiliated	A public policy research left at a university
Political-party affiliated	A public policy research organization that is formally affiliated with a political party
Government affiliated	A public policy research organization that is part of the structure of government
Quasi-governmental	A public policy research organization that is funded exclusively by government grants and contracts but not a part of the formal structure of government
For-profit	A public policy research organization that operates as a for-profit business

TABLE 1.2 Characteristics of independent and affiliated think tanks

Type of think tank	Culture	Objective	Limitations	Interest served	Example institutions
University-based	Academic	Advance knowledge	Education and knowledge creation are top priorities not politics or public policy	Academia	Asia-Pacific Research left— Stanford University
"University without students"	Academic	Bring knowledge to bear on public policy	Theoretical approach to problems, not always directly conducive (relevant) to policymaking	Academics and policymakers	Brookings Institution
Contracting/ consulting	Technocratic	Serve government	Systems and quantitative approach to policy analysis does not apply to all policy problems and client interest priorities	Government agencies and bureaucrat	RAND Corporation
Advocacy	Ideological	Promote ideology	Ideology restricts research topics and expression of opinions	Ideologues and narrow interest group	Institute for Policy Studies
Policy enterprise	Marketing	Package and promote ideas for market and market segment	Orient their research toward the interests of the market (selected donors and policymakers)	Individual market segments	The Heritage Foundation
Political party	Political	Get party elected	Party platform, party members limits range of policy options	Party	Progressive Policy Institute
Governmental	Bureaucratic	Provide information for policy production	Bureaucratic culture. Agenda set by branches of the government. Bureaucratic politics and turf issues constrains analysis and policy choices	Executive and legislative branches of government	Congressional Research Service
For-profit	Business	Expand client base	Client's interest. Business approach to policy analysis may ignore political dimension of public policy	Private	McKinsey Global Institute

TABLE 1.3 Sample classification of think tanks worldwide

Organization	Date established	Organizational type
Center for Economic and Social Development (Azerbaijan)	2005	Autonomous and independent
Institute for Security Studies (South Africa)	1990	
Peterson Institute for International Economics (US)	1981	
European Trade Union Institute (Belgium)	1978	Quasi-independent
NLI Research Institute (Japan)	1988	
left for Defense Information (US)	1990	
Foreign Policy Institute, Hacettepe University (Turkey)	1974	University affiliated
Institute For International Relations (Brazil)	1979	
The Hoover Institution on War, Revolution and Peace, Stanford University (US)	1919	
Konrad-Adenauer-Stiftung (Germany)	1964	Political party
Foundation for Political Innovation (France)	2004	
Progressive Policy Institute (US)	1998	
Development Research left of the State Council (PRC)	1995	Government
Ethiopian Development Research Institute (Ethiopia)	1999	
United States Institute of Peace (US)	1984	
Institute for Strategic and International Studies (Malaysia)	1983	Quasi-governmental
Korean Development Institute (Korea)	1971	
Woodrow International left For Scholars (US)	1968	
Think tank of Deutsche Bank Group	2006	For-profit
McKinsey Global Institute	1990	
Nomura Research Institute (Japan)	1965	

government commissions mirror some contract researchers; interest groups and public interest lobbies mirror advocacy tanks; and party research departments mirror party think tanks. As a result, it is better to think of think tanks along a continuum of structures and functions than in any set of rigid categories.

Global think tanks and think tank networks

Recent years have given rise to several new extensions of think tanks, particularly think tank networks and global think tanks. While more think tanks are appearing around the globe, individual think tanks themselves are simultaneously globalizing. Individual think tanks are executing global expansion strategies, in which a think tank establishes multiple physical operational centers, either in different domestic locations or in countries outside its headquarters. Think tanks and a variety of international actors are also responding to globalization through the "networking phenomenon." When introducing the idea of a "networking phenomena," two different but interrelated trends occurring among think tanks and the rest of the policy-interested community are described. These trends are think tank networking and the development of structurally-independent public policy networks (which will be discussed in greater detail in Chapter 2). Think tank networks are those formed by and around a think tank that are comprised of researchers, members, or partners; structurally independent public policy networks distinguish themselves by having an operating structure and management that is designed at the time of network formation and is independent from a previously-established institution.

A think tank network is created by a previously-established think tank that takes one of the following three forms: (1) research network: an integrated relatively-permanent body of researchers in separate locales that perform the organizations' central functions; (2) member network: an integrated body of members (institutional or individual) that contribute to and benefit from the organization's functions; and (3) partner network: a temporary aggregation of separate organizational partners to perform specific temporary functions. It should be noted that these networks could be domestic, regional or international in scope, with the separate researchers, members or partners being located in other domestic locations, in various regional locations or around the globe. Often, they bridge together people from all sectors of society, including the military, government, and private spheres. One example of a prominent think tank network is the Association of Southeast Asian Nations—Institute of Strategic and International Studies (ASEAN-ISIS). For decades before the establishment of ASEAN-ISIS, individual think tanks in the region conducted research on the economics of Southeast Asia and security cooperation. After the formation of ASEAN in 1967, policy analysis was necessary to understand the implications of regional policy-making, but the organization's structure could not adequately fulfill all of its functions. As a result, think tanks in the region were able to step into this role. Comprised of various think tanks in Southeast Asia, the main objective of the network is to increase cooperation among nations in the region.[11]

A global think tank establishes operational centers, field offices or outreach centers outside the country of its headquarters, or it establishes one of the three forms of think tank networks, with the qualification that the networked researchers, members or partners are outside the country of its headquarters. Additionally, the think tank would have substantial areas of research that extend beyond its country's borders and domestic issues. One example of a global think tank is KAS, which has offices scattered throughout the globe.[12]

A structurally independent public policy network is an umbrella organization that is formed to coordinate already established think tanks, international organizations, universities, research centers, non-profits, corporations and/or members of the general public ("constituents"). Such organizations create a network for one or more of the following functions: research and policy analysis, project and/or advocacy work, field-research and data gathering, dialogue and information sharing, training and/or education. This definition contrasts with that of think tank networks, emphasizing the structurally independent aspect of these networks. Regardless of how the network was originally formed, the network should be structurally independent of any national government, corporation or political party.

As such, classification systems that correspond to these definitions are necessary in order to simplify and filter the information collected on think tanks. One must be particularly careful to classify a global think tank and a structurally independent policy network first by its function and second by its discipline. The previous classification systems for networks, which have focused on classification by discipline, are limiting and ultimately not useful. These classification systems are a function of the "tyranny of academic disciplines." As academic disciplines have long been a strong source of funding for research, their inclination to fund research that only addresses that particular discipline has hindered the progress of multi-disciplinary research. Classification by discipline hinders achievement of the final goal, which is to determine the ability of these structures to influence global public policy in a multi-disciplinary way. In order to preserve the possible usefulness of classification of global think tanks and structurally independent policy networks by the areas that they research, it is necessary to conclude with a classification by "subject-focus" rather than by academic discipline (see Table 1.4).

Classification of expansion function identifies the functions performed by the global think tank through its expansion structure. These structures consist of a global physical expansion, a research network, a member network, or a partner network (see Table 1.5).

The classification of structurally-independent global public policy networks differs from that of global think tanks. First and foremost is the classification of founding body(ies). Should there be a specific institutional founder, it is important to note the founder of these networks. From the founder we can infer particular opportunities and challenges for the network (see Table 1.6).

TABLE 1.4 Global think tank function

Category	Definition
R	Research and policy analysis
P	Project work or advocacy work
F	Field research/data-gathering
D	Dialogue/information-sharing
T	Training and education
L	Liaison function/relationship building with governments or international organizations

TABLE 1.5 Global think tank structure

Category	Definition
GC	Global physical expansion
RN	Research network
MN	Member network
PN	Partner network

TABLE 1.6 Structurally-independent global public policy networks founding bodies

Category	Definition
TT	Think tank
M	Multilateral
G	Government
U	University
PP	Political party
IA	Open assembly

Classification of current constituency attempts to determine the current constituents' type and number. These types can range from think tanks, universities, foundations, political parties, corporations, governments, or multilateral in nature (see Table 1.7).

For classification by range, we look at the scope of the networks' constituents. The scope can be typically delineated between specific regions or globally (see Table 1.8).

With regards to classification by network function, we allow for classification by more than one function. These functions consist of research and policy analysis, project work and advocacy work, field research and data-gathering, dialogue and information-sharing, training and education, and liaison functions and relationship building among members (see Table 1.9).

TABLE 1.7 Structurally-independent global public policy networks constituencies

Category	Definition
TT	Think tank
M	Multilateral
G	Government
U	University
PP	Political party
F	Foundation
C	Corporation

TABLE 1.8 Structurally-independent global public policy networks constituency scope

Category	Definition
Region	Asia, Europe, Middle East & North Africa, North America, South & Central America, Sub-Saharan Africa
Global	Worldwide

TABLE 1.9 Structurally-independent global public policy networks function

Category	Definition
R	Research and policy analysis
P	Project work and advocacy work
F	Field research/data-gathering
D	Dialogue/information-sharing
T	Training and education
L	Liaison function/relationship building among members

Lastly, classification by subject focus allows for identification by multiple areas. These identifications are discipline, multi-disciplinary, tri-sectoral, or issue networks (see Table 1.10).

As discussed, think tanks are organizations that generate policy-oriented research, analysis, and advice on domestic and international issues. They conduct basic research on policy problems and policy solutions, in addition to providing advice on immediate policy concerns. They are also quite valuable in evaluating government programs, and can facilitate the exchange of ideas as well as providing timely and digestible interpretations of policies and current events for the digital and print media.

TABLE 1.10 Structurally-independent global public policy networks subject focus

Category	Definition
Discipline[1]	Discipline networks are defined by traditional academic disciplines, e.g. economics (domestic or global), security (domestic or global), governance issues, law/legal studies, politics (domestic or global), international politics/relations, environment, social policy, education policy, science and technology, health policy (domestic or global), foreign policy, development (domestic or global), finance
Multi-disciplinary	Include a range of academic disciplines and professions that are not bound by a single discipline. A cross-disciplinary approach is taking to defining and solving policy issues
Tri-sectoral	Consist of organizations and individuals from the public, corporate and nongovernmental sectors
Issue networks	Consist of members of the executive and legislative branches of government, career bureaucrats, management and policy consultants, academic researchers, journalists, foundation executive and civil society organizations who come together around issue being debated in public or before a legislative or executive body. They may not form lasting ties and the nature of their relationship is defined by their shared interested in a policy issue

[1] Subject areas of research drawn from James McGann, "Global Trends in Think Tank Impact," Think Tanks and Civil Societies Program, Foreign Policy Research Institute, Philadelphia, 2008: 21.

Notes

1 For an excellent discussion of the role of think tanks in Washington DC, see Richard N. Haass, "Think Tanks and US Foreign Policy: A Policy-Maker's Perspective," *US Foreign Policy Agenda* (November 2002), an electronic journal of the US Department of State; and for an overview of the changing role of think tanks, see James G. McGann, "Think Tanks and the Transnationalization of Foreign Policy," *US Foreign Policy Agenda* (November 2002).

2 Diane Stone, "Think Tank Transnationalisation and Non-Profit Analysis, Advice and Advocacy," *Global Society* 14, no.2 (April 2000): 153–172.

3 For example, see Brookings, *A Century of Ideas*, www.brookings.edu/a-century-of-idea s/ and NORC at the University of Chicago, *75 Years of Insight, Innovation, and Impact*, 75.norc.org/#/intro.

4 Robin Niblett, "Rediscovering a sense of purpose: the challenge for western think-tanks," *International Affairs* 94, no.6 (November 2018): 1409–1429.

5 Priscilla Roberts, from the University of Hong Kong, has surveyed the patterns of linkages between foreign policy think tanks and a broader Anglo-American, imperial, and internationalist network and relationship, discussing the recent proliferation and frequent globalization of foreign policy think tanks. Priscilla Roberts, "A century of international affairs think tanks in historical perspective," *International Journal* 70, no.4 (June 2015): 535–555.

6 Juliana Cristina Rosa Hauck, from Universidade Federal de Minas Gerais, Brazil, has sought to reduce non-specificities in the concept of a think tank. Juliana Cristina Rosa Hauck, "What are 'Think Tanks'? Revisiting the Dilemma of the Definition," *Brazilian Political Science Review* 11, no.2 (July 2017).

7 In his analysis of a total of 17,801 references, Mahmood Ahmad (Allama Iqbal Open University, Islamabad, Pakistan) and Muhammad Ayub Jan (Department of Political Science, University of Peshawar, Pakistan) found that newspapers and reports were the preferred sources of information for global think tanks' reports, instead of research or conference papers. They also found that the diversity level of think tanks' sources decreased with an increase in the number of reports produced, and the diversity level of sources increased with a higher page count. They conclude that many global think tanks are more inclined towards producing material in a timely manner that is readily available and accessible. Mahmood Ahmad and Muhammad Ayub Jan, "Diversity of information sources: An evaluation of global think tanks knowledge construct," *Research Evaluation* 28, no.3 (May 2019): 273–278.

8 In a book edited by Alejandra Salas-Porras and Georgina Murray, scholars examine topics such as the rise and decline of the business roundtable, neoliberal think tank networks in Latin America and Europe, and think tanks as key spaces in the structure of power in global politics. Alejandra Salas-Porras and Georgina Murray, *Think Tanks and Global Politics: Key Spaces in the Structure of Power* (New York, NY: Palgrave Macmillan, 2017).

9 James G. McGann, *2012 Global Go To Think Tank Index*, Think Tanks and Civil Societies Program, Lauder Institute, University of Pennsylvania, https://repository.up enn.edu/think_tanks/7/.

10 See On Think Tanks, *For-profit think tanks and implications for funders*, onthinktanks.org/a rticles/for-profit-think-tanks-and-implications-for-funders/.

11 Diane Stone, "The ASEAN-ISIS network: Interpretive communities, informal diplomacy and discourses of region," *Minerva* 49, no.2 (June 2011): 241–262.

12 Konrad-Adenauer-Stiftung, *Personen und Strukturen*, www.kas.de/personen-und-strukturen.

2

EMERGENCE OF THINK TANKS IN THE POLICY WORLD

The United States and beyond

- Theory and history
- Ideology and government institutions
- Adaptation and planning difficulties
- The emergence of think tanks
- Think tanks in the US context
- Origins and emergence of think tanks as independent actors in policymaking
- Specificity and diversity in think tank research
- Lessons from the US experience
- Adaptations of the US experience around the world
- Tools for governments
- Challenges to think tank impact

The purpose of this chapter is to bring the concept of think tanks and policy networks to life, providing detailed typology, examples, and analysis of these various institutions engaged in policy analysis today. We begin with an overview of the reasons behind the emergence of think tanks and look at the history of think tank development in the United States and abroad. We then proceed to synthesize lessons from US think tank development, compare it to the think tank phenomenon in other countries, and provide recommendations for improving the environment for think tank development in those countries. This chapter explores the origins and emergence of both think tanks and policy networks within policymaking. In particular, attention is devoted to the various types of think tanks and policy networks that have emerged since the formation of think tanks in the general sense. Current iterations of these institutions within the present policymaking process are noted and examined.

Theory and history

Why do we encounter a recent trend of different kinds or brands of think tanks being developed when, for many centuries, the governments of the world were able to manage their affairs quite well without them? The answer lies in the intersection of the policy function itself and changing philosophies of government in the 20th century.[1]

In order to govern well, governments need information, knowledge, and means of implementation that connect informed policy to the relevant theatre of social operations. Information should be distinguished from knowledge. While information is data collected from the world, knowledge comes from the integration of information into an inherited cognitive framework meaningful to human beings.[2] Think tanks are crucial in providing the necessary administrative, budgetary, and legal means to translate a policy intention into action, and to connect intellectual policy research into that which can be utilized by government. The "theatre" of issues touched upon may concern the economy, defense and foreign policy, environmental issues, public health, and any number of other public policy domains.[3]

Ideology and government institutions

In theory, how much information, knowledge, and means of implementation a government needs to function well is "sized" by expectations rooted in political philosophy or ideology. Governments operating under socialist or statist ideologies generally assume responsibility for more rather than less of what concerns their societies. Put differently, the definition of what is public as compared to what is private is relatively broad. Contrarily, governments operating under liberal ideologies (in the original 19th-century meaning of the term) rely more on a range of "invisible hands" to achieve general social governance. The presumption is that market forces shape most economic decisions while religious and philanthropic institutions care for the poor, the elderly, the ill, and the disabled.[4] Depending on particular historical and geographical circumstances, liberal governments are predisposed to subsidiary—namely, favoring decentralized local government over centralized administration for most quotidian purposes. In this schema, which is explicitly articulated by Scottish Enlightenment thinkers of the 17th century, government is conceived as a clearinghouse for the lawful adjudication of social conflict and as a vehicle for the common defense. Apart from the importance of the moral example of its leadership, government has no proactive programmatic function.

Historically, the most extreme examples of the socialist or even totalitarian tendency include the former Soviet Union, Germany under National Socialism, and China under the Chinese Communist Party. The totalitarian environment is not conducive for think tank development because think tanks, by definition, are at least semi-independent of government, and it is the nature of the socialist regime that no such semi-independent centers should exist. Societies under socialist regimes are often administered and governed by a centralized political party, often suppressing freedom of the press through censorship and stifling the possibility of independent research. At the other extreme are liberal governments that we tend to call Jeffersonian, after Thomas Jefferson's dictum that the government which governs best is the government which governs least. Pre-20th century America and Great Britain suggest themselves as examples in this domain by keeping government small and leaving social issues at the local level. Again, think tanks were not essential because the need for government policy over so vast an array of social issues simply did not arise.

In the 21st century, an unexpected convergence took place within these antithetical philosophies of government. Totalitarianism has run up against the limits of its inherent inefficiencies, and even before the fall of the Soviet Union, its leaders finally realized, as China's do now, that central planning is often more ineffective than market forces. Liberalism has faced its limits as well. Modern capitalism, distinguished by high knowledge and capital inputs, great occupational diversification, and unprecedented demands from an affluent populace for various services, requires more than a series of invisible hands to make it work smoothly.[5] One example of this requirement is the accretion of welfare state institutions in the United States beginning not, as often thought, with the New Deal, but in the Progressive era of the 1900s. Another instance is the slow evolution of British political culture throughout the 19th century and into the early 20th century—a political culture whose broad international influence has been enormous and has affected Central America, the Caribbean, Australia, New Zealand, South Africa, and many other domains.

Briefly, all modern governments face enormous and ever-shifting organizational and policy challenges. Indeed, as the late scholar Mancur Olson suggested, the institutional capacities of societies, governmental and nongovernmental, define, more than anything else, whether a government is or can be modern.[6] Governments with liberal origins now presume to do more than their predecessors ever dreamed possible, let alone considered desirable. Statist governments are evolving in ways that require them to do less, but to do it better than before. History may not have ended, and arguments over political philosophy go on, but in a gross sense, the definition of the proper ambit of government—at least in most modern countries around the globe—has grown closer together. This is what some observers, such as Anthony Giddens, mean when they refer to "third way" politics.

Adaptation and planning difficulties

Moreover, technological change that promotes economic change, which then engenders social change, seems to many, if not most, contemporary observers to be accelerating. This puts a premium on planning, as governments must be able to not only meet today's challenges, but also anticipate tomorrow's. Here we encounter a big problem: governments do not adapt or plan particularly well. There are two general reasons for this.

One reason is that governments tend to be large, internally differentiated organizations, and size alone is a surprisingly crucial variable in their functional limits. Following Nicholas Georgescu Roegen's *The Entropy Law and Economic Process*, [7] the larger an organization, the larger the transactional costs needed to keep it functioning. Moreover, as size increases, transactional costs grow not arithmetically but logarithmically. Since transaction costs are a diseconomy, it follows that diminishing returns in efficiency are bound to set in at some point as an organization grows larger. This is why the socialist planning apparatus did proportionately far greater harm in a huge place like the Soviet Union than they have done in a small country like Israel. This is also the reason why revolutionary innovations in information technology have generally positive economic implications, for they enable relatively smaller, nonhierarchical organizations to compete effectively for production and services niches.

Another example, also involving Israel, shows a common sense side of the importance of size. Both the US and Israeli militaries flew the F-16 fighter aircraft for most of the 1980s. Pilots complained that the cockpit design was deficient, noting that the combination of the seating orientation and the electronic displays created "blind spots" to left and right at acute angles behind the pilot's field of vision. Operating in a far smaller and less formalized institutional environment, Israeli pilots improvised and literally affixed the equivalent of a rearview mirror to the fuselage of the aircraft. US pilots were not allowed to tamper with their planes; instead, they had to go through bureaucratic channels to request a formal design adjustment. This involved the Air Force, Defense Department, and contractor bureaucracies as well as, ultimately, the General Accounting Office. It took nearly two years to effect a change that Israeli pilots accomplished in less than three weeks.

Not only is coordination a problem, but conflicts of interest also arise between incommensurate values as institutionalized within separate administrative and policy domains. To take a recent and pertinent US example, the State and Defense Departments are charged with protecting US foreign and security interests, but the Commerce Department is charged with promoting US trade. When it comes to the question of export controls, State and especially Defense tend to want more and more rigorous export controls, while Commerce strives for fewer and less rigorous ones. This tension is entrenched in the existing bureaucratic structure, and it will never go away. Planning for a new policy concerning, for instance, US satellite launch capability, which would have to involve the National Aeronautics and Space Administration (NASA), the Justice Department, the Congress, the intelligence community and the three executive departments noted above, is, therefore, no easy task. Unless a higher authority, in this case the President, focuses on a problem and imposes a solution, such problems are managed at best, but they are not solved.

Examples of such crosscutting interests within government are rife. The Department of Transportation, for instance, wants to promote the building of infrastructure, but Occupational Safety and Health Administration and the Environmental Protection Agency want to attach limiting conditions, so there is conflict.

When a bomb goes off in the United States, the Justice Department and the Federal Bureau of Investigation (FBI) go into prosecutorial mode, but the Central Intelligence Agency (CIA) and the Defense Intelligence Agency (DIA) want to investigate the possibility of foreign sponsorship as a national security, not a legal, issue. Does the FBI sometimes withhold information from the CIA out of fear that CIA personnel will jeopardize a pending court case? The answer is, of course, yes. Or, for another example, the Labor Department wants to maximize employment, but Health and Human Services tends to favor a higher minimum wage, which is likely to increase unemployment. Examples could be listed almost without end.

Because of such conflicts, many government policies tend to form through a process of accretion characterized by compromise and deliberate ambiguity whenever discrete departmental decision points collide. Over time, policy and attendant legal structures can develop that, if viewed from an objective outside vantage point, may seem illogical and even dysfunctional. Planning from the basis of such structures works well when interdepartmental conflict is modest, but it tends to work poorly when the level of such conflict is high. A good case example of an attempt to overcome these problems was undertaken by the Heath Government in the United Kingdom in the 1970s. It established the Central Policy Review Staff (CPRS) which was modeled after US think tanks and designed to strengthen the analytical capacity of government in an effort to improve government decision making. The objective was noble. According to Greenwood and Wilson, "The CPRS's freedom from day-to-day pressures and vested departmental interests enabled it to engage in more wide-ranging analyses than might otherwise have been possible."[8] But in the end, this noble effort to create an interdepartmental think tank lost out to egos, turf, and budget battles.[9]

Second, in high policy councils of every sort, the urgent always pushes out the merely important, and the long-term loses salience in direct proportion to the fear that the short-term will be lethal. Most governments have various institutionalized planning directorates within, with presumably appropriate research functions to aid them; however, much of the time these directorates are either fuddled by bureaucratic inertia or, more often, ignored by busy politicians who are worried about saving the day, not the next decade when they will be safely out of office.

The emergence of think tanks

Those who have worked in government, particularly in high level positions, came to recognize these problems of adaptation and planning as the US government grew in size and complexity during and after World War II. Think tanks made their mark because it was believed that they were immune to many of the problems plaguing adaptation and planning in government. They were relatively small, and as independent organizations, they had no vested bureaucratic interests and could thus take synergetic, trans-departmental perspectives on problems. They thrived on informality. Free from the pressure of immediate deadlines and line responsibilities, they could also be forward thinking. In terms of research methods and technologies, they could innovate more quickly than government. In general, because they were funded by the project and not by the hour, they accomplished things faster than government. Additionally, because many early think tanks were associated at least indirectly with prestigious universities, they carried that prestige with them as well.

Since 1945, the promise of think tanks as a means to ameliorate the short-comings of government to adapt and to plan in policy domains has been borne out for the most part. It is not that think tanks have been immune from error, from theoretical *culs-de-sac*, and from bias and fads that have affected everyone else in their day, but think tanks have done well enough to become part and parcel of the way that government works in the United States. The reasons, however, are not all obvious, and the implications are not fully understood even by the participants in the world of think tanks. It turns out that the sociological impacts of think tanks are as crucial as any other, and the deeper sociocultural origins of think tanks are more important than the obvious institutional ones.

Think tanks in the US context

The origin of think tanks in America is far more complicated than the introductory sketch given earlier suggests, and these complications deserve careful attention. In general, think tanks are very educational. While the vast majority of think tanks in the United States are focused on foreign relations and economic affairs, there is a think tank for every issue area. As more than mere advocacy groups, these think tanks unite scholars and policymakers to discuss and debate pressing issues in order to create relevant and applicable policies for the government to adapt.

Think tanks are an American invention, and their development remains largely an American phenomenon. There are about 8,200 think tanks in the world, including 1,872 located in the United States and 2,219 located in Europe. Think tanks have had, and still have, a greater influence within the US policy process than think tanks do in any other country.

Second, public policymaking in the United States is very porous to non-governmental influence compared to virtually all other countries. The reason is structural and quite obvious when noted. The US system of government features a much sharper division between the executive and legislative branches than in standard parliamentary systems, including that of Central America and the Caribbean. A prime minister acts both as the executive and the head of his party in the legislature; a president does not. In most parliamentary systems, initiative for legislation comes from an indistinct collusion between the head of the government, his party, and its parliamentary contingent. In the United States, on the other hand, initiative for legislation can and does come from both Congress and the White House.

In particular, the crucial matters of appropriations and budget authorization in the United States are, more so than in parliamentary systems, determined through an adversarial process between branches of government than between parties. This means that external influence and input can occur at many more points in the US policy process than in most others. To use an economic metaphor, there is a larger market for external inputs, and since interests rise and fall on influencing policy, that market never goes without its bidders and buyers.

This explains why the US legislative branch alone has so many large inhouse research functions. Consider just a few of them: the Congressional Research Service, the Office of Technology Assessment, the Congressional Budget Office, and the General Accounting Office. The raw research capabilities of any one of these offices is immense. Remember, too, that all of these research groups have formed associations with outside think tanks.

Third, and perhaps most important of all in explaining the continuing influence of think tanks in US political culture, is the fact that the recruitment process into and out of government in the United States is wider than it is in most other democracies. The United States does not have as closed a government class as most other political cultures. Rather, through what is known as Title C appointments, politicians can become government ministers (e.g. Les Aspin, a congressman who became the Secretary of Defense). Governors, such as Jimmy Carter and Ronald Reagan, and other local politicians can get involved in national politics. Journalists (e.g. Strobe Talbott), businessmen (e.g. Robert Rubin), and academics (e.g. Henry Kissinger) come to occupy high policy positions in far greater numbers than elsewhere.

Think tanks play an important role in this process. Some think tanks are really "holding tanks" for experts and politicians whose political leanings leave them in the opposition at any given time. Some think tanks, such as Brookings Institution and the American Enterprise Institute, are widely thought of as repositories of shadow governments whilst their political opposites are in office. Others in academia, who are members of think tanks connected to prestigious universities, are instrumental in cycling former politicians, journalists, and cabinet officials into university life. Professors such as Joseph Nye and Graham Allison at Harvard University, who have themselves occupied high government positions, regularly bring politicians such as Geraldine Ferraro, journalists such as Barrie Dunsmore, and diplomats such as Cyrus Vance into any of the several adjunct research institutions at that university. Even senior foundation personnel find themselves either coming or going from the government or the think tank world. For instance, Dean Rusk was head of the Ford Foundation before becoming Secretary of State.

Therefore, this "revolving door" is a key aspect of American think tanks and politics in general that greatly distinguishes them from their counterparts abroad. This was the case most recently with both George W. Bush and Barack Obama, who both relied on the help and expertise of think tanks such as the conservative American Enterprise Institute and the progressive Center for American Progress, respectively. In the current Donald Trump administration, The Heritage Foundation recommended some of the administration's most prominent members, with at least 66 Heritage employees hired by the Trump administration.[10] These think tanks helped shape the ideas and policy of the administration in power.[11] Indeed, many government officials participate in the "revolving door" and move between positions within the government and in the think tank community. This movement usually depends on which party is in power in the White House and both houses of Congress. The "revolving door" phenomenon is not new either; it has helped to form "governments-in-waiting" since 1961.[12] Moreover, several think tanks have even been founded by high-profile government officials, including US Presidents and presidential candidates.[13] The Hoover Institution at Stanford University is a notable example.

The ease of entry between the government sector and think tanks allows scholars and public officials to maintain a healthy balance between hectic, purely policy-focused work and more abstract, scholarly pursuits. Indeed, P.J. Crowley, former Senior Fellow and Director of Homeland Security at the Center for American Progress, who formerly served in the Department of State's Bureau of Public Affairs, explains "there's a lot more sanity in the think tank world than there is in government. You're not on the treadmill as much … It is a chance to step back, to actually think. If you're in government, you're dealing with those boundaries that have already been set. In a think tank, you start with a blank piece of paper."[14] This ends up benefitting the policy-creating process as a whole. In their own words, academics who straddle the academic and policy worlds can attest to the importance of the "revolving door": "One of the most effective transmission belts for ideas to travel from the academy to government might be called 'embedded capital' in the minds of 'in and outers' … As Henry Kissinger once pointed out, the pressure on time that bears upon policymakers means that they rely on ideas and intellectual capital created before they entered the maelstrom."[15]

Prominent journals, too, are part of the process. In the foreign and security policy domain, for example, four quarterly journals sit atop the prestige ladder. *Foreign Affairs* is a part of the Council on Foreign Relations, which is itself, among other things, a think tank with offices in New York and Washington DC. *Foreign Policy* is part of the Carnegie Endowment, which is also, among other things, a think tank located in Washington DC. *The National Interest* itself does not belong to a large institution or perform research functions, but both its editor and executive editor have worked at think tanks and served in government positions. The journal gets many of its articles from former, present, and future think tankers as well. *Orbis* is published by the Foreign Policy Research Institute (FPRI), a Philadelphia-based think tank that increasingly disseminates its research in abridged form over the internet.

In short, there is a very broad "interlocking directorate" between government, elite journalism, academia, the foundation world, and think tanks in every high-profile public policy domain in the United States. Staff move between all these areas with a regularity and speed that occurs in no other country. As a result, people "know each other" in these various domains, and it is very common for career tracks to move back and forth between two, three or even more occupational tracks. Think tanks are, to put it in a neurological metaphor, the corpus callosum of this process. They serve as filters for talent as that talent moves from one occupational domain to the next.

Lastly, in this regard, this interlocking directorate is as wide, richly talented and mobile as it is because it is sizable, meaning it has a sort of critical mass (see Table 2.1). To have become as sizable as it is, the country itself has to be not only large but cosmopolitan in its thinking, in addition to deep in the pocket.

Origins and emergence of think tanks as independent actors in policymaking

Even before the 20th century, think tanks existed, although without the label that has become so popular today. The Royal United Services Institute, established in Britain in 1831, and the Fabian Society in 1884, are considered two of the earliest think tanks. In the United States, one of the earliest meetings sharing characteristics found among think tanks occurred in 1865 when a large number of people converged on the Massachusetts State House in Boston. It was there that a number of progressives of all types (those interested in unemployment, public health, etc.) met to discuss and analyze the problems of the times. Several professional organizations, such as the American Political Science Association and the National Conference of Charities and Correction, among others, trace their origins to that meeting. Although not a think tank meeting per se, the event in Boston signified one of the first recorded times in which experts had assembled in one place to discuss current issues.[16]

As mentioned in Chapter 1, think tanks first emerged during the progressive era in an attempt to professionalize government. They were initially nonpartisan and provided government officials with unbiased policy advice. These institutions initially faced strong opposition, as President Woodrow Wilson viewed these elite experts as potential threats to the United States and, ultimately, democracy itself. This opposition was diminished when Franklin D. Roosevelt assumed office, building an administration in which his Brain Trust placed increased importance on the usefulness of experts. John F. Kennedy's New Frontiersmen continued that trend. Reagan's election victory later in the century marked a significant shift toward executive reliance on expert advice, as libertarian and conservative voices arose to greater prominence in the policymaking process. As such, a new "ideas industry" emerged as right-wing think tanks such as the Hoover Institution, the American Enterprise Institute and The Heritage Foundation assumed important positions of influence in regard to the Reagan administration. Despite the proliferation of think tanks in both the United States and Europe, the underlying objective remained largely universal: to provide governments with expert, non-partisan, disinterested advice.

In the decade following World War II, demand for defense experts and technocrats increased remarkably, leading to the development of organizations that shared close ties with governments. These organizations would serve as the foundational models for a new generation of "contract research" think tanks. The inherent objective of these institutions would be to assist in the management of defense that was established in the new security arrangements of the Cold War era.

TABLE 2.1 US think tanks by state (from highest to lowest number)

State	Number of think tanks
Massachusetts	176
California	172
New York	150
Virginia	107
Illinois	64
Texas	50
Maryland	48
Connecticut	44
Pennsylvania	43
New Jersey	36
Florida	32
Colorado	31
Michigan	31
Georgia	29
Ohio	26
Washington	24
Minnesota	23
North Carolina	23
Wisconsin	22
Arizona	21
Indiana	21
Maine	21
Rhode Island	20
Tennessee	20
Missouri	19
Alabama	17
Kansas	17
Oregon	17
New Hampshire	13
Hawaii	12
Kentucky	12
Louisiana	12
Oklahoma	11
Iowa	10
Mississippi	10
Montana	9
Arkansas	8
Utah	8
Nebraska	7

(Continued)

TABLE 2.1 (Cont.)

State	Number of think tanks
New Mexico	7
West Virginia	7
South Carolina	6
South Dakota	5
Vermont	5
Idaho	4
Nevada	4
North Dakota	4
Delaware	3
Alaska	2
Wyoming	0

More specifically, such contract research provided to governments was executed in order to further develop the defense hardware and systems installed after World War II. The emergence of the Cold War, in addition to the United States' new position as a superpower, contributed greatly to this new development. This period also witnessed the rise of "strategic" think tanks—primarily in the United States—which were comprised of "defense intellectuals," such as the RAND Corporation. These defense specialists ultimately led to the emergence of "strategic" think tanks across the world in the following decades.

The social turmoil of the 1960s and the inherent political pressures provided the foundation for the emergence of a new generation of specialized think tanks. These new think tanks were far more focused on a particular issue than their predecessors, and the 1970s revealed a Washington that had become increasingly receptive to think tank advice. As voters began to assume stances on specific issues, demand for research regarding the various viewpoints expanded. These issue-specific think tanks often established sites outside the individual country of origin and fostered formal relationships with international institutions. Their staff included specialists, advocacy experts, and academics. Not surprisingly, these think tanks blurred the lines between the original concept of a think tank (which was academic) with that of an advocacy group.

Beginning in the 1990s, think tanks started spreading around the world at an exponential rate. The spread of globalization, the growing needs of the information age, and the extraordinary complexity of global public policy problems called for an equally global strategy.[17] As globalization has evolved over the past two decades, so too has the rate at which think tanks spread across the world. From 1991 to 2000, the think tank proliferation phenomenon was at its height, with an astounding number of new institutions arising around the globe each year. Beginning around 2000, the form of public policy research globalized and gave rise to global think tanks, which formed think tank networks or physically expanded across the globe. Expansion and networking of these and similar institutions occur at the domestic, regional and global levels. In addition to its primary staff, a global think tank has a large number of collaborators, who come from a myriad of sectors such as international organizations, non-governmental organizations (NGOs), corporations, and academia, which assist the institution in its various functions. Furthermore, growth in structurally-independent public policy networks has shown similar characteristics, arguably surpassing even the global think tank phenomenon, and providing an influential alternative and/or complement to the traditional one-headquarter per think tank.[18]

Not surprisingly, the rates of proliferation differ widely across regions and time. North America, specifically the United States and Canada, along with Western Europe host the majority (51.9 percent) of the world's think tanks. Although most regions experienced a gradual increase in the number of think tanks established beginning in the 1940s, the period of largest growth occurred from 1991 to 2000. This sharp spikes in think tank establishment rates can be largely attributed to the greater democratization in formerly closed societies after the conclusion of the Cold War, increased trade liberalization, and the expansion of both market-based economies and globalization.[19] Prior to 1991, most think tank proliferation occurred in the United States and Canada. The growth of democratization and liberalization that occurred during the 1990s in effect created a more hospitable atmosphere for the rise of independent policy advisors institutionalized in think tanks. Even as China economically liberalized in the late 20th century, its think tank profile inevitably grew to influence public policy.[20]

North America, in contrast, experienced a gradual decrease in the number of think tanks established in the decade following the peak in the 1980s (see Table 2.2) and then a sharp decline at the beginning of the 21st century. The following sections will expand on the trends and context of think tanks within Western Europe, Latin America, Southeast Asia, Eastern Europe, and Sub-Saharan Africa.

Think tanks in the context of Western Europe

As mentioned earlier, think tanks inhabit a major role in determining the process of policymaking in the United States. However, in other regions of the world, their influence is much more subtle. In Western Europe, think tanks did not become a significant part of political discourse until the late 1990s, coinciding with the rise of the European Union and the need for greater policy accountability. Even then, think tanks in the area were increasingly partisan, conducting research on behalf of their affiliated political party. As scholars Rosetta Collura and Pierre Vercauteren explained, "think tanks [in Western Europe] have for long been recognized as having an active role within the decision-making process. Even if think tanks in the EU have some specificities, their main resource (knowledge) is central in the governance process."[21] With the rise of supranational organizations such as the European Union, the number of think tanks should continue to grow to protect national interests and make sure all members' needs are addressed.

TABLE 2.2 Global emergence of think tanks over time

Time period	Global	Africa	Asia (including Oceania)	Eastern Europe	Latin America	Middle East	North America	Western Europe
1701–1800	3	0	1	0	0	0	1	1
1801–1900	18	0	1	0	0	0	8	9
1901–1910	16	0	1	0	0	0	12	3
1911–1920	25	0	0	1	0	0	19	5
1921–1930	39	1	3	4	0	0	22	9
1931–1940	36	1	4	0	1	0	20	10
1941–1950	117	2	17	8	6	0	54	30
1951–1960	196	3	24	8	18	3	70	70
1961–1970	340	10	50	15	28	13	127	97
1970–1980	476	30	76	6	54	24	248	38
1981–1990	956	42	113	50	96	31	417	206
1991–2000	1,248	110	135	249	85	63	348	258
2001–2010	414	30	48	61	34	24	89	128
2011–2018	1617	62	592	159	301	178	60	265

Some of the most well-known think tanks in the area are Chatham House in the United Kingdom and KAS in Germany. Primarily focused on international security and economics, Chatham House has conducted numerous research projects dealing with global threats such as ultranationalism and food security, in addition to focusing on energy and the environment, global health, and regional studies. As an independent, non-profit organization, Chatham House has drawn praise from leaders around the world for its quality research output and its international forums to encourage global cooperation. While KAS is a political party-based think tank associated with the German Christian Democratic Union, its work and impact around the world cannot be understated. With the expansion of the European Union within the past decade, KAS has been providing policy advice and other means of research to foster European integration and better trade relations around the world. While they are often regarded by the European public as irrelevant to their daily lives, these think tanks are nonetheless indispensable to Europe's changing relations with its neighbors. However, though, ideally, the number of think tanks in Western Europe would continue to grow, following the explosion in the proliferation of think tanks worldwide in the 1990s there was a sharp contraction and significantly decreased proliferation after 2000. There are several reasons for the decrease, namely that Western European think tanks remain underfunded and have a limited influence in domestic policy. Given economic difficulties in the early 21st century, there was little incentive to keep these institutions growing.[22]

Think tanks in the context of Latin America

In Latin America, it is important to note the severity of state repression during the period of think tank growth expansion. Authoritarian governments, which were prominent among Latin American countries during the mid to late 20th century, stunted the formation of think tanks. The concept of independent research institutions threatened the control of these regimes. When think tanks ultimately formed throughout the region, strong ties to governments and public officials were their defining characteristic.[23] This phenomenon is most apparent in the realm of foreign affairs.

Due to the authoritarian regimes which marked significant periods of 20th century Latin America, the political culture of this region is one in which the central governments act with a higher level of autonomy than in a country such as the United States. As a result, track two diplomacy was often hard to come by, or nonexistent, in these countries. Today, there are only approximately ten think tanks in Latin America that are focused on foreign affairs, which is a slight growth from the three that were prominent in 1993.[24] While the number of these research institutions are growing, they are still primarily administered by political insiders. Furthermore, think tanks in the region struggle to receive outside funding, which increases their dependency on government and its funding.[25]

This reliance on government underscores the development of think tanks in Latin America. Although most countries in the region have shifted away from authoritarian regimes to a more democratic style of government, the quality of these democracies is lesser than those in Western Europe or the United States. "Hybrid" democracies based on the principle of neopopulism have begun to sprout in certain countries.[26] Moreover, major think tanks in the region, such as the Argentine Council for International Relations (CARI) and the Brazilian Center for International Relations (CEBRI) were created by government officials.[27] As a result, these think tanks are sometimes used to confirm the beliefs and theories of the political party that controls them. The lack of autonomy found in these think tanks is a repetitive characteristic of institutions in this region.

Think tanks in the context of Southeast Asia

Similar to the structure of Latin American politics, governments in the Association of Southeast Asian Nations (ASEAN) maintain a strong autonomy over political affairs. Think tanks in the region struggled to gain access to policymaking during the early years of ASEAN. However, divergent from Latin America, ASEAN has now been able to force cooperation between think tanks in Southeast Asia.[28] Unlike many other regions, this level of cooperation has fostered a relationship between the think tanks in Southeast Asia, and the economic and security policy they produce, that benefits nations in Southeast Asia as a whole. However, this proximity of think tanks to government has posed problems; think tanks in ASEAN countries often fall into "entrapment," in that they solely offer research which bolsters the politician's point of view.[29]

Think tanks in the context of Eastern Europe

In regions such as Eastern Europe, the scope of think tanks is more significant. The numbers of think tanks rose during the 1990s, in part to due to globalization and the increase of democratic regimes. The disbanding of the Soviet bloc allowed private research institutions to flourish. With Western support, think tanks began springing up throughout Central and Eastern Europe. Due to the lack of stable and accountable governments in the newly democratic states, think tanks quickly became the means to fill the power vacuum, and political parties had no choice but to accept the advice of these think tanks to develop policies. Institutions such as the Albanian Center for Economic Research and the Center for the Study of Democracy in Bulgaria became some of the most successful think tanks to come out of the Cold War Era, formulating liberal policy and helping to ease democratic reforms to the public. As described by Juliette Ebélé and Stephen Boucher, "by acting as guardians of the liberal orthodoxy, many think tanks became part of the policy establishment, and were adopted as the West's favourite partners."[30]

However, think tanks in the area have faced sustainability issues during the early 21st century. Like their Western European counterparts, think tanks in Eastern Europe face significant developmental obstacles due to lack of funding and decreasing public trust. With funding shortages in the wake of the European financial crisis of 2006, most think tanks have been limited to foreign donations. The funding is just enough to enable them to keep their heads above water, but not enough to encourage them to pursue new and innovative policy projects. In light of the expansion of a resurgent Russia during the Putin administration, civil society organizations in the former Eastern Bloc have become the targets of public scrutiny and ridicule.[31] As Russia expands its sphere of influence, the future for think tanks in Eastern Europe is in jeopardy.

Think tanks in Sub-Saharan Africa

Think tanks in Sub-Saharan Africa are currently in crisis. Although think tanks have historically had critical moments of influence, especially in democratic and liberal regimes such as Ghana, Guinea, and South Africa, think tanks in countries across Sub-Saharan Africa are currently over-reliant on international donors, and those international donors are currently pulling out their funding at a dizzying pace. One indicative example of this predicament is the Think Tank Initiative (TTI). Launched in 2008 and managed by Canada's International Development Research Centre (IDRC), TTI is a partnership between five donors—the William and Flora Hewlett Foundation, UK Aid, the Bill & Melinda Gates Foundation, the Ministry of Foreign Affairs of the Netherlands, and Norad. The program concluded at the end of 2019. Although the program sought to nurture the long-term sustainability of think tanks across developing nations, research by the Think Tanks and Civil Societies Program (TTCSP) at the University of Pennsylvania, including interviews with some of the African think tanks involved in the program, underscored how the influx of funds from TTI had resulted in inflated budgets and staff sizes. While project-specific staff and researchers were increased, staff for core operations, such as communications and development, were left underdeveloped. Now, as the TTI funding ends at the end of 2019, no African think tank involved with TTI has been able to fully replace the funding that they lost at the end of 2019, resulting in fears of lay-offs and some fearing closure. The Ethiopian Development Research Institute (EDRI), one of the TTI participants and a leading think tank in Ethiopia, is already set to close.[32]

Specificity and diversity in think tank research

The 21st century has ushered in an era of heterogeneous think tanks. Some, such as the Washington Institute for Near East Policy, focus on specific functional or regional issues. Others, such as the Center for Strategic and International Studies, examine entire fields such as foreign policy. A select few, such as the RAND Corporation or the Brookings Institution, can incorporate research on an extremely diverse range of areas, anything from foreign policy to economics.[33] In this sense, specific distinctions begin to emerge: full service, multi-issue, and single-issue. Full service think tanks conduct research on a diverse and large number of issue areas, whereas multi-issue think tanks are not as broad in overall scope but still incorporate multiple policy domains. Lastly, single-issue think tanks focus their efforts and research solely on a single topic. This diversification broadens funding sources as well. Some think tanks base much of their budget on government funds while others operate primarily through contract work (either in the public or private sector). Still others rely on grants, membership fees, and individual donations.

To be more specific, in the United States there are not just three or four but three or four dozen world class universities. There are not just two or three but well over a dozen intellectually serious weekly, monthly, and quarterly policy-oriented national publications. The research function within government is huge; every cabinet position has permanent research staff at whose pinnacle stands one permutation or another of an interlocking directorate such as that described above. And, as noted, the number of foundations with permanent staff that monitor and interact with academia, government, think tanks, and the publishing world is unprecedented—and so is the amount of cash that foundations are willing to spend on activities that are not directly for-profit.

What this means, among other things, is that, because people move around so much, the transference of knowledge into policy is to some degree personalized. Very often an expert at a think tank will write a report, publish a study and evaluate a program that government policymakers will read, or which they themselves have contracted. But frequently the think tanker himself or herself is either temporarily or more permanently taken into government to implement his or her own ideas. Sometimes, at the higher levels, this happens via the Title C route, but it happens more routinely, at many other levels, via the dynamics of the interlocking directorate described earlier.

The wider implications of this sort of mobility are major. Bringing intellectually vested and often prestigious individuals into policymaking circles shakes up those circles, revivifies and redirects them on an episodic basis. Obviously, there is a price to be paid for such disruptions, for the institutional memory of a bureaucracy is as much a precious thing as its inertial and self-interestedly closed tendency is a bad thing. In the United States, however, there is a similar kind of "creative destruction" in policy research functions—thanks to think tanks and their influence—as there is in market capitalism itself. The "mixing it up" to which think tanks contribute so much ensures that ideas get generated and are exchanged, that they are flung into the appropriate professional arenas for debate and that, at times, they are launched out of a professional arena and become politicized through the media. In short, think tanks contribute to the relative democratization of policy debates. On balance, this is a healthy process despite the downsides that occasionally occur.

What are those downsides? As already noted in passing, not all think tanks are composed of disinterested intellectuals backed by purely charitable foundations. Some think tanks are oriented toward advocacy rather than dispassionate analysis. They may be so oriented on the basis of ideology (e.g. the American Enterprise Institute, which is conservative) or commercial interests (e.g. USA Engage, which is a recently formed ad-hoc business lobby with a modest research function dedicated to overturning US unilateral economic sanctions). Sometimes, debate can be imbalanced through the power of money. Occasionally, rather half-baked ideas (supply-side economics, many would argue) can assume disproportionate influence due to the interlocking directorate described earlier. Sometimes, it is not wise to short circuit the professional work of bureaucracies and place in their stead political appointees with popular but dubious notions about how to solve an important national problem. Sometimes, in the "creative destruction" of a think tank-driven policy process, one gets more destruction than creation.

Moreover, sometimes government agencies use think tanks not to learn about policy, but to gain leverage over bureaucratic rivals. Many studies have been financed with taxpayer money for the purpose of hammering home a preconceived point designed to gain a government agency more money, personnel, clout or prestige in intergovernmental competitions. Sometimes, think tanks are used because government cannot hire the personnel necessary to perform a task in a timely fashion. Sometimes, government faces hiring ceilings and must go outside for help. In other times, it is not cost-effective for government to staff up for temporary projects. But in all these cases, it does not follow that outsiders unfamiliar with policy routines will necessarily do a better job than a fully-staffed bureaucracy. Quite the contrary is true much of the time.

As suggested earlier, think tanks have made serious mistakes. Quantitative analysis is good for understanding some sorts of problems but downright misleading when (mis)applied to others. The positivist bias of social science and the social science bias of think tanks after World War II led to many epistemological atrocities and wastes of money. To be sure, Senator William Proxmire's famous "Golden Fleece" awards often bore a serious point. The conservative critique of the think tank mentality of the 1960s and 1970s—that it neglected the importance of values, and that it shared a pro big-government social engineering bias—was essentially, if not always and entirely, correct. And for all their genius and independence of mind, where are the think tank studies from 30 and 40 years ago that told of the impact of commercial television on "deep" literacy, that forecasted the impact of the national highway systems on the viability of urban neighborhoods or that warned of the general social and public health implications of widespread female contraception? Think tanks missed many of the biggest issues, just like nearly everybody else.

Furthermore, given that think tanks often rely on donors such as companies or individual philanthropists for their funding, they can become too dependent on fragmented, project-specific funding to sponsor their growing operations. In this process, they lose their potential for innovation as they research or recommend policy on specific issue areas outlined by their donors. This dependence upon project specific funding is an increasing challenge for the US think tank community because the core operations are underfunded. Another growing challenge is the sheer number of think tanks, lobby groups, and other civil society organizations all working to affect government policy. In the new age of the internet, it has become exceedingly easy for all of these organizations to share and broadcast their goals and ideas, thereby forcing think tanks to find increasingly more creative means to gain the attention of the public and government officials.

Still, compared to bureaucracy alone, think tanks have helped governments to think. Knowing their limits, however, wise American policy managers seek the best mix between innovation and steadfastness, between think tank/external input and bureaucratic/internal input. It is not an easy task to create and maintain such a balance, and, as always, it comes down to having talented and experienced people in the right place to do so. But at least in the American experience, the challenge signifies that there is a choice.

Alas, most other countries, including most other democracies, simply do not have such a choice, and they increasingly feel that problems are outrunning the capacity of government to keep up with them—whether it concerns drug abuse, environmental despoliation, poverty, the corruption of world financial markets or international terrorism by whatever means. Furthermore, when the reaction of besieged policymakers to a sense of mounting problems leads to more government rather than more innovative government, it only makes the disadvantages of operating through large, inertia-prone and hierarchical organizations even worse.

This situation deteriorates further when information (which is easier than ever to collect due to its limitless abundance) is equated with knowledge (which is still as difficult as ever to acquire). There may also be a disconnection between knowledge and the means of implementing policy. Since government can more easily collect information than process it, and since ideas are more abundant than are the means to change existing operations, the tendency often enough is for each stage of the policy function to drown the successive one. The result often is, to recall Herbert Lindbloom's well-turned phrase, "muddling through," if one is lucky, or outright paralysis if one is not. Despite all of its problems, think tank culture offers the chance to cut through such debilities. Even in their various and confusing forms, think tanks have this key advantage.

Lessons from the US experience

Think tank culture offers a chance to get around governmental inertia for six reasons:

1. They can be and often are more future oriented than government research functionaries, who work in an environment in which efforts at creative disruption are rarely rewarded, if they are tolerated at all;
2. They are more likely to generate reconfigured policy agendas, while bureaucracies thrive on the security of standard operating procedures;
3. They are better able to facilitate collaboration among separate groups of researchers for a common purpose because they have no permanent vested interest in any one domain;
4. Moreover, they promote the intellectual synthesis that comes from breaking down bureaucratic barriers;
5. They can better disseminate relevant policy research within government than government agencies themselves, which are occasionally subject to bureaucratic politics and "turf" wars; and
6. Often, they can telescope the policy function from data collection to formation of knowledge to conceiving a means of implementation better than government bureaucracies, which may be internally segmented along functional lines.

It is not possible in a short report to fully document these policymaking innovations, which comprise our six subthemes. Nor, obviously, is it the case that think tanks always outperform bureaucracies. Work in large think tanks such as the RAND Corporation has been routinized to the point that a small Defense Department office (Net Assessment) regularly comes up with more creative analyses of problems than RAND, which is a hundred times its size. As noted earlier, policy intellectuals often err by allowing ideas to become disconnected from means of implementation—"little things" such as not having the money, the staff or sometimes even the law on one's side. The think tanks that work best are those whose senior managers have been in government and know the practical limits to what can be done.

This report about think tanks has limits, too. This space limits us to the use of case studies and examples in order to show how think tanks have fulfilled their promised function along each of the six subthemes noted earlier, and to note a few instances in which they have not. As suggested, bureaucracies have trouble planning very far ahead unless they are specifically charged with doing so. Even then, they do not always succeed. One needs to look no further than Net Assessment in the Pentagon or Policy Planning in the Department of State for accessible examples. One reason is budgetary; managers do not know how much money they will have to work with. Planning beyond two or three fiscal years very quickly begins to seem "theoretical" to those inside the system. Bureaucratic culture also drives shortsighted policy planning. Bureaucracies thrive on predictability and a stable environment, and they tend to project those qualities onto the things they study and deal with. To predict a radical discontinuity "out there" implies a need for some big shake-ups "in here," which bureaucrats are rarely, if ever, able to do. When political appointees brought in from the outside try such things, they often meet stiff resistance. This threat to a newcomer's reputation precludes most attempts to enact reforms.

Moreover, political appointees do not last as long in their jobs as career bureaucrats usually do, so inertia wins by out waiting. Likewise, political leadership in democracies is more limited in time than the typical bureaucratic life, and some things take more than four years of effort to really change in large organizations.

Another reason is, as noted earlier, that the urgent drives out the important. Large as some bureaucracies are, the action of the moment is generally more interesting, rewarding, and prestigious than thinking about what will happen in five years' time. For those who aim to be of importance in their jobs, there is usually no time to think about the future beyond a few weeks or months.

A final reason for a lack of future-orientation is that large organizations, covetous of budget share and stability, do not like rocking the larger government boat for fear of getting on the wrong side of protectors and patrons. They tend to focus on process and methodology, not on evaluation or reevaluation of goals. They count computer power, personnel and petty cash, but they do not as readily audit their own larger purposes, which requires looking into the future. They generate order without reference to design. The typical government agencies, as Blackstone and Plowden put it, are "pluralistic, divided, under informed, shortsighted, only partly in control of their own processes, and unable to guarantee the outcomes which they promise. There are enormous gaps, and sometimes no linkages at all, between realities, perceptions, decisions, actions, and consequences."[34]

Think tanks, on the other hand, have always put a premium on planning and forecasting. The RAND Corporation was something of a prototype in this regard. After all, it takes years to get from the design stage of a new weapons system to its actual integration into a military force. One simply has to plan ahead, technically, financially, and administratively. Herman Kahn of the Hudson Institute, a spinoff of RAND, was known for this futurology. Indeed, he practically invented futurology in its current form. Later on, the Club of Rome, Earthwatch and other environmental groups also put a premium on calculating the future. Thinking ahead has not only been accepted in think tank environments, it has also been their bread and butter, stimulated by government contracting agents aware of think tanks' huge competitive advantage in this area.

To give just one example, the United States Army regularly (every five years) undertakes a project called ALREF (Army Long-Range Environmental Forecasting). The Defense Intelligence Agency, as well as Army Intelligence, does not perform this research, which projects social, economic, and political trends throughout the world for five- and ten-year periods. It hires a think tank to do the work instead. Years ago, the Hudson Institute, the FPRI and the Arroyo Center of the RAND Corporation did this work.

These think tanks were allowed to use "secret" data the Army had available, but this data turned out not to be very useful to the research. What was useful was a future-oriented state of mind and the willingness to derive scenarios and assign a probability to the likelihood of their happening. The Army, with vastly larger institutional and financial resources, could not perform the task because it lacked a willingness to adopt a contingent attitude—as opposed to an arch conservative, straight-line extrapolation-based attitude—toward the future. A review of these studies shows that, while think tankers' probability assignments did not always predict the future accurately, their scenarios rarely missed the mark altogether.

Bureaucracies do not typically call into question their own goals or basic internal organization except in institutional emergencies, or through a process of protracted absentmindedness. An example of the former is the International Monetary Fund after 1971, when its original function determined at Bretton Woods was eclipsed by the birth of a floating exchange rate system. It drifted from that task into that of being an advocate for extensive economic reforms and, more recently, appears to have become a lender of last resort. An example of the latter is the General Accounting Office, which gradually moved from a clerical function—essentially checking and filing purchase vouchers—to being a great engine of program evaluation. Most of the time, though, bureaucracies do not reinvent themselves; think tanks do.

Think tanks, when they are doing what they are designed to do, can think "beyond the frame." A good example from municipal government concerns a tariff rate debate over storm sewer tariffs in the city of Philadelphia. Some years ago, the City of Philadelphia tried to raise commercial tariff rates to finance storm sewer maintenance and construction. This was undertaken by the office of the water commissioner in the city. Some store owners complained that the basis of the tariff was unfair, for it was assessed according to those properties that had water meters. This was unfair, it was claimed, for two reasons: some properties were subdivided and so had more than one meter, subjecting the same physical space to double or triple charges, and businesses without meters, especially parking lots, were not charged at all, despite that fact that the impermeable surface of parking lots far exceeded those of "improved lots" and thus contributed far more water to the streets. The city resisted these complaints, a suit was brought in court, the city lost, and the court ordered the city to refigure the way it calculated its storm sewer tariff rates.

The city, though its bureaucracy is large, claimed that it lacked the technical expertise to do so. So, it contracted the court order out to a small think tank that was itself a spinoff of the School of Public and Urban Policy (SPUP) at the University of Pennsylvania. The think tank, in turn, subcontracted part of the study to one of its former graduates, then a science museum educational specialist (another nonprofit), who was charged with the task of looking at how other cities handled this particular problem. The sub-subcontractor studied how 26 other US cities managed the problem, and concluded, among other things, that most combined storm sewer and sewage tariff rates despite the fact that most cities had two separate systems to channel and treat these types of waste fluids. Since the latter rates are higher because they require more costly services, this created a revenue pool large enough to handle storm sewer repair and maintenance.

Among the recommendations to the city, eventually accepted, was that it reorganize itself bureaucratically to combine storm sewer and sewage tariffs and create a special tariff for properties without either water meters or plumbing. The separate little enclaves in the city bureaucracy never would have hit upon a functional merger as part of the solution; the think tank report to the court made it seem obvious.

Bureaucracies sometimes collaborate, and sometimes the collaboration is institutionalized to some degree. Thus, it is obviously impossible, say, to develop an overall US policy toward China without input from the Departments of State, Defense, Commerce, and Labor, as well as the White House National Security Council (NSC) staff, the relevant congressional committees, the CIA, and so forth. Within the executive branch, interagency groups are formed, usually under NSC guidance, to take care of such matters.

But not all matters are subject to effective collaboration; this is where think tanks can help. About two years before the first edition of this book, the Foreign Ministry of Japan approached a Washington-based, Middle East-oriented organization to study political succession in four Arab countries plus the Palestine Liberation Organization (PLO). The Japanese Foreign Ministry concluded that it did not have the expertise to do this task and did not wish to collaborate with other governments for reasons of diplomatic sensitivity.

The particular think tank chosen was originally a spinoff of an advocacy think tank—the American Israel Public Affairs Committee (AIPAC). Over the years, under two directors, it had managed to build an independent image of impartiality and research excellence. The think tank got its money from individuals, foundations, and government research contracts, illustrating the mixed nature of many think tanks in their funding. It agreed to do the work for the Japanese Foreign Ministry but turned to an adjunct associate of the think tank to actually draft out the work. The think tank helped by putting the researcher, a PhD in the relevant area of political analysis and area studies, in touch with other experts who would have been hard to find otherwise. The researcher, while a particular expert in two of the five cases, needed help on the other three.

Now, this researcher also happened to be employed part-time at another think tank (not exclusively focused on the Middle East) in a different city and was, more regularly, the executive editor of a prestigious foreign policy journal, also financed by individuals and foundations. As it happened, the researcher also taught one course a semester at the School of Advanced International Studies of Johns Hopkins University, located in Washington. The researcher had business relations with the head of the think tank through all three of his means of employment. The infrastructure of this particular project, then, vividly illustrates the interlocking directorate of think tanks, government, academe, foundations, and elite journalism.

The researcher performed the study, the Washington-based think tank packaged and presented the product, the sponsor was pleased, and the money was split and paid out according to prior arrangement. The think tank then used the study to raise money from US-based foundations in order to hold a series of closed seminars on each of the five cases. The best experts that could be found from within and outside the US government were invited to the seminars. The researcher and the think tank head served as co-chairmen of the meetings.

At these meetings were midlevel (not Title C) representatives of the Departments of State and Defense, the CIA, the executive branch's office of intelligence liaison, and others. Journalists, academics, and observers from foreign governments were also in attendance. Several of the government participants noted that they had never before been assembled in one place at one time to discuss the crucially important subject of the day: "What will happen, and what should the US government be prepared to do, after [Arafat, Asad, Mubarak, Fahd, and Hussein]." Indeed, most of the US government officials found the cumulative impact of the discussion with so many diverse participants to be revelatory. The government itself was unable to establish such interagency coordination about a subject of the future at the working level. But a think tank, now in the second cycle of a project started by a foreign government, could do so.

After the five seminars were completed, the results were written up by the co-chairmen. The report eventually was purchased by an agency of the US government as a proprietary document at the request of some of the government employees who had attended the seminar. What this example shows, among other things, is that once a project is launched, it is never clear exactly what its future and its impact may be. It sometimes happens that the most important and the most beneficial consequences are entirely unanticipated at the outset. This is a function of the interlocking directorate and "critical mass" of a "democratized" policy discussion in the world of think tanks.

There is a close relationship between physical segmentation and intellectual truncation in government, or in any large organization. Such segmentation and truncation are of course necessary; if, in a large organization, everyone was responsible for everything and everyone talked to everyone else, nothing of worth would ever get done. But every organization has a transcendent design as well as a standard operating procedure pattern, and it is the job of those responsible for the design function to ensure that the bureaucracy as a whole does what it was intended to do. The accretions of incremental changes over time, whether within the bureaucracy or in the external environment (or usually both), can fuddle an original design. Sometimes it takes a disaster to force a rethinking.

For example, in October 1983, a bomb exploded outside the US Marine contingent in Lebanon near Beirut airport, killing 241 US soldiers, and the political/security mission itself turned into chaos. Why? Because a truck with the bomb was able to drive right up against the side of the dormitory compound. A simple concrete pillar placed in the right spot would have prevented the disaster, or at least forced the assailants to think of another, less certain way of wreaking havoc.

But consider: the Marine contingent in Lebanon was part of Centcom (Central Command), whose base was in Tampa, Florida. The Marine contingent in Lebanon operated through the auspices of the 7th Fleet, whose base was in Italy. The commander on the ground in Lebanon thus had to go to Italy for some authorizations and all the way back to Florida for others.

This is of critical importance, for the chain of command evolved within the overall structure of planning and deploying US military forces in the Mediterranean, which were part of an even larger structure designed to fight a world war against the Soviet Union should strategic deterrence fail. Nowhere in the design of Centcom or the 7th Fleet was any consideration given to the potential problem of a single Shi'a Muslim guerilla warfare cell in Lebanon. This was not unreasonable, for that is something one would tend not to worry about—all else equal—in the context of global warfare with a superpower adversary.

In the Lebanese context, however, this meant that attending to security measures such as concrete pillars as a deterrent to guerrilla warfare attacks was no one's job— no one's standard operating procedure. And so, the job was not done. As the Lebanon mission was being planned, someone in charge of mission design should have thought of this—or hired a think tank to puzzle over the differences between the original design and the ad hoc design of using US forces in Lebanon. But that job was not done either.

An example of a successful alteration of design in the planning stages involves a triangle of precision-guided munitions design, reactive armor, and a think tank in Philadelphia. The Defense Advanced Research Projects Agency (DARPA), a technology research office in the Department of Defense, is responsible for thinking up new concepts in weapons design. Other offices are responsible for military intelligence, counterintelligence, and surveillance. In the mid-1970s, DARPA, in conjunction with the US Army and several contractors, was designing the "fire and forget" anti-tank munitions. These munitions were designed to fire a barrage of missiles from a distance, using what was then a newtech infrared homing signal to guide the missiles to their targets. The advantage of the system was in its range: it could hit enemy armor from a distance beyond the reach of its enemy counterparts.

The relevant contracting office in the Defense Department hired a man at a Philadelphia think tank to try to spoof or defeat the system. This was no ordinary man, however. An Israeli by birth and experience, he had, 15 years earlier, designed the Gabriel naval missile system, one of the most effective of its kind (here, too, is an example of a think tank being useful because it has specialized, even unique, talent unavailable to government). Had the researcher not had acquaintances in the right places, the contract probably never would have been negotiated, so the informal network, in this case an international one, was the key to the arrangement.

The researcher's methodology was unorthodox. He did not rely primarily on computers or sophisticated technical engineering analyses. He simply thought from his own experience and tried to put himself in the place of a Soviet planner faced with the fire and forget problem. He reasoned that the system could be easily spoofed—after its first surprise success—by running Soviet tanks and other armor through an inexpensive Styrofoam bath. This would interfere with the infrared tracking system, because the metal of the tank would no longer give forth its characteristic infrared signal. He also reasoned that the system would not work well in combat in sandy or dusty conditions for the same reason; as a war veteran, he could imagine actual combat conditions in a way that DARPA scientists simply could not. Furthermore, he reasoned that destroyed tanks sitting in a desert would give off infrared signals similar to working tanks, so that the fire and forget missiles would, before long, start homing in on vehicles that had already been destroyed or disabled. What this meant, on balance, is that if the Army invested the bulk of its research and development funds in this area in the fire and forget program, only to find that it didn't work as planned in combat, US forces would be left virtually naked in the face of Soviet conventional forces, to their advantage.

Lastly, the researcher reasoned that the size of the munitions, which had to be made small in order to accommodate a barrage type of delivery mechanism, could also be defeated by reactive armor—a means of insulating a tank so that a small internal explosion deflects the blast of an incoming projectile on contact. The researcher knew that Israeli designers were thinking about reactive armor for the new Merkava tank, but he did not know whether the US government had yet hit upon the possibility.

This last conclusion was particularly startling to the Defense Department, because in fact it too was working on the notion of reactive armor,[35] but it had never thought in terms of the impact of one of its programs (reactive armor) on another of its programs (fire and forget). It had been thinking in a segmented, bureaucratic fashion that kept the two parts of the same problem apart, and since both the programs were top secret, the segmentation was reinforced by a designed lack of communication. The researchers working on getting missiles to hit tanks never thought about the effect of possible enemy countermeasures—that was someone else's job. The think tank researcher's report forced the segmentation to break down and synthesis to occur. Both programs went ahead, but more slowly, more carefully, and in connection with each other.

As noted earlier, information is common, but knowledge is rare. Policymakers are frequently besieged by more information than they can possibly use, complaints from constituents, reports from international agencies or civil society organizations, advice from bureaucrats, lobbying by interest groups, exposure of the problems of current government programs in the popular or elite media, and so forth. The problem is that much of this information is unsystematic; some is unreliable, and some is tainted by the interests of those who are disseminating it. Some may be so technical or simply voluminous that generalist policymakers cannot understand or use it. Some information may be politically, financially or administratively impractical, or not in the interests of the policymakers who must make decisions. Other information may not be useful because it differs too radically from the world view or ideology of those receiving it.

Policymakers and others interested in the policymaking process, in short, need information that is understandable, reliable, accessible, and redacted for use in reasonable timescales. There are many potential sources for this information. Government agencies may provide it, as may university-based academics or research centers. International agencies are another potential source of information, especially on such basic data about how the world works as trade flows. But think tanks can do it too, and an excellent example comes from the Center on Budget and Policy Priorities.

The US budget is a truly monstrous document. It is very unlikely that anyone ever reads the entire thing. Summarizing the budget so that it is intelligible, though obviously not an entirely disinterested project, is a difficult but necessary task. The Center on Budget and Policy Priorities has been performing such a task for several years.

Staffed by experienced budgeteers, the summaries of the budget prepared each year are especially useful to members of the press, who have to report on the budget but have little time to read it themselves. Similarly, the government itself, in its various interested agencies, is forced to rely on think tank summaries, because no one has time to digest the entire document so as to see what it portends for public policy as a whole. And, oddly enough, government agencies are more inclined to trust a think tank, even one that admits an ideological agenda—one that is liberal and pro-government action on behalf of the poor, for example—than to trust a rival agency whose bureaucratic interests oppose its own.

Even more important than disseminating information is disseminating knowledge. The government has vast resources to collect information, far more than most think tanks. Think tanks, however, can sometimes more readily tell government what the information means. Not surprisingly, the US Geological Survey maintains a huge database about the physical country of the United States. When Landsat began augmenting our information about geology some two decades ago, new and important information about mineral and hydrocarbon deposits accumulated much faster than anyone in the government could evaluate it. Think tanks filled the gap. They did not provide the Survey with information, but instead with what the information meant in practice, in terms of areas to exploit, to protect, and to restudy.

At the outset of this report, pains were taken to distinguish information from knowledge, and to emphasize the importance of means of implementation in policy. One helpful thing that think tanks can do is design micro-experiments that integrate these three elements of policy innovation. An excellent example is RAND's Health Insurance Experiment of the 1970s.

The Health Insurance Experiment was designed as a major policy research effort that integrated project design, data collection, data analysis, and application all in one. It was a 15-year, $100 million effort that enrolled over 2,700 families at various places around the United States to see how various health insurance plans ranging from free care to 95 percent copayment would affect medical care and costs. The key purpose of the project was to observe the effects of various means of financing health care, both on the demand placed on the health care system and on the overall health of the participants. Because the project was an end-to-end integrated experiment going from data collection to analysis within a real-world but controlled environment, its conclusions were authoritative. What it found was that when families had access to free health care, they used the medical facilities about 50 percent more often than families who had joined cost-sharing systems. Yet, on average, the health outcomes were much the same. Also, surprisingly, the elasticity of demand for health services did not vary proportionately according to the cost of the copayment that families had accepted to pay; rather, plateaus were revealed that varied logarithmically with cost.

Between 1982 and 1984—the period following the professional publication of the study's findings—the number of major employer health plans with deductibles for hospitalization increased from 30 percent to 62 percent, and those with deductibles of $200 or more increased from 4 percent to 21 percent. Both corporations and unions used the study (legitimately, it would seem) to argue that cutting medical fringe benefits to some extent would not undermine workers' health.

Adaptations of the US experience around the world

Most countries in the world are not as large or as wealthy as the United States. They also do not have the same problems and needs, particularly in the defense/military/foreign policy domain. However, some lessons can be distilled from the US experience with think tanks that apply to the countries in the region. These lessons break down into four interrelated categories: markets, legal environment, political culture, and intellectual environment.

Markets

For think tanks to fulfill their mission of improving public policy in any country, they must operate in two distinct but overlapping markets: a market for funding and a market for policy advice. These markets sometimes overlap, for example, when government agencies responsible for a policy sector contract with a think tank for advice on a specific policy problem. More frequently, however, the funders of policy advice and the audience for that advice are distinct, for example, when a foundation or international development agency funds a study that is intended to inform the decisions made by a national government.

Where markets do not exist but are desired, they can be created through incentives. This may take time or may happen more quickly than one expects. If governments wish to bring into being a think tank-friendly environment, one way to go about it is to buy it. And one does not have to create something from nothing through incentives either. For example, in the absence of a strong standing corporate philanthropic tradition, a government can privatize some of its own internal research functions. It can, in short, spinoff some of its own government researchers to augment the private, independent think tanks that already exist. This may be particularly useful for policy areas in which private, independent think tanks are scarce or nonexistent.

But the market works two ways. Not only must research be paid for, but research must also have a target. That may be other government agencies or the intelligent engaged public in general. It is wiser to start with RAND-like contract research first, for that ensures an audience, and to think of more general dissemination as a secondary product. A different balance can evolve over time.

Think tanks can also be created through higher education policy. University faculties are often skeptical of policy research, but not all are. Create the right incentives, and they will serve. Countries in the region have many fine, first-rate universities, and the creation of university-affiliated research institutions is not an impossible task. Of course, universities must cooperate in this, but, in Central America and the Caribbean, universities are often heavily subsidized by the state; thus, this should not prove an impossible task.

An example: some US cities have several major universities within a small physical area (New York, Philadelphia, Chicago, Boston, and several others). In many of these cities, "science center" areas have been carved out for professors to wear a second hat. It works like this: the universities cooperate to buy real estate and build buildings and laboratories to rent to their own faculties. The professors use their university affiliations to attract research money, either on a nonprofit or for-profit basis, which filters back to the university not directly but in the form of rent for facilities. Universities set rules as to how much of a professor's earnings can be made "outside the classroom." But because the relationship is indirect, mediated through the science center arrangement, universities can avoid the difficulties of direct work for government. Everyone wins: faculty can augment their income, as can the university, and a new resource is developed for government and public policy use. It follows that today more young elites are being sent for international education and training. Already, international consortiums of graduate education, such as the Global Public Policy Network, aim to prepare some of the world's most able graduate students to assume global leadership roles in the coming decades.[36]

It is also worth pointing out a number of trends influencing the market for policy advice after the end of the Cold War. Both political and technological developments have transformed economic, social, and political debates in many countries, which, in turn, have created a greater demand for policy advice. The marketplace has become increasingly globalized in recent years. Major funders of policy research, such as foundations and international development agencies, are increasingly operating across national boundaries, while think tanks and other policy research organizations are also carrying out their work transnationally. Policy fads purveyed by think tanks and other advice-giving organizations have also become almost instantly global in scope, especially when endorsed by major fund-giving organizations.

Lastly, in this regard, because the academic market in Central America and the Caribbean is smaller than its academic production, many scholars have taken up professional residence outside their own country. Some of these professionals, as foreign nationals, would involve themselves in think tanks of intergovernmental organizations as subcontractors, or more, if the opportunity to do so existed. Governments should consider making an inventory of such professionals for this purpose. Indeed, a broader inventory of nationals who are PhDs or other professionals is not too much to do, and it would give the government useful knowledge of its own human raw materials.

Legal environment

Two of the devices used in the United States to maintain a healthy environment for public service philanthropy are the legal and tax codes. The nonprofit sector as a whole in the United States is supported by making it economically rational to give money away for certain purposes. While this reduces government revenue, the long-term benefits outweigh the costs. Clearly, if a government wishes to move from an initial situation in which government itself is the major source of funds for new think tanks to a more "democratized" and privatized situation more like that in the United States, then it must make it both legally possible and economically rational for a larger nonprofit sector to arise. Since rates of taxation in the region are fairly low, the possibilities of adjusting the code are many. Perhaps it would be wise to hire a domestic policy think tank to work out the possibilities in detail. Perhaps then, too, these institutes would not be under pressure to go hat in hand to raise large shares of their operating funds each year that their endowments cannot cover.

Political culture

Earlier in the chapter, a strong emphasis was placed on the importance of the informal, interlocking directorate that binds together government, academia, foundations, elite journalism, and think tanks. It is this sizable and intellectually active policy elite that each country needs to augment if it wishes to create an innovative, intellectually vital sector to help government think. In the United States, this fluid exchange between government and civil society is known as the "revolving door." This suggests a few things to do, and a few to avoid.

First, getting academics into the policy world, insofar as that is possible and appropriate, is essential. One way to do this is to create government fellowships to exchange workers. So, for instance, two or three managers in public health services go for a year to a relevant university department to do research and possibly to teach, while two or three academics take the seats of the government workers to learn how policy operates. This does not need to be very costly, for one is simply exchanging one professional salary for another.

Second, similar exchanges can be made between academics and journalists. Harvard University has the Nieman Fellowship, for example, which brings prestigious journalists into academia for a semester or year. Academics can be farmed out to newspapers and magazines as well. These exchanges can also try to mimic what the US government and the Council on Foreign Relations (CFR) do together. The CFR has a fellowship program where a select group of younger scholars from think tanks or academia intern in government agencies for a year. This has the effect of circulating promising personnel in and out of the various parts of the interlocking directorate, and it works well. One CFR fellow, Condoleezza Rice, went on to serve in the NSC and as Secretary of State in the Bush Administration, and she is now working at a think tank—the Hoover Institution (in addition to being a professor at Stanford University). Another moved from the CIA to academia and then to the State Department as a result of the fellowship.

Thus, it might be beneficial to mix up the categories and professions to make sure they get to know one another and appreciate the synergies between what they do for a living. Therefore, when deciding where to physically locate new think tanks, fellowships and the like, it makes sense to put them where such synergies can most easily take place. Do not do what the Australian government has done: it located its publicly-supported research facilities in out-of-the-way places such as Canberra, while the swirling, active talent of the country lives in Sydney and Melbourne. While "think tanks" originally conveyed some safe, secure, isolated place away from the outside world, this is, sociologically speaking, the opposite of what one should strive for today.

Intellectual environment

The United States was founded and populated by a more than typical share of nonconformists. US political culture and its intellectual environment have put a premium on individuality and self-reliance. The traditions of the countries in the region share some similarities, but the role of government as a strong force in social and economic life is somewhat different in the US experience. Think tanks, ideally speaking, should be independent and freestanding if they are to do their job well. Too much connection to government, or to political parties—as is the case in Germany—makes it next to impossible for institutions to establish their own research agendas. Direct government funding also means that organizations must live essentially from project to project, resulting in a failure to secure new projects in a timely fashion, which spells organizational disaster.

The role of government in society in Germany goes back to three traits of its political culture, which are reflected in the intellectual environment. First, there is no public service philanthropic tradition. That tradition as a whole is weak, and, where it does exist, it tends to avoid public policy and all controversial issues to focus on "good works." Even the wealthiest foundations are pale compared to their US counterparts in this respect. Second, the adversarial tradition vis-à-vis government is weak in countries in the Central European region. While there is less volunteerism and self-reliance compared to the United States, there is also more trust in government institutions. Third, the intellectual climate as a whole is less intense and less ideological; concern about political issues is simply less widespread in the population than in the United States.

These are not things that can change overnight, nor should they be. But the spirit of debate, of argument, of criticism, and of emotional and moral engagement in the public realm is necessary to support a vibrant, independent, intellectually serious think tank sector. It is important because "mere" positivist social science is not enough to sustain such institutions, for such positivist social science itself carries an ideological agenda. The real point of having think tanks to help governments think is not to have them be mere technical adjuncts to the bureaucracy, but to have them be a probing, critical, independent spirit in society that is part of the process of holding government accountable to a democratic polity. Indeed, think tanks are best thought of as part of civil society—that space between the private lives of individuals and the business of government. Think tanks perform what is, in essence, a social process, not a technical one.

Tools for governments

While things cannot be changed overnight, the governments in the region have several options with respect to pushing the future along. Some have been noted above by way of tax law changes, international funding and audience, and fellowship programs. But another way to promote the exchange of knowledge about how large and public policy-oriented think tanks in the US work, with the objective of adapting this knowledge to other countries and contexts, would be for each country's embassy in Washington to host an array of individuals from government, academia, and the media for an extended period of time. The embassy could contact the major Washington think tanks and ask that its representatives be invited to meetings and seminars, something with which most think tanks would gladly comply. Over time, each country would build up a network of knowledgeable and connected institutions, which would have an intimate sense of how the interlocking directorate works. They would also learn how to appeal and make proposals to foundations to secure funding. The lessons from these interactions can be used to build up the think tank environment in the home country.

Yet another option is to ask one or several American think tanks to develop partnerships with countries in the region and help build capacity in existing institutions and seed new think tanks. This has happened before. When the states of Central and Eastern Europe became independent from the USSR, a huge public policy vacuum was created. In one case, the newly formed Institute of International Relations in Prague was matched with a US think tank (the FPRI), with funds from the Pew Charitable Trusts, to observe the methods by which FPRI publishes a journal, sets up its filing system, keeps records and contracts for various services, writes proposals, deals with the press, and formats and distributes publications. The option of pairing new think tanks with more established ones could allow for "increasing availability of foundation support and development aid" and open a gateway to "cheap flows of information." Most importantly, this transnationalization could lead to the expansion of international agendas.[37]

Challenges to think tank impact

While think tanks can assume vital roles in the policymaking process within their respective regions, they do suffer from various limitations that affect not only how they operate, but also how "successful" they are in influencing policy decisions. As mentioned previously, think tanks are subjected to problems and challenges both in the United States and around the world including, but not limited to, issues of funding, political acceptance, culture and language barriers, and competition for idea management.

Perhaps the most universal issue confronting think tanks today, regardless of international location, is, as we have already discussed, funding problems. A considerable percentage of the world's think tanks rely on donations from individuals, corporations or other public and private enterprises to constitute a majority of annual funds. As such, these institutions can easily become dominated by the interests of the donor and therefore concentrate on isolated and specific issue areas as opposed to maintaining a broad capacity for research. This project-specific funding negatively impacts the potential for innovation. Moreover, the severe budget constraints as well as the "fiscal restraints and state entrenchment"[38] that affect many think tanks leave them unable to appropriately staff and subsequently conduct the necessary research for policymakers to utilize. Think tanks are also facing increased competition for less funding, particularly in regard to foreign sources, reducing their ability to substitute for and diversify domestic funding. Already-scarce domestic funding resources exacerbate competition and, in some cases, create an inability to fully function without foreign support. Increased competition creates more partnerships and dependencies that lead to questions of whether the think tank remains truly independent and autonomous.

Political acceptance and access to policymakers, the media and the public are also important considerations for any think tank desiring to influence the policymaking process, as with all civil society groups.[39] These issues are particularly relevant for many European think tanks, which have not been engaged by the media and, likewise, do not seek to attract media attention. They are also largely ignored at the policy level due to perceptions that they act primarily as research-oriented institutions (so-called "universities without students") rather than vehicles for innovative policy recommendations and solutions. In some respects, these issues are inter-related with funding problems. Many think tanks simply do not have the resources available to actively pursue the media. European think tanks (and think tanks elsewhere, especially in the Middle East) also tend to be affiliated with political parties or government more often than their American counterparts (although affiliation does exist to some degree in the United States; for example, Progressive Policy Institute is affiliated with the Democratic Leadership Council).[40] These connections, therefore, create further complications of establishing independence from external influences. Some governments use or establish their own tightly-controlled think tanks to conduct research that furthers the political agenda rather than putting forth new and innovative policies. As a result, institutions that obtain funding from governments or political parties run the risk of being excluded entirely from the policymaking process if their affiliated political party or government is replaced by a rival.

While less of a problem for US think tanks, cultural and language barriers represent a critical current and future challenge for such knowledge-based institutions. This is particularly the case for the rise of global (many of which are US-based) or pan-European think tanks, which must familiarize themselves with new civil society and policymaking structures in the countries or regions of their global or international expansions. Without a global political system and global political parties, think tanks face the challenge of re-learning policy influence techniques from the ground up each time they enter a new international location, and these techniques may be incongruous with previous techniques or ideals. Additionally, think tanks looking to make a global impact may have to learn how to deal not only with governments, but also with international organizations and global governance institutions, which operate in different ways.[41] These issues are exacerbated by advances in information technology, which allow for greater global availability and accessibility of ideas. The global spread of the personal computer, RSS feeds, networking sites such as Facebook and Twitter, electronic libraries, and the internet in general have exponentially increased the capacity for think tanks to project their innovative policies and ideas beyond their own national or regional boundaries or borders. The challenge has shifted from being able to broadcast these ideas in a general sense to how to properly and appropriately adapt them to new civil society norms. Away from headquarters, there could be a lack of familiar media or proper representative policymakers, or there could be political parties with different ideologies. All of these considerations can have potentially strong negative impacts on a think tank's ability to influence the policymaking process not only within its respective region, but also internationally.

In certain aspects, the very "information tsunami" that drives policymakers to seek out think tanks to provide them with concise, timely, and accurate policy recommendations constructed from the churning sea of available information also creates fundamental issues regarding the competition for idea management. Specifically, the market of ideas is becoming increasingly crowded. Think tanks are not the sole producers of innovative ideas, as universities and businesses also perform policy thinking.[42] These institutions, especially the mega-corporations and other business firms and conglomerates, may have already established a global reach and reputation that easily rivals that of the largest internationally-active think tanks. As such, think tanks are challenged to assess the work and mode of operation of these competitors or partner institutions, and to maintain their policy-setting niche in order to communicate knowledge and values globally. As mentioned previously, advances in communication and information technology have allowed more streamlined and accessible methods of communication, but think tanks are not the only institutions to benefit from them. The sheer number of think tanks, lobby groups, and other civil society organizations around the world attempting to affect government policy represents one of the strongest challenges, both current and future, for any given think tank regardless of size and power.[43] The digital revolution has also, as stated before, facilitated the exchange of information between organizations, thereby compelling think tanks to explore new means of gaining the attention of the public and government officials.

Ultimately, think tanks have been, and will continue to be, increasingly crucial in assisting policymakers in managing the flood of information and policy issues on a global scale. Nevertheless, just like any other institution, they suffer from inherent flaws and challenges that affect how they operate and how successful they are in influencing the policymaking process. The flaws, limitations, and challenges mentioned above, as well as others, will be discussed in greater detail in Chapter 5

Notes

1 The American think tanks often mentioned as coming before World War II—the Brookings Institution (1927), the Russell Sage Foundation (1907), and the Carnegie Endowment for International Peace (1914)—were really less think tanks than advocacy groups coming out of the Progressive movement. Brookings was something of an exception and, in its day, was quite unique. The US government's research function also arose in earnest in the interwar period. Others suggest that the term was first used to describe the secure environment in which the Allies planned the invasion of Europe during World War II. The National Academy of Science was founded in the 19th century, and even a cursory familiarity with the themes of the Philadelphia 1876 Centennial Exhibition shows that the idea of harnessing applied science to government was already around. But it was not until the Wilson Administration and the experience of America in World War I that the government's own research function set roots. For an excellent summary, see Carol H. Weiss, *Organizations for Policy Analysis: Helping Governments Think* (Newbury Park, CA: Sage, 1992), 12.
2 Fred I. Dretske, *Knowledge and the Flow of Information* (Boston, Massachusetts: MIT Press, 1981).
3 James G. McGann, *2018 Global Go To Think Tank Index Report*, Think Tanks and Civil Societies Program, Lauder Institute, University of Pennsylvania, https://repository.up enn.edu/think_tanks/16.
4 Craig Murphy, "The Emergence of Global Governance," in *International Organization and Global Governance*, ed. Thomas G. Weiss and Rorden Wilkinson (Abingdon, Oxon: Routledge 2018), 29–30.
5 Julian Germann, "Marxism" in *International Organization and Global Governance*, ed. Thomas G. Weiss and Rorden Wilkinson (Abingdon, Oxon: Routledge 2018), 170–180.
6 Mancur Olson, *The Rise and Decline of Nations* (New Haven: Yale University Press, 1982).
7 Nicholas Georgescu Roegen, *The Entropy Law and Economic Process* (Cambridge: Harvard University Press, 1971).
8 John Greenwood and David Wilson, *Public Administration in Britain* (Crow's Nest: Allen & Unwin, 1984), 50.
9 For an excellent examination of this case see T. Blackstone and W. Plowden, *Inside the Think Tank: Advising the Cabinet 1971–1983* (London: Mandarin, 1992), 12.
10 Jonathan Mahler, "How One Conservative Think Tank Is Stocking Trump's Government," *New York Times*, 20 June 2018.
11 Lee Michael Katz, "American Think Tanks: Their Influence is on the Rise," *Carnegie Reporter* 5, no.2 (Spring 2009).
12 James McGann, *Think Tanks and Policy Advice in the US* (London: Routledge, 2007), 92.
13 Ibid., 124–125.

14 Lee Michael Katz, "American Think Tanks: Their Influence is on the Rise," *Carnegie Reporter* 5, no.2 (Spring 2009): 6.
15 Joseph Nye, "Bridging the Gap Between Theory and Policy," *Political Psychology* 29, no.4, (2008): 600.
16 James A. Smith, *Idea Brokers: Think Tanks and the Rise of the New Policy Elite* (New York: Free Press, 1993).
17 Craig Murphy, "The Emergence of Global Governance," in *International Organization and Global Governance*, ed. Thomas G. Weiss and Rorden Wilkinson (Abingdon, Oxon: Routledge 2018): 28.
18 Jan Scholte, "Civil Society and NGOs," in *International Organization and Global Governance*, ed. Thomas G. Weiss and Rorden Wilkinson (Abingdon, Oxon: Routledge 2018), 351.
19 James G. McGann, *Think Tank Impact Assessment Report* (Philadelphia, Pennsylvania: Foreign Policy Research Institute, 2008).
20 Xufeng Zhu, *The Rise of Think Tanks in China* (New York: Routledge, 2013).
21 Rosetta Collura and Pierre Vercauteren, "Theoretical Perspectives on Think Tanks on European Governance," *Studio Europea* 1, no.62 (March 2017): 48.
22 Tatyana Bajenova, Think Tanks in Europe: Rising, Peaking, or Declining?, *Observatoire Européen Des Think Tanks*, www.oftt.eu/think-tanks/generalites/article/think-tanks-in-europe-rising-peaking-or.
23 Daniel C. Levy, "Latin America's think tanks: The roots of nonprofit privatization," *Studies in Comparative International Development* 30, no.2 (1995): 3–25.
24 Argentina, Brazil, Chile, Colombia, the Dominican Republic, Mexico, Paraguay, Peru, Uruguay, and Venezuela have foreign policy think tanks.
25 Federico Merke and Gino Pauselli, "In the shadow of the state: Think tanks and foreign policy in Latin America," *International Journal* 70, no.4 (2015): 613–628.
26 Elisabeth Jay Friedman and Kathryn Hochstetler, "Assessing the third transition in Latin American democratization: representational regimes and civil society in Argentina and Brazil," *Comparative Politics* 35, no.1 (2002): 21–42.
27 Federico Merke and Gino Pauselli, "In the shadow of the state: Think tanks and foreign policy in Latin America," *International Journal* 70, no.4 (2015): 613–628.
28 Without the ability to share and analyze findings, regional bodies such as the Pacific Trade and Development Conference (PAFTAD) and the Pacific Economic Cooperation Council (PECC) could not have been formed. Diane Stone and Helen E. Nesadurai "Networks, second track diplomacy and regional cooperation: the experience of Southeast Asian think tanks," in *Inaugural Conference on Bridging Knowledge and Policy* (Bonn, Germany: 1999).
29 Amitav Acharya, "Engagement or entrapment? Scholarship and policymaking on Asian regionalism," *International Studies Review* 13, no.1 (2011): 12–17.
30 J Ebélé and S. Boucher, *Think Tanks in Central Europe and Eurasia: A Selective Directory* (Budapest: Freedom House, 2006), 14–27.
31 Saskia Brechenmacher, *Civil Society Under Assault: Repression and Responses in Russia, Egypt, and Ethiopia* (Washington DC: Carnegie Endowment for International Peace, 2017), 9.
32 For more about the plight of African think tanks, read the *2018 Africa Think Tank Summit Report*, Think Tanks and Civil Societies Program, Lauder Institute, University of Pennsylvania, https://repository.upenn.edu/think_tanks/16/ and the *2017 Africa Think Tank Sustainability Forum Report*, Think Tanks and Civil Societies Program, Lauder Institute, University of Pennsylvania, https://repository.upenn.edu/ttcsp_summitreports/20/.
33 Richard Haass, "Think Tanks and U.S. Foreign Policy: A Policy Maker's Perspective," *US Foreign Policy Agenda* (November 2002).
34 Tessa Blackstone and William Plowden, *Inside the Think Tank: Advising the Cabinet 1921–83* (London: Heinemann, 1988).
35 Walter Hahn and Hans Joachim Maitre, *Paying the Premium: a military insurance policy for peace and freedom* (Westport, CT: Greenwood Press, 1993).
36 Diane Stone, "Global Public Policy, Transnational Policy Communities and their Networks," *Policy Studies Journal* 36, no.1 (February 2008).

37 Diane Stone, "Think Tank Transnationalisation and Non-Profit Analysis, Advice and Advocacy," *Global Society* 14, no.2 (April 2000): 153–172.

38 Ibid., 153–172.

39 Jan Scholte, "Civil Society and NGOs," in *International Organization and Global Governance*, ed. Thomas G. Weiss and Rorden Wilkinson (Abingdon, Oxon: Routledge 2018): 354.

40 R. Kent Weaver, "The Changing World of Think-Tanks," *PS: Political Science and Politics* (September 1989): 563–78; and Dr Martin Thunert, "Organization/Structure of Think Tanks" (Konrad-Adenauer-Stiftung, June 2008).

41 Jan Scholte, "Civil Society and NGOs," in *International Organization and Global Governance*, ed. Thomas G. Weiss and Rorden Wilkinson (Abingdon, Oxon: Routledge 2018): 354.

42 Francesco Grillo, "Think Tanks in the Global Marketplace of Ideas," *openDemocracy*, 5 September 2001.

43 Jan Scholte, "Civil Society and NGOs," in *International Organization and Global Governance*, ed. Thomas G. Weiss and Rorden Wilkinson (Abingdon, Oxon: Routledge 2018): 362.

3

NEW INSTITUTIONAL STRUCTURES

Global think tanks and policy networks

- Origins and emergence of policy networks in policymaking
- Transnational advocacy network
- Transnational executive networks
- Knowledge networks or epistemic communities
- Issues networks
- Networking among think tanks
- Global think tanks: context and structure
- The role and utility of think tank networks
- Atlas Network
- Global Development Network
- Global policy networks: forms and emergence
- The proliferation and expansion of global think tanks
- The emergence of regional think tank hubs
- Achieving success: individual cases
- Outlooks for the future
- Current trends in global think tank research

The purpose of this chapter is to introduce and explore global think tanks and policy networks in detail. Specifically, this chapter explores the origins and emergence of both global think tanks and policy networks. In particular, attention is placed on the various stimuli and underlying foundations that have enabled the rise of these entities. Brief discussions on the past and current challenges facing both transnational think tanks and policy networks, as well as what the future holds for both, are included, although the Chapter 4 will explore those areas in much more detail. A small number of select individual cases that have been quite successful are included as a point of reference.

The idea of Global Public Goods (GPGs) is emerging on the international agenda with an increased recognition of and attention to cross-border social problems among policymakers, civil society actors, and the public. GPGs are nonexcludable (everyone can use them), nonrival (impossible to be depleted from overuse), and have benefits that transcend population, time and political barriers. Knowledge has been used by Joseph Stiglitz as an example of a GPG.[1] GPGs have increased drastically as issues that were typically of national concern have now grown too big for any one nation to handle by itself. Most public goods, according to Kaul et al., suffer from under provision, as individual actors deem it in their best interest to enjoy the free benefits of letting others deal with the problem.[2] This phenomenon is known as the "free rider" problem. It occurs when consumers benefit from public goods without contributing to their production. It is a result of selfish, individualistic thinking. An example would be the climate crisis, such as how some countries may not partake in emission cutting programs even though they benefit from other countries doing so and cutting worldwide CO_2 levels.[3] The United Nations Development Program described the challenges of facing this phenomenon: "Sometimes a good may be lacking. Instead of peace, conflict and war may prevail, ravaging people's lives. And sometimes a good may exist but be shaped in such a way that it entails costs for some people or countries while benefiting others. For example, procedures for managing international financial crises have at times placed a heavier burden on borrowers than on lenders. So, it is not only the level at which goods are provided that may affect people's lives: the way in which they are provided matters too."[4]

Think tanks and policy networks aim to find solutions to these "externalities" that arise from GPGs, searching for feasible policy options that serve to limit the effects of self-interested, nationalist thought. Globalization and the expansion of the global marketplace of ideas as well as a rapid increase in information technology have catalyzed the growth of global policy networks, global think tanks, and global think tank policy networks (essentially a combination of the two) as a new form of public discourse, authority, and intellectual exchange.[5]

Origins and emergence of policy networks in policymaking

Within this explosion of international organizations and institutions in today's global public sphere, networks are garnering increased attention from scholars and even non-academics. Their ability to realize social goals in particular makes them universally attractive.[6] Given the flow of services and capital globally, global public policy networks have not only become possible but also desirable due to their role as social mechanisms that can work across social, governmental, and geographical boundaries. In this sense, policy networks can build bridges that bring together a diverse range of actors, including governments, businesses, and civil society. These policy networks are not simply networks among already-established institutions such as think tanks; they often exist as structurally-independent entities as well. This section follows the development of networks—of both forms—in policymaking.

With regard to their origins, policy networks experienced rapid proliferation and growth during the 1990s. As the Cold War ended and globalization began, it became exceedingly obvious that there were issues that no single actor could or should resolve alone. Advancements in technology and communications have made network creation simple, thereby allowing policy networks to fill in the gaps and roles left vacant by governments. Similarly to think tanks, these networks began to encompass a wide variety of issues, not only in terms of research but also of structure; their focus is not limited to one area.

Globalization, then, greatly facilitated this proliferation of policy networks. Two specific factors in particular fueled their growth: increased political and economic liberalization and the technological revolution. Economic liberalization has expanded market and labor access across the world.[7] Increased political liberalization has allowed for the growth of civil society organizations, which, in turn, have created transnational relationships and connections. The technological revolution, initially confined to the private sector, soon reached the public sector in the form of a massive increase of global linkages and communication.

Within these emerging policy networks, tri-sector networks represent a unique divergence from that of a typical network. Typical networks generally fuse the civil society sector with the strong financial resources of businesses, as well as the enforcement and rule-making power of states and international organizations. A tri-sector network, however, consists of states, international organizations, civil society actors and the private sector, all of which collaborate in order to resolve issues that they would each be unable to do individually.[8] In this sense, transnational bridges are created, and, considering they can combine a varied number of groups and resources, think tanks are incredibly diversified. This diversity is the key element in enabling these networks to resolve these issues. Global policy networks, then, are unique in that they can manage and maintain such a varied range of actors.

Most policy networks have emerged during the past decade and, due to their diversity, flexibility, and ability to garner political attention and support, have established themselves as one of the social phenomena of our time. That being said, however, they are still comprised of dependent links on the already-established foundation and collection of individual civil society organizations, governments and international organizations. Thus, policy networks have yet to emerge as fully independent, particularly regarding funding. Currently, the member-funded model continues to rely on outside patronage. This outside patronage often involves financial support from international organizations such as the World Bank or the World Health Organization or big, private, international foundations such as the Ford Foundation and the Rockefeller Foundation. These private and public international donors are directly responsible, at least in part, for the rapid proliferation of policy networks within the past decade. Accordingly, these organizations form the backbone of the policy networks in that they provide funding, personnel, advisory services and other resources in order to promote collective action responses.[9]

The fundamental goals of policy networks, then, are multi-layered. Policy networks operate with the drive to push new issues into the public sphere and ultimately on the global agenda while assisting in the construction and implementation of global standards. Specifically, they work towards incorporating all parties that have a vested interest in a particular issue, promote transparency and adopt a tri-sector model while placing time restrictions in order to encourage agreement and avoid a gridlock. Policy networks also aim to accumulate and disperse knowledge and are well assisted in this venture by overall advancements technology and communication methods, which allow them to easily acquire and disseminate vast amounts of knowledge to ever-expanding audiences.

Given the growing ability to access and disperse knowledge to expanding audiences, policy networks have permeated all sectors of society and reached all levels of scope. Domestic policy networks comprise of clusters of actors focused on an issue that is purely limited to the domestic sphere and often unique to the individual area. They can also be regional in scope and commonly found in areas where they can link political parties and social movements into an advocacy function, such as in Latin America. Founded in 2010, the Latin America Initiative for Research on Public Policies is comprised of 12 think tanks across Central and South America. Its goal is for Latin American societies to achieve true economic, social, political, and institutional sustainable development.[10] Regional networks are also particularly adept at addressing specific regional policy issues such as democratic transformation or economic growth. By limiting themselves to a more appropriate scope, these regional policy networks may perhaps be more effective than the global ones depending on the subject, issue or function addressed. This may be because they have greater first-hand knowledge and experience with these elements and can sustain a perception of being intricately tied to and invested in the issue—something that a global network may not be able to do.

Global public policy networks operate between and above nation-states. They are "alliances of government agencies, international organizations, corporations and elements of civil society that join together to achieve what none can accomplish alone … and give once ignored groups a greater voice in international decision making."[11]

Differences in structure and overall scope among policy networks highlight the various types of networks as defined by their function. Their function illuminates different trends in policy networks' modes and methods of impact on global policy. These broad groups of policy networks are defined by their function as transnational advocacy networks, transnational executive networks, knowledge networks or epistemic communities, and issues networks. Each of these five types of global policy networks will now be examined more closely.

Transnational advocacy network

A transnational advocacy network incorporates relevant actors working internationally on a particular issue. They are called advocacy networks because "advocates plead the causes of others or defend a cause or proposition."[12] These actors are bound by a shared set of values, a common discourse and intense exchanges of information and services. Accordingly, in attempts to further a common goal, information is exchanged rather than produced. In this sense, networks function as a form of assembly. As civil society organizations, networks are a potential means for civic engagement and an effective device for expanding participation. In addition to their advocacy function, they can provide dialogue/information-sharing and liaison functions. They can also provide training and education for their members with the inherent goal of increasing the capacity for advocacy work. Above all, the primary objective of a transnational advocacy network is to raise global consciousness. As such, they are usually comprised of civil society groups and states that combine forces to lobby intergovernmental organizations, other states, and the private sector. The media is often employed to draw public attention to their cause, and advocacy networks will often phrase their missions as morally superior, thereby rendering most opposition ineffective. However, transnational advocacy networks are generally not well integrated into policymaking and tend to operate more like "outsider groups."[13] Examples of such networks include the International Campaign to Ban Landmines, the International Federation for Human Rights and Amnesty International.

Transnational executive networks

Transnational executive networks are networks of government officials, ranging from policy investigators to financial regulators to legislators and judges. Their primary goal is to expand regulatory reach, thereby allowing national government officials to keep abreast of corporations and civic organizations.[14] These networks perform information-sharing, dialogue and liaison functions with members within as well as outside actors, particularly professionals. The executive networking function can often be observed in the structural form of both a think tank network and a structurally-independent public policy network. Examples of such are the International Association of Insurance Supervisors or the Center for Financial Studies, both of which are think tanks that have associated professional networks of individuals.

Knowledge networks or epistemic communities

Knowledge networks or epistemic communities are networks that bring together policy actors who have a shared set of norms and seek change in specific areas of policy. These networks contribute heavily to the diversity, shape and equality of the global marketplace of ideas. Unlike the other network types that are directly political and policy-oriented, knowledge networks invest strongly in the dialogue and information-sharing function. In accordance with their name, these networks focus primarily on knowledge creation and dissemination, often promoting research based on a specific political theme. An example of an epistemic community or knowledge network is the Centre for European Reform (CER), which will be further discussed in this chapter.

Issues networks

Issue networks are a unique case of policy networks. They arise not as permanent fixtures but in response to a specific, urgent issue. The exact nature of the issue varies widely; issues could be as small as a local educational campaign or as large as issue networks that arise on a global scale, which tend to include grass-roots actors. They are thereby inherently multi-sectoral in order to provide for a stronger foundation for action and advocacy.

It is important to note that the agendas of global think tanks and global policy networks have developed in conjunction with globalization, shifting to exhibit an international focus and an emphasis on "trans-border policy problems."[15] Think tank research is increasingly available and accessible digitally, due largely to the advances in communication technology, such as social media, and the increasingly ambitious goal of think tanks to reach a worldwide audience.

Networking among think tanks

When discussing global think tanks, the idea of a "networking phenomenon" emerges. Two distinct but interrelated trends are inherent within this phenomenon: think tank networking and the development of structurally-independent public policy networks.

Undoubtedly, globalization and improvements in communications technologies facilitate networking. Social media platforms such as Facebook, Twitter and Instagram enable greater international collaboration and dissemination of information. At least in principle, it is quite possible for policy research organizations to disseminate their work globally with very limited resources. International consortia of like-minded think tanks have appeared to share ideas and promote subsequent adoption in policy sectors. In the first edition of this book, we noted that the growth of cyber communications had made it much more difficult for authoritarian governments to restrict the inflow of information and opinion from cyberspace. However, with the increase in internet monitoring in countries such as China, this is perhaps not as true as it once was.

Another aspect of the current international landscape is the expansion of policy problems beyond borders. Conflicts and problems are no longer confined to specific physical borders. Terrorist threats, natural disasters and health epidemics require coordinated and rapid policy responses across countries. Financial and environmental regulation requires thoughtful planning and policy design that incorporate actors regardless of physical borders or functions. Policy networks can link institutions and governments together irrespective of physical distance, thereby facilitating policy design and implementation.

The increased need for multi-sectoral participation in the policy process is yet another driver of the networking phenomenon. As policy problems become more complex, especially on a global scale, the body of essential actors expands from governments and think tanks to include universities, international organizations, nonprofits and other civil society organizations, political parties, social movements and even corporations and the private sector. In a dynamic global environment, formal government institutions such as the United Nations simply cannot fulfill all the social responsibilities placed upon them. Civil society organizations, private actors, and businesses must work in partnership with public actors to enable states and international organizations to meet their goals.

Networking has established itself as an appropriate tool for aggregating the input and resources of these disparate actors. Think tanks can increase the importance and accuracy of their policy analysis by incorporating geographically, ideologically and functionally disparate actors into their researcher, member and partner networks. Structurally independent public policy networks are a collective, rather than think tank-driven, response to the need for multi-sectoral contributions to the policy process.

As new and different think tanks crop up in every region around the globe, these think tanks need a means of coordinating functions and sharing information in order to intensify policy impact and increase operational efficiency in the policy arena. Think tank partner networks address both issues, providing a means for think tanks to gain and share information and to pool resources for a particular policy agenda. Structurally independent public policy networks can also arise as a result of think tank proliferation, connecting independent think tanks on a level playing field through an independent coordinating body.

As think tanks establish local centers in areas with new forms of policymaking and new civil society norms, they must quickly accustom themselves to the environment and make connections in order to function efficiently and attain policy impact. Think tank networks are a natural means of an institution's integration into a new policymaking environment and civil society. As think tanks reach out for locally-based researchers, members, and partners, they increase their local information-gathering functionality, gain access to new policy perspectives, gain new local resources, and increase legitimacy in the new policymaking environment.

Global think tanks: context and structure

Global think tanks tend to be context-specific and aim to have an impact on policy in specific countries. Based on a critical analysis of the previous literature, a global think tank is one that establishes operational centers, field offices or outreach centers outside the country of its headquarters. Additionally, a think tank can qualify itself as global if it establishes one of the three forms of think tank networks (research, member or partner), with the qualification that the networked researchers, members or partners are outside the country of its headquarters.

Global think tank networks, which emerged over the past two decades as a particular form of think tank globalization, have become one of the most prominent social phenomena of our time. The distinction between global policy networks and think tank networks lies in the characteristics of their members and in the similarity of their members' policy positions. First, we assert that a policy network differs from a think tank network in that think tanks are not the only type of actor. Think tank networks are composed only of research institutes and policy centers that share similar organizational structure and general objectives. Raymond Struyk extends this distinction between a think tank network and a policy network to observe functional differences; he asserts that policy networks are primarily created to mediate among members with differing interests, while think tank networks typically are composed of research organizations with a shared perspective in order to pursue similar research goals. An example of such a network is The Global Development Network (GDN), which, composed of various policy and research institutions, aims to promote "the generation, sharing, and application to policy of multidisciplinary knowledge for the purpose of development."[16] The emergence of think tank networks across the globe occurred alongside a development in regional think tank cooperation as well. For example, Southern Voice, established in 2012, focuses on the Sustainable Development Goals of the UN and is comprised of think tanks across Latin America, Africa and Asia.[17]

Raymond Struyk also divides think tank networks based on four classifying criteria: objective or primary goal, incentives for participation, basis for membership, and network coherence.[18] Struyk defines network coherence as the extent to which policies creating working relationships and a shared sense of community are implemented by the networks. Although policy networks tend to experience greater problems of network coherence due to their more volatile nature, think tank networks remain subject to the same considerations. More specifically, Struyk suggests that coherence may be much greater in networks where members meet on a consistent basis, participation is relatively stable and the agenda is of genuine interest to the members.[19] Incentives for participation are of particular importance because they share a correlation with the think tank's visibility. Strong participation incentives among knowledge networks lead to more submissions and contributions, thereby increasing overall visibility and credibility within think tank and public policy communities.

The role and utility of think tank networks

It is evident from an examination of the Atlas Network, formerly known as the Atlas Economic Research Foundation, and GDN that these networks are integral entities that can serve a variety of roles for think tanks. Through an overview of each organization's mission, organizational and funding structures, activities, publications, and affiliations, it may be assessed that these networks act to: (1) enhance the financial stability of their affiliated think tanks; (2) increase these think tanks' ability to disseminate their research and policy prescriptions; (3) provide organizational and managerial advice; and (4) facilitate information exchange and thus advance these think tanks' and the actual network's mission. It is through these four common services that networks can act to strengthen the capacity of their members.

Financial support

Whereas think tanks that operate in isolation may often confront difficulties in raising funds, diversifying their donor base or retaining financial contributors over the long-term, networks, such as those listed above, can act to increase the abilities of their affiliated think tanks to locate funding opportunities, maintain their donors and diversify the character of their contributors. For instance, the Atlas Network includes within its guiding priorities the objectives, "to develop and support [intellectual entrepreneurs] in the establishment and growth of organizations with the potential to advance [Atlas'] mission" and "to alert institutes about potential funding opportunities."[20] Additionally, Atlas commits financial resources that are long-term in nature to new and innovative institutes and programs in order to encourage their development, and it subsequently monitors these organizations and programs in order to safeguard their success.

GDN also serves to enhance the financial stability of its regional affiliates and partner organizations by opening these institutes to a large funding base. Specifically, it currently receives financial support from a variety of different types of donors. Governments comprise the bulk of GDN's funding, providing 45 percent of the network's revenue source. Strategic Institutional Partnerships and Multilateral Agencies contribute 29 percent and 14 percent of the funding, respectively. Foundations and other types of income provide the remaining 12 percent of the Network's revenue. These sources of revenue are including but not limited to, the World Bank, the International Monetary Fund (IMF), USAID, the United Kingdom Department for International Development, the Swiss Agency for Development and Cooperation, the Sweden Ministry of Foreign Affairs, the Department for Global Development, and the Japan Ministry of Finance. Consequently, while their affiliated think tanks may be confronted with funding challenges on their own, their involvement in GDN increases their financial capacity.

Increasing dissemination

Networks can prove highly effective in increasing the dissemination capacity and reach of their partnered think tanks by providing these institutions with a broader audience. In addition, networks often possess regional and international recognition, and, as a result, the prestige of affiliated think tanks may also increase. With regard to the former, the four networks examined all evidenced a commitment to disseminating research findings and policy prescriptions on a consistent basis and to a broad audience, as well as a commitment to engaging state, regional and international civil society through their activities and reports.

In this regard, the Atlas Network positions dissemination as a key element of its overarching objectives by stating that it is necessary, "to support the dissemination of our work to current and potential opinion leaders." Formerly called *Highlights*, *Freedom's Champion* is the Network's quarterly journal used to publish the findings of its think tanks and disseminate these findings to a wider audience. Atlas believes that "building independent think tanks that can produce and disseminate credible and principled research is the best way to affect a long-term change in the climate of ideas," and its network priorities reflect this sentiment.

The GDN evidences a similar goal. Developed in December 1999, the Network seeks to "improve development outcomes and livelihoods through high-quality, policy-oriented research in the social sciences, produced in developing countries and connected globally."[21] In order to do this, the organization works to "support researchers with financial resources, global networking, as well as access to information, training, peer review and mentoring." To this end, it maintains a dedication to publicizing the research and policy advice of state think tanks on a regional and global level through an online database (GDNet) of scholarly reports and think tank publications. In addition, it notes as one of its primary objectives to make "a world in which evidence and scholarly knowledge inform and inspire development and policy decisions."[22] Combined, these aims serve to increase the ability of its partnered think tanks to disseminate their research to an external audience as well as to court the attention of state policy-making communities.

Organizational and managerial advice

One of the principal capacity building values provided by networks is their ability to support and sustain the think tanks they are affiliated with by providing organizational guidance. This aim is reflected in the publications and objectives of three of the four networks examined. Specifically, the Atlas Network works to "discover, develop and support intellectual entrepreneurs worldwide who have the potential to create independent public policy institutes and related programs, which advance our vision; and to provide ongoing support as such institutes and programs mature."[23] Consequently, committing resources to emerging think tanks and monitoring their development is a key activity of the Network. To this end, Atlas offers advisement to "young think tanks and institutes," hosts workshops and networking events, administers prize programs and undertakes projects to bring more resources to local institutes.

Similarly, the GDN adheres to a non-hierarchical organizational structure which enables the Network to coordinate and support the efforts of its multiple institutions and promotes information sharing in order to offer a more conducive framework for think tank development. Through these efforts, GDN seeks to build the research capacity of its think tanks and, by strengthening these institutions, solidify the mission and international position of the Network.

Information sharing

A final service provided by networks is their ability to facilitate information sharing between and among their partnered think tanks. In that a primary goal of think tanks is to produce research and analysis that is succinct, timely, accurate, and relevant to policymakers and the public, the ability of networks to provide for information exchange increases their value. Toward this end, the four networks examined for this review all position information sharing as a central objective in their effort to produce and disseminate credible and valuable policy advice.

The GDN aims to properly inform institutes and disseminate information to a wide range of organizations through publications and conferences. Operating in accordance with its motto, "Local Research for Better Lives," the Network aims to "facilitate knowledge sharing among researchers and policymakers" and "promote multidisciplinary collaboration." This is pursued through its three categories of partnerships—regional network partners, partner institutes, and donors—all of which collaborate on research projects and activities and thereby increase communication between and among various think tanks and financial contributors. In addition, GDN seeks to involve policymakers in these activities as well as provide a resource of scholarly reports and affiliated articles through its website and blog.

It is evident from an examination of the Atlas Network and GDN that these organizations play an integral role in enhancing the funding and organizational capacity of think tanks, increasing these institutes' national, regional, and international prestige, and contributing to a more informed policy dialogue. Consequently, it may arguably be affirmed that networks can serve to strengthen the capacity of their think tank members.

Atlas Network

Mission

The Atlas Network is guided by an overarching mission to increase "opportunity and prosperity by strengthening a global network of independent civil society organizations that promote individual freedom and remove barriers to human flourishing." The organization works to achieve this mission by implementing programs within its "Coach, Compete, Celebrate" strategic model. This model of "coaching through training programs, fostering friendly competition via grants and awards, and then celebrating partners' achievements at our world-class events" is meant to foster innovation and efficiency in promoting the freedom movement.[24]

Structure and personnel

Located in Arlington, Virginia, the Atlas Network was established in 1981 by Sir Anthony Fisher for the purpose of enhancing the level of public policy debate by providing credible and timely research and analysis, and in so doing increasing the number of "intellectual entrepreneurs" in civil society. After 30 years of discovering, developing, and supporting intellectual entrepreneurs worldwide, the Atlas Economic Research Foundation rebranded as the Atlas Network. In pursuit of its goals, the Network has adopted a strategic model consisting of Coaching, Competing and Celebrating individuals and organizations. Through the Atlas Leadership Academy, the Network offers credit-based courses to *coach* and improve basic managerial and communication skills. In 2017 alone, Atlas trained nearly 1,000 individuals in skills that will transfer to the development of their think tanks. The Network awards grants and prizes to organizations that *compete* in a competitive selection process to earn funding. Over five million dollars was awarded to a variety of organizations in 2017. The events organized by the Network are aimed to *celebrate* excellence and connect the different think tanks in the Atlas Network. Atlas uses its staff—which totals about 30 individuals who have played many roles and have had years of experience within the think tank movement—to direct their research and guide their efforts.[25]

Target audiences and political and ideological orientation

The target audience of the Atlas Network includes academics, state, regional and global think tanks, policymakers, the public, and the media. The Atlas Network considers itself nonpartisan and independent and seeks to secure the legitimacy of this characterization by refusing to accept or recruit government funding. Atlas describes itself as pro-free enterprise and is often cited as a libertarian network.[26, 27, 28]

Research priorities

In addition to assisting and working with independent think tanks, the Atlas Network also seeks to involve academics in their effort to improve public understanding of the causes and consequences of freedom. One such effort, termed the Atlas Leadership Academy, aims to educate individuals in the field in management, communication, and funding. Alumni of the Academy are able to receive special opportunities, including participation in Atlas' Think Tank Shark Tank, which awards a $25,000 project grant to the winner.[29]

Key activities

The Atlas Network works to commit resources to new and innovative institutes and programs and monitor these investments (which are long-term in nature) in order to improve their chances of success. In addition, the Network offers advisement to young think tanks and institutes, hosts workshops and networking events, administers prize programs, and undertakes special projects to bring more resources to local institutes. These objectives are primarily achieved through the Atlas Leadership Academy

Publications

Atlas publishes *Freedom's Champion* quarterly, which, when including the active years of its predecessor *Highlights*, is the longest-running newsletter dedicated to examining developments among the international network of market-oriented think tanks. In addition, the Network publishes a newsletter titled *World10*, which features "the top ten happenings around the world in the global freedom movement, showcasing the work of Atlas Network partners." Atlas also provides a variety of tools, such as Roadmaps (publications to help advance individual professional development) and online information-sharing tools including a Global Directory (which includes over 500 think tanks that are like-minded in their dedication to the values of a free society), a calendar of events and archives of every *Freedom's Champion* and *Highlights* quarterly. These are offered as a convenient way for people to access information about global networks.[30]

Formal and informal affiliations

To build a stronger freedom movement, Atlas Network helps existing partners; launches new efforts; and fosters collaboration.[31] In keeping with this sentiment, Atlas not only funds but also partners informally with nearly 500 tanks worldwide, including the American Enterprise Institute, the Cato Institute, the Competitive Enterprise Institute, the Fraser Institute, The Heritage Foundation, the Hayek Institute in Austria, the Manhattan Institute, and Libertad y Desarrollo in Chile, among others. Atlas believes that "the strengths of our partners have created some of the world's greatest improvements in freedom."[32]

Funding

In order to maintain their independent posture, Atlas does not seek or accept government funding. The Network's programs and expenditures are funded, primarily, by voluntary contributions from foundations, individuals, and corporations. In addition, a smaller portion of their revenue is generated from conference registration fees and the sale of publications and videos. Atlas is a nonprofit, tax-exempt educational foundation under Section 501 (c) 3 of the Internal Revenue Code; it does not have an endowment, and maintains reserves that are adequate to operate the organization for six- to twelve-month periods.[33]

Governance

While over a thousand individuals participate in the Atlas Network through the various think tanks and organizations that partner with it, there are only 30 individuals who work specifically for the Atlas Network. About 30 benefactors comprise the Network's Advisory Council, which is "a community of global leaders in entrepreneurship, business, investment, academics, and philanthropy" aimed at advising and guiding the Network. Its Council of Mentors is a group of 23 experts in nonprofit management and free-market policy reform, who are generous in helping Atlas Network's partners. The Network is guided by 14 board members, who share the Network's values of enhancing the freedom movement.[34]

Social media

Since the emergence of social media in the early to mid-2000s, the Network has capitalized on new forms of communication to share news, events, videos, and more. As of spring 2019, Atlas has amassed over 12,000 followers on Twitter, nearly 3,000 YouTube subscribers, and over 60,000 followers on Facebook.[3536] The Network uses these platforms to promote its own programs such as training courses and webinars. It also shares its research articles and findings on these sites to reach a larger audience.

Global Development Network

Mission

GDN is a worldwide network of research and policy institutes working to provide a fresh and relevant perspective on current development challenges. The Network believes in "a world in which evidence and scholarly knowledge inform and inspire development and policy decisions."[37] As a result, GDN aims to generate research at a local level by connecting local research institutions and providing financial and networking resources in developing and transitional countries.[38] In 2001, GDN became an independent unit with the goal to "improve development outcomes and livelihoods through high-quality, policy-oriented research in the social sciences, produced in developing countries and connected globally."[39] To achieve this aim, the Network lays out a three-pronged strategy: (1) strengthening research in low-capacity environments through funding; (2) joining hands for global excellence to promote the advancement of research around the world; and (3) putting development research to better use by connecting research advisors to policymakers in government. Through connecting and aiding research institutes in developing countries, GDN hopes to achieve its goal by facilitating and advocating policy advice from the bottom up.[40]

Structure and governance

In December 1999, GDN was established as a subsidiary of the World Bank to aid in international economic development. After becoming independent in 2001, it created its own chain of command of policy advisors and academics to help with research efforts. François Bourguignon, former Chief Economist of the World Bank and Emeritus Professor of the Paris School of Economics, heads the GDN Board of Directors. This Board, which consists of 15 members and a Vice-Chair, meets twice a year and "remains the driving force behind GDN by developing and directing policy decisions at the Network."[41] The board members are representative of all regions of the world as well as various social science backgrounds. In addition, GDN also consists of a general assembly comprised of various ambassadors from other countries, as well as staff members from advisors of the Indian government.[42] The structure of the organization is non-hierarchical and, as a result, enables the Network to efficiently coordinate the efforts of multiple institutions. Within the Washington, DC office itself, GDN houses only a few staff members; however, its nine regional partners link the Network to hundreds of researchers around the world. GDN's main office and a majority of its staff is currently located in New Delhi, India.

Target audiences and research priorities

In its effort to alleviate poverty and aid in global development, GDN seeks to influence and disseminate its research and policy prescriptions to academics, think tank scholars, the think tank community, funders, and policymakers. GDN aims to: (1) raise awareness about evidence and research-based analytical work with various stakeholder groups; (2) stream local academic research as a unique way to provide both evidence and robust methods of analysis; (3) explore various options in a sound analytical and critical way and shape policy judgment; and (4) raise the voice of developing-country researchers in the global debate to successfully address global challenges and sustainable development goals.[43]

Key activities

To achieve its vision, the Network maintains multiple programs dedicated to expanding developmental policy research. Four of these programs include: (1) Annual Global Development Conferences, which the organization has hosted since 1999, gathering researchers and political leaders to interact and discuss a common platform for global development; (2) Doing Research, a program which partners various research institutions in developing countries and linking access to social science research systems; (3) the Global Development Awards and Medals Competition, which represents the largest international annual conference for researchers on issues of development; and (4) the newly-formed Applied Development Finance Program, which partnered GDN with the European Investment Bank to study the impact of developmental aid and project investment around the world.[44]

Publications

GDN utilizes the internet as its primary means of information dissemination, distributing its research through its website and its blog, GlobalDev. In this manner, GDN is able to enhance communication and research dissemination as well as support between and among regional institutes, partners, organizations, and the broader global community. Its most prominent research topics include aid effectiveness in Sub-Saharan Africa, natural resource management, governance and public service delivery, and public finance and expenditure management.[45]

Formal and informal affiliations

The partners of GDN primarily fall into three categories—Funding Partners, Knowledge Partners, and Policy Stakeholder Partners. Policy Stakeholder Partners serve to implement GDN programs and activities in their local areas, connect the numerous research institutions affiliated with each partner to the network, and facilitate contact with policymakers. They include organizations such as the African Economic Research Consortium, the Economic Research Forum (Middle East and

North Africa), the Center for Economic Research and Graduate Education-Economics Institution (Eastern and Central Europe), the Economics Education and Research Consortium (Russia and CIS), the East Asian Development Network, the South Asia Network for Economic Research Institutes, the Latin American and Caribbean Economic Association, and the Oceania Development Network. Its partner institutions collaborate with GDN to "support high-quality, policy-oriented social science research in developing countries."[46] These include the Institute of Development Studies, the IMF, the Institute for the Relations between Italy and Africa, Latin America and the Middle East, Merck & Co, One World, and the National Institutes of Health Competition on Health, Economics, and Health Finance in Developing Countries, among others. Knowledge Partners include various other think tanks and educational institutions such as the Central European University, Peking University, Tulane University, Results of Development Institute and TTI. As of 2018, GDN has supported more than 4,000 researchers and grantees from around 140 developing and transition countries.[47]

Funding

Governments compile the bulk of GDN's funding, providing 45 percent of the network's revenue source. Strategic Institutional Partnerships and Multilateral Agencies contribute 29 percent and 14 percent of the funding, respectively. Foundations and other types of income provide the remaining 12 percent of the Network's revenue. Currently, GDN receives financial support from more than forty donors, including, but not limited to, the World Bank, the IMF, USAID, the European Investment Bank, IDRC, the Bill & Melinda Gates Foundation, Department for Global Development, and the Inter-American Development Bank. In 2017, GDN accrued more than $4 million from international donations and external funding.[48]

Social media

GDN also maintains a fairly strong social media following on Facebook, Twitter, YouTube, and LinkedIn. As of April 2018, it accumulated over 70,000 Facebook "likes," over 1,600 Twitter followers and nearly 1,000 LinkedIn followers. Primarily used to promote events and new research publications, GDN used online social media to advocate for new policy initiatives and programs.

Global policy networks: forms and emergence

The phenomena of global policy networks and global think tanks, particularly with the advent of global think tank networks, are often hard to distinguish from one another. The literature offers a variety of definitions and frameworks in order to pinpoint the differences and classify these institutions by function and scope. The best definition of a policy network (rather than typology or classification system) offered by the literature is "a conceptual category to describe coordinated patterns of interaction to inform or make policy at local, national and transnational levels."[49] This definition identifies a policy network by its function, not form. Other literature introduces classification systems for policy networks. Policy networks can be categorized based on the different actors among which the network mediates: Global Public Policy Networks, Transnational Advocacy Networks, Transnational Executive Networks, and Knowledge Networks and Epistemic Communities.[50] Specifically, we identify global policy networks as structurally independent public policy networks whose constituents are based in international locales and whose functions are oriented toward global policy issues.

Policy networks can take many different forms and include many different constituents for the international dissemination of ideas. They operate on the fundamental principle that cooperation among a diverse group of actors is necessary for an effective resolution to the issue at hand. No single group or actor can address the problem alone. The best ones often aim to be trisectoral by bringing together actors from government, civil society, and private sector partnerships.[51] Thus, as political, social, and economic activity is diffused among actors in both the public and private sectors, policy networks are becoming increasingly important in the area of policy formulation and implementation due to their ability to convene and mediate among actors from multiple sectors. As such, "multi-sectoral networks are able to reflect the changing roles and relative importance of each of the actors involved in combining their resources to solve a particular problem."[52]

Policy networks "serve to enhance the quality of research by enabling greater interdisciplinary and cross-sectoral collaboration." Not only do they help "build the skills of individual researchers, but whole professions within a region," but policy networks can also "broaden policy horizons by introducing new concepts, approaches or 'ways of thinking' into research and policy fora."[53] According to Witte et al., the goals of policy networks consist of: (1) placing new issues on the global agenda (e.g. advocacy networks); (2) facilitating the negotiation and settlement of global standards (working with all parties to reach a compromise solution); (3) gathering and disseminating knowledge; (4) making new markets where they are lacking and deepening markets that are failing to fulfill their potential (e.g. bridge the gap between supply and demand); and, lastly, (5) to act as innovative implementation mechanisms. The first goal of bringing attention to neglected issues is one all kinds of networks attempt to do, especially advocacy networks. These networks attempt this by phrasing their message in a way that has maximum impact (such as naming an organization the International Campaign to Ban Landmines), as well as by using the media and influential sources. The second goal of facilitation and negotiation in order to reach a fair and equitable compromise necessitates the involvement of representatives from all sectors of the issue at hand. The World Commission on Dams (WCD) is an example of how including all stakeholders, building trust and consensus, allowing for considerable transparency and setting a time limit for agreement all combine to form a successful coalition and solution. The third goal is one that some networks make their primary objective. Because of the recent explosion in communication technology, gathering information and knowledge from all relevant sectors of society is easy and fast, allowing easy contact between entities working on a similar issue. In pursuit of the fourth goal, many policy networks attempt to achieve their objective by creating an economic incentive for it to be accomplished. For example, the Medicines for Malaria Venture (MMV) has tried to get pharmaceutical companies to have it be in their self-interest to produce vaccines for developing countries. Lastly, the fifth goal of some global public policy networks is to make certain that intergovernmental treaties are adhered to. An example of such action can be seen in the Global Environment Facility's (GEF) deeds when it restructured its organization by focusing less on the intergovernmental input and more on NGO input.

Policy networks combine the driving forces of globalization: economic and political liberalization as well as technological change. They do this in order to establish and support a particular agenda.[54] Given the dynamic environment in which they operate as well as the often-changing nature of the issues at stake, networks are able to update and evolve their structures in response to failures and successes.

The proliferation and expansion of global think tanks

Global think tanks (along with their think tank networks) amass an international constituency, utilizing scholars, experts, and other civil society actors from diverse fields and locations to pursue their institutional aims. The agendas of global think tanks have developed in time with globalization, shifting to exhibit an international focus and an emphasis on "trans-border policy problems". Think tank research is also increasingly available on the internet—a testament both to the advances in communication technology brought about by globalization and to the growing intent of think tanks to reach a worldwide audience.[55]

Another testament to globalization is the rapid proliferation of think tanks that the world has experienced over the past couple of decades. Between 1991 and 2000, the world saw an average of 124.8 think tanks established per year. This trend was observed most prominently in Africa, Eastern Europe, and the Middle East. It is important to note that since the turn of the century, there has been a dramatic decrease in the growth of think tanks, perhaps due to the fact that there are so many and the world has reached a "carrying capacity" for such organizations.[56] However, within the past decade, the spread of global think tanks has increased dramatically, with more think tanks around the world expanding their focus toward international affairs and wider economic development as opposed to solely domestic issues.

The rise of American think tanks, many of which have global reach, has certainly been influenced by the increasing demand for research-based information in Washington. More specifically, legislators and those who have the ability to influence policy can incorporate research-based information from an "outside" source with minimal cost in their beliefs regarding policy options and alternatives, thereby elevating their credibility.[57] The opportunity to affect legislative policy by becoming a sought-after source for research-based and evaluative information thus creates powerful incentives for the establishment and organization of think tanks. Since 1970, the number of think tanks in the United States has almost quadrupled and is expected to grow in the following decades. Perhaps corresponding with increasing partisanship and distrust among Washington policymakers, ideological think tanks became one of the most common types of think tanks to emerge in the 21st century.[58]

The emergence of regional think tank hubs

Table 3.1 set out the cities where the action is in the seven major regions of the world. Each city in the table contains a significant number of influential think tanks and has become a center in its respective region for policy discourse.

Achieving success: individual cases

Certain global think tanks lead the pack in terms of global expansion. The Carnegie Endowment for International Peace (CEIP) has dubbed itself as the United States' "first foreign policy think tank," opening its sixth office abroad in New Delhi in 2016.[59] This think tank is also exemplary in "internationalizing" the composition of its leadership by securing various well-known diplomats and policymakers around the world to specialize in certain global areas, including a new institute in the Middle East. The International Crisis Group (ICG), another global think tank addressing humanitarian crises, has regional offices in Bogota, Dakar,

TABLE 3.1 Regional think tank hubs

Region	Location
Asia	Sydney, Australia
	Kuala Lumpur, Malaysia
	Tokyo, Japan
	Singapore
Eastern Europe	Budapest, Hungary
	Kiev, Ukraine
	Warsaw, Poland
Western Europe	Brussels, Belgium
	Berlin, Germany
	London, United Kingdom
Latin America and the Caribbean	Buenos Aires, Argentina
Middle East and North Africa	Tel Aviv, Israel
	Istanbul, Turkey
East, West, and Southern Africa	Nairobi, Kenya
	Dakar, Senegal
	Cape Town, South Africa
North America	Washington, DC, United States

Islamabad, Istanbul, London, Nairobi, New York, and Washington, DC. ICG is notable for its expansion in the form of field offices, which serve as outsourcing bases from which to draw real-time data and knowledge abroad. Currently, it has field offices in over forty countries to monitor incoming signs of internal distress or conflict.[60]

Policy networks face many challenges as they try to achieve their goals, but there are certain networks that can serve as successful examples for other networks. The first of these success stories is the Global Call to Action Against Poverty (GCAP), a global coalition of community groups, trade unions, NGOs, individuals, faith groups, and campaigners from all over the world that raises awareness on the importance of the achievement of the Millennium Development Goals. Structurally, GCAP decided not to create many procedures and rules. Instead, it chose to allow decentralization and autonomy to its members. The network focused on small, localized campaigns with multiple civil society organizations formed into groups called National Coalitions. These coalitions are responsible for individual issues most relevant to their respective countries, while also tapping into larger global movements. Subsequently, GCAP has managed to become an actor with a loud voice that has reached high-level political spaces.[61] To promote funding for its members, GCAP provided promotional materials and global communication to its partners around the globe and also helped open the door to different sources of sponsorship. Being part of a global network helped participating members convince donors of their ability to have impact.[62]

The Fédération Internationale des droits de l'Homme, or the International Federation of Human Rights (FIDH) is another global network that can serve as a successful example to other networks. It is comprised of 182 organizations from 112 countries devoted to the advancement of human rights around the world.[63] It achieves its objectives by bringing together multiple organizations involving human rights, supporting networking and new research, and pursuing policies of advocacy work that will influence donors, statewide policymakers, and international corporations. Combined together, the organizations form a sort of Congress that dictates the policies of FIDH and bears the responsibility to develop and implement a program of initiatives to advocate at the international level. It is a movement for global change, combined with an elected international bureau and an international secretariat overseeing its operations. FIDH's leadership structure has proven highly effective, with the international secretariat based in France working in coordination with delegations from other supranational institutions such as those based in The Hague, as well as the European Union and the United Nations.[64]

Lastly, the CER is an epistemic community, or knowledge network, that is particularly successful at making its ideas relevant in a wider political context. The CER has greatly influenced the United Kingdom's views on European armaments and defense cooperation and has affected the UK's interests and desired role in Europe.[65] However, in recent years, the CER has re-focused its efforts on internal policies of the European Union and strengthened its role in the international community. Since the United Kingdom has voted to leave the European Union, the CER promoted the idea of European integration as a force for good, and researched ways in which the

European Union can be more accountable to its member states and safeguard Europe's collective security. Its research topics include European politics, economics and EU foreign relations with other states.[66]

Outlooks for the future

Globalization, the advancements in communication technology and the rise of social media, along with the spread of misinformation have all transformed the think tank sector and encouraged many to go global themselves in order to reach out to different sectors. The vast amounts of hybridization and model blending that are occurring have resulted in increasingly diversified organizations that incorporate a multitude of voices, perspectives, actors, and expertise. Furthermore, hybridized institutions and networks tend to behave like regulated organizations rather than extensions of administrative agencies under legislative control. Hybrid entities, given their private, informal and "delegated authority" status, are also intrinsically less responsive to the political preferences of their political masters and publics.[67]

Fortunately or unfortunately, globalization has also created truly global issues that require a unified, multilateral approach to resolve. Global think tanks, with their ability to function as international idea managers and brokers, find themselves in a prime position to affect policy. Simply put, policymakers cannot even begin to fully comprehend the vast amount of information that is available to them. In order to do so, they are increasingly relying on outside sources and entities to effectively and efficiently interpret and analyze that information avalanche and subsequently produce clear and comprehensible policy recommendations and solutions.

The globalization of think tanks has also inspired a necessary collaboration effort between think tanks. One example of this was the gathering of over a dozen think tanks "from Beijing to Brasilia" in a Global Leadership Consortium. These think tanks convened to discuss how think tanks could successfully globalize and collaborate to meet the "challenges facing humanity." The Global Leadership Consortium is intended "to serve as a learning and action network of solution-oriented leaders and their institutions to address the new reality that no single nation – and no single think tank – can be an effective problem-solver."[68] In addition, TTCSP has also held a number of global think tank summits in recent years. In 2018, it hosted 15 summits with its think tank partners, bringing together a wide range of established and think tanks around the world.[69] Its largest think tank summit to date, the 2018 Global Think Tank Summit brought together over 100 think tank executives and leaders in Brussels, Belgium, and the TTCSP's annual "Why Think Tanks Matter" movement consisted of over 330 events in 89 countries.

The real question is not whether global think tanks can assume positions of influence in affecting global policy. The answer is quite clear that they can. Instead, the true question is whether going global can become a truly widespread phenomenon and not just limited to a Euro/US-centric perspective. Given the intense competition on everything ranging from funding to idea management, the answer is not clear at this point.

Current trends in global think tank research

Since the beginning of the global physical expansion of think tanks worldwide, these institutions have gone global in a number of different ways. These differing launch methods have resulted in a considerable diversity of existing global think tanks. While these institutions are alike in their capacity for worldwide influence, they differ greatly in many areas, including structural organization, methods of operation, budgets, staff numbers, mission statements and goals, and research topics. Despite these differences, however, certain trends within global think tank research can be observed.

The existing global think tanks can be grouped according to a number of characteristics, but perhaps the most understandable is research focus. This categorization by research focus generally entails three main distinctions: single issue, multi-issue or distinctive. While these categorizations are somewhat broad and not all global think tanks fit squarely within one particular distinction, these three types can serve as a potential foundation for greater understanding in regard to global think tanks as catalysts for ideas and action. It is important to note that several "location" trends can be observed and applied to all three classification categories. Specifically, think tanks—regardless of where they are based or what their specific research focus may be—maintain a bias in their research toward their home country. Second, global think tank research is potentially, although certainly not always, affected by the organization's location.

The first categorization within global think tank research types are single issue think tanks. These organizations deliberately choose to specialize and focus their research on specific topics. Although these organizations typically fall into broader or more general research categories, such as economics, security, human rights, and civil society, there is considerable variance in the mission statements, outlooks, and goals of the individual institutions.

Multi-issue think tanks generally cover a wide range of topics, amassing a broad range of expertise on various issues but not concentrating specific or sole focus on any one of them. Such think tanks generally pursue regional research projects in addition to research regarding common and broad themes, either domestically or internationally. They also examine common fields including security, the environment and natural resources, economics, health, and poverty and development.[70] Examples include the Centre for Policy Studies (CPS) in the United Kingdom and the Brookings Institute and Roosevelt Institute in the United States, each of which lays out a general goal or ideology to focus its research.

Today, a considerable number of global think tanks can be designated as single-issue global think tanks. This simply means that these organizations focus their research around a certain broad topic instead of covering many different international issues. They tend to focus their research on one of seven main categories. Within these eight main research fields, global think tanks choose to specialize in different subcategories and often have contrasting research approaches and missions. The eight main research fields are: economics, security, peace building, human rights and civil society, sustainable development, the promotion of democracy, freedom and liberal values, and science.

The global think tanks that research economics all tend to have research divisions in the fields of globalization, international finance or macroeconomics, international trade, and investment and development. Economically oriented think tanks have also recently adopted sections devoted to the global economic crisis and the possible means to recover from it. Some, however, search for more practical solutions to economic problems and follow a rather pragmatic path of research. The Peterson Institute for International Economics (PIIE) is an example of a more classical approach to the study of economics. PIIE concentrates on international trade and investment, international finance and exchange rates, macroeconomic policy and crisis response, and globalization and human welfare, as well as current "hot topics" that relate directly to economic theory.[71] However, others look for innovative solutions in the field of economics and research areas that do not traditionally fall under the discipline of economics. The Kiel Institute for the World Economy is one such example, as, in addition to research on more traditional economic topics, it also investigates globalization and the environment, climate and energy, poverty reduction, equity and reforming the welfare society, and other issues pertaining to sustainable development around the world.[72]

Security-oriented single-issue think tanks tend to structure their research around two themes. First, these institutions have issue-based research that generally revolve around themes such as nonproliferation and disarmament, major power relations, counterterrorism and de-radicalization, conflict and defense. As a second layer of their research, security-based think tanks tend to have regional concentrations in certain areas, spanning Asia, the Middle East, Russia and Eurasia, South Asia, Europe, Africa, and the Americas. The International Institute for Strategic Studies (IISS), for example, provides regular reports on current international conflicts and terrorist campaigns while its defense analysis program focuses on rethinking military concepts, structures, and technologies based on current threats to global security. In addition, it also expanded its scope to include cyber security and energy security as technology in the fields progressed.[73]

Many of the peace-building single-issue think tanks follow the same general framework as those that are strictly security oriented. Peace-building think tanks have both theme-based research and regionally concentrated research. These themes are focused on: coping with and resolving crisis, peace and state building, and the responsibility to protect. Regional concentrations tend to be generally narrower and usually include Africa, Asia, and the Middle East. Meanwhile, single-issue think tanks that conduct their research in the field of human rights and civil society have a much more scattered set of research topics. While their areas of research are not always uniform, they are all related in that they choose their topics based upon pertinence to human rights.

Think tanks that focus on the topic of sustainable development often have similar goals as those that focus on human rights and civil society. Both groups tend to be focused on the promotion of social well-being, but think tanks in this particular category emphasize growth and progress initiatives rather than fighting social injustice. These organizations frequently focus on areas such as economic growth, climate change and environment, and inequality.

In a manner similar to the two previous subcategories, think tanks that concentrate their research around the promotion of democracy, freedom, and liberal values reflect common goals rather than common sub-areas of research. Although there are large degrees of variation, most tend to engage more heavily in advocacy and action than think tanks in other categories. As mentioned before, advocacy and issue-based think tanks are becoming increasingly influential in the United States. Some of these organizations conduct research with the aim of promoting and sustaining democracy, freedom, and liberal values where they currently have a strong backing and foundation, while others work towards spreading these values in areas where such norms are weak or nonexistent. Some do share certain characteristics with those in the economic subcategory in that they conduct research on promoting free market systems. Still others resemble human rights think tanks in that they focus on promoting social welfare. The fundamental goal of promoting democracy through advocacy and action is the key element that links these think tanks in this particular subcategory.

The think tanks that can be classified under science and technology are ones that aim to benefit society as a whole through the use of scientific knowledge. These organizations hope to solve the grand challenges faced by society, science, and industry through developing technological innovations. They generally aim to promote economic development and industry while still considering social welfare and the environment. The Helmholtz-Gemeinschaft in Germany is one such example in that it strives to improve human life by working on the challenges faced by society in the fields of science and industry. It works toward innovative technological developments in order to provide for the future. These types of think tanks can also be exclusive, elite, and closed to deliberative decision-making. For instance, the discourse and techno-scientific language as well as professional credentials of those within these knowledge networks can act as "gatekeepers" that block entry to the network.[74]

The majority of today's global think tanks choose not to specialize in one single field, but, rather, cover a large number of different topics in their research. Such organizations frequently divide their research into two sections. First, these organizations usually have regional projects in which they study the problems faced by high profile regions in the world today. Second, the multi-issue global think tanks have research groups devoted to a number of broad topics with a global reach. These topics roughly coincide with the research done by single-issue global think tanks.

Although each multi-issue global think tank may conduct research in different locations depending on where the think tank itself is located—think tanks tend to do more research in their own region—there is a common set of regions that tend to be researched in some capacity by all of these organizations. These regions coincide closely with the areas studied by security-oriented, single-issue think tanks and include the Middle East and North Africa, Russia and Eurasia, the Americas, Africa, South Asia, and Europe.

Furthermore, the broad topics covered by researchers at multi-issue global think tanks are very similar to the eight main research topics covered by single-issue global think tanks. In addition to studying the fields of economics, security, peace building, human rights and civil society, sustainable development, the promotion of democracy, freedom and liberal values, and science, multi-issue think tanks frequently cover topics such as the environment and natural resources, health, and poverty and development. It is important to note that, although multi-issue and single-issue think tanks will often overlap in research focus, multi-issue think tanks sport full-fledged, well-funded and distinct programs, whereas a single-issue think tank will focus most, if not all, resources into a particular broad subject area.

A small portion of today's global think tanks do not fit into the single-topic or multi-topic research categories because the work that they do is in some way unique or innovative. They tend to be innovative and multi-disciplinary and, as such, defy being categorized into traditional disciplinary, functional, or geographic groupings. These think tanks either have unique research topics included in their overall output or take an uncommon approach to their research in general.

Lastly, two overarching location trends can apply to all three of the research categories that are defined above. These two trends, which we will call "home country bias" and "geographically determined focus," may seem rather obvious and similar but are in fact two distinct entities that require explanation. The former refers to the idea that, regardless of its research focus, a think tank will be biased in its research toward its "home country"—the country where it was established and generally has headquarters. The latter trend refers to the idea that, in many but not all cases, a think tank's location determines the focus of its research in general.

When global think tanks have a "home country bias"—and most of the organizations do—it means simply that, while their research is global, there is a greater emphasis on certain fields of research as they relate to the home country. The intensity of this bias ranges. Some global think tanks conduct the entirety of their research on how global trends affect their country or region. For example, various foreign policy think tanks in Canada have been criticized for hiring only Canadian experts and producing research only pertinent to its interests.[75] Others may have certain research areas that are truly global and unbiased but also have topics devoted to their home country. It is important to note that this trend is not to be considered in a negative light, as it is natural and does not diminish the research done by such institutions.

The geographically determined focus trend is one that does appear with some consistency but is not universal. This trend suggests that many think tanks are affected by their location at a deeper level than simply having a research bias toward their home country. In this sense, it is possible that the location of a think tank is a key determinant in the overall focus of its research. This trend seems natural when broken down: think tanks are created to research and help solve the specific problems facing that area, and so, when these think tanks become global, they maintain a research focus in their original field.

The breakdown of the identified global think tanks into the aforementioned categories reveals that there may perhaps be certain incentives for global think tanks to focus their research agendas into single-issue areas, however broad, for a number of reasons. These reasons might be purely financial in that it may be easier to secure and maintain a funding network if efforts and research are concentrated in a single broad issue area instead of cast over a diverse array of topics. In the same vein, there also might be the perception that focusing on a single issue raises overall efficiency and effectiveness; in this sense, a global think tank might be more influential in impacting global public policy if it identifies itself as a single-issue think tank instead of branching its research agenda into different spheres of interest.

Ideas are powerful, but, in a world of increasingly diverse and globalized sources of information, especially from overwhelming flows of information from social media such as Twitter, the good ideas can be lost. Policymakers often suffer not from a lack of information, but from an "avalanche of information" (and more recently, disinformation). This problem may be reflected in the organization and research focus of think tanks themselves. Specifically, the avalanche of information may be a strong factor in determining whether a think tank that is going global will choose to pursue either the single-issue area or become a multi-issue think tank. Since there is such an overload of information, and since it is by no means easy to widely and effectively disseminate timely and accurate information that is often coupled with policy suggestions, solutions, or recommendations, think tanks may feel constrained and therefore choose the single-issue route. This might be done under the assumption that focusing on one issue area will enable the organization to compete more efficiently with other voices, such as international organizations or other advocacy groups, which are all attempting to garner the attention of policymakers. In this sense, the belief that targeting a single-issue area as the primary research agenda or focus is much more conducive to securing any means of impact or influence over the policy-making process may actually inhibit the greater proliferation of more multi-issue global think tanks.

While they do share some commonalities, such as global challenges and opportunities and the overall goal of affecting the policymaking process and global public policy, the next chapter will illuminate how each global think tank uniquely pursues its own agenda. In order to do so, we will examine a selected number of successful global think tanks as well as one regional think tank in order to demonstration how hybridization has blended previously-defined boundaries and transformed the global think tank into an amalgam of policy research, advocacy, political affiliations and academics.

Table 3.2 sets out the leading think tanks in the world that have a global orientation, meaning that their research program and/or their operations are transnational.

TABLE 3.2 Global think tank name, location of headquarters, and structural orientation

Global think tank	Location of headquarters	Structural orientation	Date of establishment
Adam Smith Institute	United Kingdom	Independent and autonomous	1977
Alexander von Humbolt-Stiftung/Foundation	Germany	Independent and autonomous	1860
Aspen Institute	United States	Independent and autonomous	1949
Atlantic Community	Germany	Independent and autonomous	2007
Brookings Institution	United States	Independent and autonomous	1916
Bruegel	Belgium	Independent and autonomous	2005
Canadian International Council	Canada	Independent and autonomous	1928
Carnegie Endowment for International Peace	United States	Independent and autonomous	1910
Carter left	United States	University-affiliated	1982
Chatham House	United Kingdom	Independent and autonomous	1920
left for Economic Policy Research	United Kingdom	Independent and autonomous	1999
left for Financial Studies	Germany	Independent and autonomous	1967
left for Global Development	United States	Independent and autonomous	2001
left for International Private Enterprise	United States	Government-affiliated	1983
left for Strategic and International Studies	United States	Independent and autonomous	1962
left on International Cooperation	United States	University-affiliated	1996
Centre d'Etudes Prospectives et d'Informations Internationales	France	Government-affiliated	1978
Club of Rome	Switzerland	Independent and autonomous	1968
Demos	United Kingdom	Independent and autonomous	2000
Deutsche Forschungsgemeinschaft	Germany	Quasi-governmental	1951
EastWest Institute	United States	Independent and autonomous	1980
European Council on Foreign Relations	Germany	Independent and autonomous	2007

Fondazione Eni Enrico Mattei	Italy	Independent and autonomous	1989
Fraunhofer-Gesellschaft	Germany	Quasi-governmental	1949
Freedom House	United States	Independent and autonomous	1941
Institut français des relations internationals	France	Independent and autonomous	1979
Friedrich-Ebert-Stiftung	Germany	Quasi-governmental	1925
Friedrich-Naumann-Stiftung für die Freiheit	Germany	Independent and autonomous	1958
German Marshall Fund of the United States	United States	Independent and autonomous	1972
Hanns-Seidel-Stiftung	Germany	Quasi-governmental	1966
Helmholtz-Gemeinschaft	Germany	Quasi-governmental	2001
Heritage Foundation	United States	Independent and autonomous	1973
Hoover Institution	United States	University-affiliated	1919
Hudson Institute	United States	Independent and autonomous	1961
Human Rights Watch	United States	Independent and autonomous	1978
Institut de Relations Internationals et Stratégiques	France	Independent and autonomous	1991
Institute for International Economic Studies	Sweden	University-affiliated	1962
Institute for Policy Studies	United States	Independent and autonomous	1961
Institute of Developing Economies	Japan	Quasi-governmental	1958
International Crisis Group	Belgium	Independent and autonomous	1995
International Development Research Centre	Canada	Government-affiliated	1970
International Institute for Strategic Studies	United Kingdom	Independent and autonomous	1958
International Institute for Sustainable Development	Global	Quasi-governmental	1990
International Peace Institute	United States	Independent and autonomous	1970
International Relations and Security Network	Switzerland	Quasi-governmental	1994
Kiel Institute for the World Economy	Germany	Independent and autonomous	1914
Konrad-Adenauer-Stiftung	Germany	Quasi-governmental	1955

(Continued)

TABLE 3.2 (Cont.)

Global think tank	Location of headquarters	Structural orientation	Date of establishment
Overseas Development Institute	United Kingdom	Quasi-governmental	1960
Peterson Institute for International Economics	United States	Independent and autonomous	1981
RAND Corporation	United States	Independent and autonomous	1948
Robert Bosch Stiftung	Germany	Independent and autonomous	1964
Royal United Services Institute	United Kingdom	Independent and autonomous	1831
Transparency International	Germany	Independent and autonomous	1993
United Nations University	Japan	Quasi-independent	1973
Urban Institute	United States	Independent and autonomous	1968
Woodrow Wilson International left for Scholars	United States	Independent and autonomous	1968

Notes

1 Joseph E Stiglitz, "Knowledge as a Global Public Good," *Global Public Goods* (July 1999): 308–326.
2 Inge Kaul, Isabelle Grunberg and Marc A. Stern, *Global public goods international cooperation in the 21st century* (New York: Oxford University Press, 1999).
3 Matthew Hoffman, "Climate Change," in *International Organization and Global Governance*, ed. Thomas G. Weiss and Rorden Wilkinson (Abingdon, Oxon: Routledge 2018): 659.
4 Inge Kaul and Pedro Conceição, *Providing Global Public Goods Managing Globalization* (New York: Oxford University Press, 2003).
5 Jan Schalte, "Civil Society and NGOs" in *International Organization and Global Governance*, ed. Thomas G. Weiss and Rorden Wilkinson (Abingdon, Oxon: Routledge 2018): 351.
6 Charlotte Streck, "Global Public Policy Networks, International Organizations and International Environmental Governance," *The Road to Earth Summit 2002* (New York, 20 April 2001): 1.
7 Nigel Haworth and Steve Hughes, "Labor," in *International Organization and Global Governance*, ed. Thomas G. Weiss and Rorden Wilkinson (Abingdon, Oxon: Routledge 2018): 357.
8 Ibid., 357.
9 Jan Martin Witte, Wolfgang H. Reinicke and Thorsten Benner, "Beyond Multilateralism: Global Public Policy Networks," *International Politics and Society* 2 (2000): 10.
10 ILAIPP, *About ILAIPP*, ilaipp.org/sobre-ilaipp/.
11 Wolfgang H. Reinicke, "The Other World Wide Web: Global Public Policy Networks," *Foreign Policy* 117 (2000): 44–57.
12 Margaret Keck and Kathryn Sikkink, *Activists Beyond Borders: Advocacy Networks in International Politics* (Ithaca, NY: Cornell University Press, 1998).
13 Ibid.
14 Vanesa Weyrauch, "Weaving Global Networks: Handbook for Policy Influence," CSGR Working Paper no. 219/07 (February 2007).
15 Ibid.

16 The Global Development Network, *About Us*, www.gdn.int/about-gdn.
17 Southern Voice, *About Southern Voice Think Tank Network*, southernvoice.org/about-southern-voice/.
18 Raymond J. Struyk, "Management of Transnational Think Tank Networks," *International Journal of Politics, Culture, and Society* 15, no.4 (2002): 626–627. For further distinctions between global policy networks and think tank networks, see Diana Stone, "The New Networks of Knowledge: Think Tanks and the Transnationalization of Governance," *The Social Science Research Council* (September 2008).
19 Raymond J. Struyk, ibid., 626–627, 636.
20 Atlas Network, *Vision and Mission*, www.atlas-fdn.org/vision/.
21 Global Development Network, *About GDN*, www.gdn.int/about-gdn.
22 Ibid.
23 Atlas Network, *Vision and Mission*, www.atlas-fdn.org/vision/.
24 Atlas Network, *About*, www.atlasnetwork.org/about/our-story.
25 Ibid.
26 Atlas Network, *Important Facts About Atlas Network*, www.atlasnetwork.org/about/faq-for-journalists#fact-4-atlas-network-is-pro-free-enterprise-not-pro-business.
27 Lee Fang, *Sphere of Influence: How American Libertarians Are Remaking Latin American Politics*, theintercept.com/2017/08/09/atlas-network-alejandro-chafuen-libertarian-think-tank-latin-america-brazil/.
28 Aram Aharonian and Alvaro Verzi Rangel, *Atlas Network, the right-wing libertarians*, peoplesdispatch.org/2018/08/29/atlas-network-the-right-wing-libertarians/.
29 Atlas Network, *Atlas Leadership Academy*, www.atlasnetwork.org/academy.
30 Atlas Network, *Resources*, www.atlasnetwork.org/media/resources.
31 Atlas Network, *How We Can Help*, www.atlasnetwork.org/partners/how-we-can-help.
32 Atlas Network, *Global Directory*, www.atlasnetwork.org/partners/global-directory.
33 Atlas Network, *Annual Reports & Financials*, www.atlasnetwork.org/about/annual-reports.
34 Atlas Network, *Our People*, www.atlasnetwork.org/about/people.
35 Atlas Network, *@AtlasNetwork*, twitter.com/atlasnetwork.
36 Atlas Network, *Facebook*, www.facebook.com/atlasnetwork.
37 Global Development Network, *The Read Ahead: Strategy 2017–2022*, www.gdn.int/sites/default/files/GDN%20Strategy%20Brochure%20Jan%202017.pdf.
38 Global Development Network, *About GDN*, www.gdnet.org.
39 Ibid.
40 Global Development Network, *The GDN Mission: Home-Grown Solutions for Home-Grown Policies*, www.gdnet.org.
41 Global Development Network, *GDN Board of Directors: The Credible Face of Research Worldwide*, www.gdnet.org.
42 Global Development Network, *Who's Who*, www.gdn.int/topic/who_s_who.
43 Global Development Network, *The Read Ahead: Strategy 2017–2022*, www.gdn.int/sites/default/files/GDN%20Strategy%20Brochure%20Jan%202017.pdf.
44 Global Development Network, *Programs*, www.gdn.int/program.
45 Global Development Network, *Topics*, www.globaldev.blog/topics.
46 Global Development Network, *Partners*, www.gdn.int/partners.
47 Global Development Network, *2018 Fact Sheet*, www.gdn.int/sites/default/files/GDN%20Factsheet%202018.pdf.
48 Global Development Network, *Financial Statements and Report of Independent Auditors* (June 2017).
49 Diane Stone, "The New Networks of Knowledge: Think Tanks and the Transnationalization of Governance," *The Social Science Research Council* (September 2008): 1. For alternative definitions of policy network, see Peter Hayes, "The Role of Think Tanks in Defining Security Issues and Agendas," Global Collaborative Essay produced by *Northeast Asia Peace and Security Network* (21 October 2004): 1–11; Tanja A. Börzel, "Organizing Babylon—On the Different Conceptions of Policy Networks," *Public*

Administration 76, no.2 (1998): 253–273; Wolfgang H. Reinicke, "The Other World Wide Web: Global Public Policy Networks," *Foreign Policy* 117 (2000): 44–57; and Julius Court and Enrique Mendizabel, "Networks and Policy Influence in International Development," *Euforic Newsletter* (May 2005): 1–5.
50 Vanesa Weyrauch, "Weaving Global Networks: Handbook for Policy Influence," CSGR Working Paper no. 219/07 (February 2007). For other frameworks of policy network, see Jiri Schneider, "Globalization and Think-Tanks; Security Policy Networks," SAREM International Seminar (Istanbul, 30 May 2003): 3; Raymond J. Struyk, "Management of Transnational Think Tank Networks," *International Journal of Politics, Culture, and Society* 15, no.4 (2002): 628–631; and Tanja A. Börzel, "Organizing Babylon—On the Different Conceptions of Policy Networks," *Public Administration* 76, no.2 (1998): 253–273.
51 Jan Martin Witte, Wolfgang H. Reinicke and Thorsten Benner, "Beyond Multilateralism: Global Public Policy Networks," *International Politics and Society* 2 (2000).
52 Charlotte Streck, "The Role of Global Public Policy Networks in Supporting Institutions: Implications for Trade and Sustainable Development," *Institute for International and European Environmental Policy* (June 2009).
53 Terri Willard and Heather Creech, ed., *Public Policy Influence of International Development Networks: Review of IDRC Experience (1995–2005)*, International Development Research Centre, 2000.
54 Charlotte Streck, "The Role of Global Public Policy Networks in Supporting Institutions: Implications for Trade and Sustainable Development," *Institute for International and European Environmental Policy* (June 2009).
55 For literature that deals with the emergence and evolution of global think tanks and policy networks, see Diane Stone, "Think Tanks Across Nations: The Networks of Knowledge," *NIRA Review* (Winter 2000): 34–39; Diana Stone, "Think Tanks and Policy Advice in Countries in Transition: How to Strengthen Policy-Oriented Research and Training in Vietnam," *Asian Development Bank Institute Symposium* (Hanoi, 31 August 2005); Francesco Grillo, "Think Tanks in the Global Marketplace of Ideas," *openDemocracy* (5 September 2001), 1–3; Vanesa Weyrauch, "Weaving Global Networks: Handbook for Policy Influence," CSGR Working Paper no. 219/07 (February 2007); and Bob Deacon, "Global Social Governance Reform," *Globalism and Social Policy Program*, Policy Brief No. 1 (January 2003): 1–8.
56 Diane Stone and Andrew Denham, eds., *Think Tank Traditions Policy Analysis Across Nations* (New York: Manchester University Press, 2004).
57 Anthony Bertelli and Jeffrey Wenger, "Demanding Information: Think Tanks and the US Congress," *British Journal of Political Science* 39, no.2 (November 2008): 225–242, 232.
58 John A. Hird, *Policy Analysis in the United States* (Chicago: Policy Press, 2018), 284.
59 Carnegie Endowment for International Peace, *About*, carnegieendowment.org/about/.
60 International Crisis Group, *Global Operations*, www.crisisgroup.org/how-we-work/operations.
61 Global Call to Action Against Poverty, *What is GCAP?*, gcap.global/about/.
62 Vanesa Weyrauch, "Weaving Global Networks: Handbook for Policy Influence," CSGR Working Paper no. 219/07 (February 2007).
63 FIDH, *International Federation for Human Rights*, www.fidh.org/en/about-us/What-is-FIDH/.
64 FIDH, *Our Organization*, www.fidh.org/en/about-us/our-organisation/.
65 "Going Global," *The Economist* (17 January 2008). For excellent case studies of global think tanks and policy networks, see Julie Kosterlitz, "Going Global," *National Journal* (29 September 2007): 67–68; Thorsten Benner, Wolfgang H. Reinicke and Jan Martin Witte, "Global Public Policy Networks: Lessons Learned and Challenges Ahead," *Brookings Review* 21 (2003): 18–21; and Jan Martin Witte, Wolfgang H. Reinicke and Thorsten Benner, "Beyond Multilateralism: Global Public Policy Networks," *International Politics and Society* 2 (2000).
   Diane Stone, "Global Public Policy, Transnational Policy Communities and their Networks," *Policy Studies Journal* 36, no.1 (February 2008).

66 Centre for European Reform, *Mission Statement*, www.cer.eu/mission-statement/.
67 Diane Stone, "Global Public Policy, Transnational Policy Communities and their Networks," *Policy Studies Journal* 36, no.1 (February 2008).
68 Mark Gerzon and Dale Pfeifer, *Event Report: Global Leadership Consortium*, www.ewi.info.
69 James G. McGann, *2018 Global Go To Think Tank Index Report*, Think Tanks and Civil Societies Program, Lauder Institute, University of Pennsylvania, repository.upenn.edu/think_tanks/16/.
70 Andrew Rich, *Think Tanks, Public Policy, and the Politics of Expertise* (Cambridge: Cambridge University Press, 2005), 17.
71 Peterson Institute for International Economics, *About PIIE*, piie.com/about-piie.
72 Kiel Institute for the World Economy, *About the Kiel Institute*, www.ifw-kiel.de/institute/about-the-kiel-institute/.
73 International Institute of Strategic Studies, *IISS: About Us*, www.iiss.org/about-us.
74 Diane Stone, "Global Public Policy, Transnational Policy Communities and their Networks," *Policy Studies Journal* 36, no.1 (February 2008).
75 Yuen Pau Woo, "On the future of foreign policy think tanks in Canada," *International Journal* 70, no.4 (December 2015): 632.

4

IMPACT OF EMERGING TECHNOLOGIES ON GLOBAL THINK TANKS AND GLOBAL GOVERNANCE

- Global governance and emerging technologies
- Emerging technology applications for global think tanks
- New competitors for global think tanks
- Bias within data: risks of artificial intelligence for global governance

Since the first edition of this book, the world has experienced endless and accelerating advances in disruptive technology that have transformed policy flows and greatly increased the velocity of information. The purpose of this chapter is to analyze the effects, opportunities, and challenges of emerging technologies on global governance and global think tanks. As global governance is challenged by a tumultuous world of constant flux, faced by drastic and fast-paced worldwide technological advancements, global think tanks have an impetus to keep up to date with these advancements to both: (1) provide timely advice to policymakers on increasingly urgent and global technological matters; and (2) utilize the speed, accuracy, and nontraditional data sources that emerging technologies unlock so as not to be overtaken by global technology companies that are moving into the traditional spaces of global think tanks. Simply put, emerging technologies have the potential to revolutionize the world of research or to wipe out global think tanks, and they have the potential to support democratic institutions and global governance or to be globally catastrophic.

Global governance and emerging technologies

The advent of emerging technologies has further increased the global velocity of information flows and transformed society in ways that affect global security and stability. One of the key aspects of emerging technologies is the impact that a country's presence in the market can have on their growth and potential dominance in data and infrastructure control. China, in particular, is poised to gain significant ground in the application of artificial intelligence (AI). Using the private sector as an extension of its military has proved an effective method and caused troubles in distinction which the United States is having trouble to address. For example, China currently has ten times the number of 5G towers as the United States, leaving Europe and the United States to assess whether to contract Chinese companies to build their 5G infrastructure affordably, risking handing over a huge amount of data and leverage to the Chinese government, or to bear a high cost burden to build up such infrastructure themselves. Given that 5G will become the nervous system of both the United States and Europe, the stakes are remarkably high. Already, China has achieved domestic surveillance, commercial, and economic dominance. Such dominance is transformative in the power that China wields on the global stage and its presence within the global community.

China is not alone in its understanding of this new and emerging global governance dynamic. Russia is using technology to disrupt Western democracies. India has used technology for sustainable development. For the United States, emerging technologies in the frame of national and global security is most pressing. Meanwhile, Europe is moving to attempt to take the lead of the regulation and ethics of AI. At the global level, as countries increasingly outsource political decision making to AI algorithms due to their accuracy and efficiency, there will be an increasingly opaque understanding of the reasoning behind decisions. If an algorithm predicts that one country is preparing to invade another, but no human analyst can explain why that is the case, what is the way to proceed? It is critical for global governance institutions to strategize and manage the challenges and opportunities in this new policy landscape.

Emerging technology applications for global think tanks

This chapter cannot cover every possible application of and type of emerging technology; indeed, one of the points of this chapter is how many possibilities there are. Among researchers, the definition of emerging technologies itself is not a consensus. Given that the term attempts to capture novel, radical technology, what is included within the definition is also constantly changing. For instance, we have yet to see the effects of quantum computing and quantum cryptography, both of which have the potential to be devastating to the existing global cybersecurity infrastructure. This chapter will build on work by Daniele Rotolo, Diana Hicks, and Ben R. Martin,[1] who combined a basic understanding of the term and the concept of "emergence" with a review of key innovation studies dealing with definitional issues of technological emergence.[2]

Given the challenges and importance of emerging technologies for global governance, and the fact that most global think tanks are lagging far behind in their utilization of such technologies, what follows is an analysis and set of concrete recommendations for technologies which we have identified as particularly relevant and salient in regard to the work of global think tanks. This section will identify possibilities in: (1) data collection; (2) analysis of data; and (3) strategic communication. This is pressing. Large, global technology companies such as Google have been exceptional in terms of collecting data, aggregating data, and disseminating information. It is now going into data analytics. This is an existential moment for global think tanks. What is the need for global think tanks if Google can do it better, faster, and with more data? Global think tanks must meet this challenge, get ahead and survive in order to help global democratic institutions survive.

Broader methods for data collection: mobile survey tools

Compared to domestic think tanks, global think tanks are in a particularly advantageous position to take advantage of new methods of data collection; with hubs around the world, they are ideal agents for increasingly global survey collection. Just as advances in communication technology made global think tanks possible, advances in data collection methods should make them increasingly relevant and desirable.

The prime illustration of this is the rise of mobile surveys. With mobile surveys, people can self-report from remote locations in real time, and there is no significant impact on the quality of responses.[3, 4] Increasingly: (1) emerging technology capabilities, such as mobile survey tools, are causing once locally-focused organizations to look globally; and (2) these agents do not have the infrastructure to implement their tools without partners in the vicinity of their target audience. Global think tanks, with worldwide hubs, have the potential to act as intermediaries and partners between organizations that are producing technology and those that they are attempting to reach. With hubs and infrastructure, and a deep knowledge of local context, global think tanks are poised as ideal partners for the actualization of mobile survey tools.[5] It is crucial that global think tanks frame themselves as open to these opportunities. Not only might global think tanks have a vast impact on the ground of their local communities in this context, but such a venture might also provide a significant source of revenue. In regards to global governance, and incorporating the global rise of populism, mobile survey tools, and the use of machine learning to process the results in real time,[6] this means that it is now possible to reach populations which were previously unreachable, to hear voices that were previously unheard, and to leverage advanced technologies in order to improve lives globally and strengthen global governance.[7]

Unlocking nontraditional data: natural language processing

Global think tanks now also have the opportunity to utilize technology for global governance by unlocking new nontraditional data sources. Not advancing in this area leaves global think tanks vulnerable to becoming outdated and not relevant, overtaken by global technology companies. Particularly pertinent to global think tanks' research is web scraping[8] and natural language processing. These tools: (1) allow global think tanks to keep a thumb on the heartbeat of global changes in sentiment on democracy, global governance, and other key trends; (2) help research to be quicker, more accurate, and broader in the topics covered; and (3) have a direct impact in the numerous local communities that global think tanks are nestled within.

Social media, in particular, is a new data source to be utilized. As much as social media has become a powerful dissemination tool for think tanks,[9] social media also provides a goldmine of data in regard to the sentiment of populations. This data source is increasingly global, though adoption varies widely across countries; according to the Pew Research Center, across the five Middle Eastern and North African countries it surveyed, a median of 68 percent say they use social networking sites. Across the seven Latin American countries surveyed, none of which is considered an advanced economy, 59 percent use social media, compared with 55 percent across the ten European countries surveyed, all of which are considered developed.[10] With those caveats in mind, social media use is increasing globally, and it provides an incredible opportunity to research populations across borders at minimal cost, anticipating trends and attitudes across nations.

Scraping and analyzing tweets, in particular, has become an increasingly common and effective entry point for global think tanks to have access to a wealth of global information. The Urban Institute, an influential US think tank, is particularly cognizant and advanced among think tanks in regard to its data science capabilities. One example of its numerous projects utilizing social media includes using a sample of geocoded Twitter data for the metropolitan area of Chicago to address: (1) whether spatial mobility patterns of Twitter users and their tweets are similar to the patterns of physical segregation along the lines of race, income, and education; and (2) whether Twitter users' friend networks are related to the demographic characteristics of the neighborhoods in which they reside.[11, 12] Such a study is an illustration of how natural language processing might have the potential be used to understand issues of justice, ethnic conflict and political oppression in otherwise hard-to-survey (or hard-to-understand) areas.

The role of web scraping and natural language processing extends well past social media. Natural language processing is being proposed as a new evaluation technique to measure innovation,[13] to identify media bias in news articles,[14] and to predict the rehospitalization risk of patients,[15] among much more. These tools have a wide array of applications, which are constantly expanding. For global think tanks, these applications are particularly salient due to their potential to connect global think tanks to their various communities in more impactful ways. A powerful example of the possibilities for these tools to have a direct, tangible impact, in addition to their research potential, is the Sex Trafficking Operations Portal (STOP), created and operated by NORC at the University of Chicago. The portal gathers adult escort ads from various websites, parses and analyzes the information within those sites, and displays the information back to end users to assist law enforcement officers in identifying and helping victims.[16] It is not hard to imagine the breadth and multiplication of impact should a program such as STOP be created and implemented by a global think tank due to its presence on the ground across the globe. Doing so also has another benefit for global think tanks and their work: it would combat the scrutiny that global think tanks face for often being disconnected from the day-to-day realities of local populations (as mentioned in Chapter 2 and Chapter 3) and improve relationships between global think tank hubs and their local government.

Advancing analytics: cloud-powered microsimulations

Advances in AI are transformative for the quality and gravitas of global governance decision making. Machine learning for predictive analysis, for example, allows researchers to greatly speed up the process of their policy research and expand the number of variables that can be considered. Again, the use of such tools is wide; for instance, they are being used to predict global health epidemics[17] and to predict the preferences of television viewers in order to inform interactive television.[18] Most pertinent to global think tanks are the prospects of cloud-powered microsimulations, computer programs that mimic the operation of government programs and demographic processes on individual ("micro") members of a population, such as people, households or businesses.[19] Such microsimulation models allow researchers to test "what if" on *thousands* of variations of a policy proposals, instead of for two to three, as has been common practice due to the time-intensity of such pursuits. This allows for a much higher quality of decision making—a capability which is crucial within a time of increased information flows and disruptive technology.

The Urban Institute serves as an interesting case study in this area as it has been leading think tanks in the development of this technology and has developed and maintained four microsimulation models,[20] the most advanced of which is the Tax Policy Center Microsimulation Model.[21] Utilizing the cloud to be able to expand its processing capabilities, the Urban Institute ran thousands of separate tax plans, allowing it to rapidly analyze the United States' recently-passed Tax Cuts and Jobs Act's trade-off and alternatives. Analyzing over 9,000 plans, each with different changes to several core individual income tax law elements that are affected by the Tax Cuts and Jobs Act, the Urban Institute was able to calculate the change in revenue for the federal government and the change in taxpayers' after-tax income for each iteration. Such a tool allows policymakers to choose their desired outcomes (outputs) and work backwards towards what the required policy specifications (inputs) would be, instead of charting out the effects two or three policy options.

As global think tanks struggle to find their niche in the global marketplace of ideas and to balance conflicting agendas, advanced microsimulation models provide an attractive solution, regardless of competition. Crucially, due to the power of such microsimulations and the ease they create for policymakers, these advancements pose a threat to think tanks that are not evolving and utilizing cloud-powered microsimulations while others are. Through their focus on data, and capacity for so many iterations, cloud-powered microsimulations are a tool that can appeal to conflicting agendas while maintaining quality and independence.

Conveying data through strategic communication

Beyond the increasing back-end power of think tanks to produce research, advances in application programming interfaces, and data visualizations provide critical new ways for global think tanks to put data in the hands of the public and combat the global increase in fake news and disinformation. The simplest reason to use emerging technologies for strategic communication is that it is effective.[22] Creative, innovative, well-designed, and interactive multimedia promotes readership and memorability within a crowded global marketplace of ideas.

The global think tanks profiled in this book do currently use a range of static multimedia, and the Carnegie Endowment for International Peace currently has two interactive application programming interfaces[23] both of which are illustrative of the prospect for interactive graphs to convey data and analysis. However, the creation of such interactive features is sparse and underdeveloped by global think tanks. Global think tanks are lagging behind other policy research organizations that are developing user-friendly interactive data portals,[24] virtual reality applications and videos,[25] and video games[26] for their data and analyses. As has been continuously stressed throughout this book, global think tanks must be agile and thoughtful in regard to their choice of dissemination techniques. In an increasingly populist world, where think tanks are increasingly distrusted, and where disinformation is on the rise, it is both in the self-interest of think tanks and in the public good for think tanks to utilize the improved tools that are available to them—even if it requires stepping out of a global think tank's comfort zone and expanding its expertise.

New competitors for global think tanks

As a whole, global think tanks have not been agile enough in utilizing emerging technologies. An analysis of top think tanks (not only global think tanks), as ranked by the *2018 Global Go To Think Tank Index*, revealed that well-respected and highly-ranked think tanks have placed a much larger emphasis on studying cyber and AI policy than on using it. While such work is clearly crucial, the lack of utilization of advanced data science by think tanks: (1) raises the question of whether think tanks have human capital with enough technological expertise to make informed recommendations and policy; and (2) whether they will be able to keep up with the pace of the technological advancements themselves. Even the Brookings Institution, the highest-ranked think tank in the world, has a well-respected AI policy program yet lacks programs, papers or methodologies that utilize natural language processing or machine learning, save for their joint program with the Urban Institute, the Tax Policy Microsimulation, the technology component for which is created and managed by the Urban Institute.

However, while global think tanks face "stickiness" institutionally (see Chapter 3 and Chapter 6), our analysis revealed that academic think tanks are on the rise in the emerging technology space due to: (1) the interdisciplinary capabilities of universities; and (2) the wealth of financial resources available at universities. In the realm of technology and policy, academic think tanks flourish from the accessibility of engineering (and design) schools. Whereas the promise of interdisciplinary research from traditional think tanks was largely unrealized, academic think tanks have resources within arm's reach to pursue research in the inherently interdisciplinary field that is technology policy. With a deep understanding of the technology itself, these institutions are able to create smart policy to nurture, guide, and regulate it.

Not only do universities have the knowledge resources that are prerequisites of creating smart technology policy, but they also have the financial backing. Compared to the larger landscape of think tanks pinched for funds, as detailed earlier in this book, universities have deep pockets to fund technology-oriented think tanks with. These deep pockets make exclusive, expensive datasets within the reach of academic think tanks, giving an advantage to these policy institutions. Larger budgets also mean that academic think tanks have the ability to scout for competitive talent and leaders in relevant fields. Combined with the massive talent pool at the university itself, which comes at a relatively inexpensive cost, academic think tanks have a large human capital potential. Universities, because of these factors, are logical centers for technology policy research and the utilization of AI for policy.[27]

What is the implication for global think tanks? Universities are valuable partners in the technology and policy space. As noted earlier in this book, global think tanks are increasingly partnering with universities across the globe; when looking to implement the recommendations made earlier in this chapter on the utilization of natural language processing, AI, and interactive data visualizations, a logical first step is global university partnerships.

Bias within data: risks of artificial intelligence for global governance

The rise of emerging technologies has been accompanied by a growing literature on the bias perpetuated through AI. In other words, it is now widely understood that using limited data sets in machine learning models can unintentionally perpetuate the existing bias that already exists in society. Given that this chapter urges global think tanks to embrace emerging technologies, it concludes with a strong word of caution on the pitfalls of such technologies, a point of entry for thinking about incorporating ethical use tools into policy research and the importance of diversity within think tanks and think tank leadership. Without such safeguards, AI has the potential to harm global governance to an even greater degree.

Ethical use tools

As global think tanks work to improve global governance through data-driven research and to improve the speed and accuracy of doing so using AI, safeguards are vital to ensure that the "improved accuracy" in research is an accuracy free from, limited in or—at the very least—aware of, and responsive to, bias. In addition to the standard bias detection tools, which typically analyze the data set and outputs of an algorithm to determine whether there is over-, under- or mis-representation of any group,[28] global think tanks must think beyond bias detection into mitigation and other negative impacts of AI research. As a timid example of this, the Urban Institute, with the knowledge that web scraping can slow down the host site's response time, developed SiteMonitor to allow web collection programs to be responsive to the host site, calculating whether a search is slowing down the host site's response time and adapting appropriately.[29] It is developments such as these, and the awareness that led to them, that are key for the responsible use of AI by global think tanks, where the stakes are high and the reach is far. This is particularly relevant in regards to securing sensitive data.

While the use of emerging technologies and AI is crucial for global think tanks to remain relevant and impactful, it also has the potential to degrade a think tank's reputation if done poorly, or without the safeguards in place to securely manage sensitive data. Awareness of these issues is also critical for think tanks which are aiming to inform technology policy. Indeed, using AI and experiencing the pitfalls firsthand may very well make a think tank better suited to make smart technology policy recommendations.

Role of diversity

As global think tanks navigate the hazards of emerging technologies, the need for a diverse workplace and leadership increases. There is a large body of literature supporting the benefits of diversity in the workplace (e.g. see a McKinsey study that found that companies with more diverse top teams were also top financial performers[30] and Lu Hong and Scott E. Page's 'Diversity Trumps Ability" Theorem[31]), but here, crucially, diversity becomes indispensable, for diversity in itself acts as a tool to safeguard against discrimination and bias within AI.

This quote from Tracy Chou, an American software engineer and prominent diversity advocate in the field, eloquently summarizes the predicament:

> Products tend to be built to solve the problems of the people building them, and that's not a bad thing, necessarily. But it means that in the Valley lots of energy and attention goes into solving the problems of young urban men with lots of disposable income, and that much less attention goes to solving the problems of women, older people, children, and so on.[32]

As so many different populations are impacted by the work of global think tanks, it is crucial to ensure that a diverse set of voices are contributing to a diverse set of research agendas, and watching out for stakeholder groups in potential AI discrimination. Global governance must have global inclusivity. Recent US tech company diversity data disclosures were dismal—only between 10 and 20 percent of workers in technology positions were women, and one study found that 45 percent of Silicon Valley companies did not have a single female executive.[33] Global think tanks cannot make the same mistake. The opportunities for greater reach, impact, and sustainability are available and waiting.

Notes

1 The resulting definition identifies five attributes that are features of the emergence of novel technologies: (1) radical novelty; (2) relatively fast growth; (3) coherence; (4) prominent impact; and (5) uncertainty and ambiguity. Daniele Rotolo, Diana Hicks and Ben Martin, "What Is an Emerging Technology?" *Research Policy* 44, no.10 (February 2015): 1827–1843.

2 Likewise, the definition of artificial intelligence (AI) is used in a variety of ways by researchers and has changed over time. This chapter will use the core sense of the term: a sub-field of computer science that focuses on how machines can imitate human intelligence, which, for the purposes of this chapter, includes machine and deep learning. For more on this, see Bernard Marr, "The Key Definitions of Artificial Intelligence (AI) That Explain Its Importance," *Forbes* (14 February 2018), www.forbes.com/sites/berna rdmarr/2018/02/14/the-key-definitions-of-artificial-intelligence-ai-that-explain-its-imp ortance/#d4da1854f5d8.

3 Take, for example, the mobile survey tool designed by the Center for Public Health & Human Rights at Johns Hopkins Bloomberg School of Public Health. The mobile survey tool is designed to track incidents of attacks on health care facilities, personnel, transports, and patients in circumstances of conflict. The tool has been adapted for a mobile platform (Magpi), which is usable on a phone, tablet or laptop and has security, database, and report-generating features. The tool was developed in Burma and is currently being tested by the Syrian American Medical Society. Christopher Antoun, Mick P. Couper and Frederick G. Conrad, "Effects of Mobile versus PC Web on Survey Response Quality," *Public Opinion Quarterly* 81, no.S1 (2017): 280–306.

4 For a brief but thorough review of the literature on this subject, see Richard Pankomera and Darelle Van Greunen, "A Model for Implementing Sustainable mHealth Applications in a Resource-constrained Setting: A Case of Malawi," *The Electronic Journal of Information Systems in Developing Countries* 84, no.2 (March 2018).

5 Note that such survey tools require the ability to house sensitive data securely, and those think tanks with adequate infrastructure are at a particular advantage.

6 For a powerful example of this, see the FoodAPS-2 study being conducted in the United States by Westat, a domestic statistical survey nonprofit. To better understand what foods Americans' acquire and have access to, the US Department of Agriculture's Economic Research Service sponsored the FoodAPS-2 study, for launch in 2021. Respondents will use a smartphone app designed to reduce respondent burden and increase data quality in order to provide information on their food acquisitions. In-person interviews will be conducted via computer-assisted personal interviewing (CAPI), and participants will be able to upload their receipts, take pictures of food items, and scan barcodes with smartphones or a barcode scanner connected to a computer or tablet. Multiple databases will support this system, allowing scanned food items to be recognized and registered in real time.

7 Such mHealth transformations are particularly concentrated in Sub-Saharan Africa. For a discussion on the scale and sustainability of mHealth approaches in Sub-Saharan Africa, see Johanna Brinkel et al., "Mobile Phone-Based mHealth Approaches for Public Health Surveillance in Sub-Saharan Africa: A Systematic Review," *International Journal of Environmental Research and Public Health* 11, no.11 (November 2014): 11559–11582.

8 "Web scraping" or "scraping" is an automated data collection technique employed to extract large amounts of data from websites whereby the data is extracted and saved in table (spreadsheet) format.

9 Juan Luis Manfredi-Sánchez, Juan Antonio Sánchez-Giménez and Juan Pizarro-Miranda, "Structural Analysis to Measure the Influence of Think Tanks' Networks in the Digital Era," *The Hague Journal of Diplomacy* 10, no.4 (October 2015): 363–395.

10 Jacob Poushter, Caldwell Bishop, and Hanyu Chwe, "Social Media Use Continues to Rise in Developing Countries but Plateaus Across Developed Ones," *Pew Research Center* (2018): 1–45.

11 Joan Wang, Graham MacDonald and Solomon Greene, "Connecting Digital and Physical Segregation: Do Online Activity and Social Networks Mirror Residential Patterns?," *The Urban Institute* (2018): 1–28.

12 A similar study by the Urban Institute employed over one million automated mouse clicks in order to study criminal background checks.

13 Sheela Pandey, Sanjay K. Pandey and Larry Miller, "Measuring Innovativeness of Public Organizations: Using Natural Language Processing Techniques in Computer-Aided Textual Analysis," *International Public Management Journal* 20, no.1 (February 2016): 78–107.

14 Felix Hamborg, Karsten Donnay and Bela Gipp, "Automated Identification of Media Bias in News Articles: An Interdisciplinary Literature Review," *International Journal on Digital Libraries* (November 2018): 1–25.

15 Christopher Norman, Thu Van Nguyen and Aurélie Névéol, "Contribution of Natural Language Processing in Predicting Rehospitalization Risk," *Medical Care* 55, no.8 (August 2017): 781.

16 Using a cloud server, the application first scrapes HTML data from a series of targeted webpages. It then extracts, parses, and analyzes the resulting data for patterns likely to represent information of interest to law enforcement including the title of the ad, the date when the ad was posted, the location of the ad (typically given as a city/state), the age of the escort, links to any images associated with the ad, and the text of the ad itself. Since phone numbers and email addresses in escort ads are obfuscated to avoid detection, NORC wrote custom software and algorithms to detect, interpret, and standardize that information. STOP is deployed in the cloud to construct a three-tiered system comprising a web server, mass storage system, and a database. NORC also built a user interface for STOP using the Django web framework for Python. David A. Herda and Glen Szczypka, "Sex Trafficking Operations Portal (STOP)," *NORC at the University of Chicago*, www. norc.org/Research/Projects/Pages/sex-trafficking-operations-portal-stop.aspx.

17 Matt Hartigan and Matt Hartigan, "How This Algorithm Detected the Ebola Outbreak Before Humans Could," *Fast Company* (6 April 2015), www.fastcompany.com/ 3034346/how-this-algorithm-detected-the-ebola-outbreak-before-humans-could.

18 Victor M. Mondragon et al., "Adaptive Contents for Interactive TV Guided by Machine Learning Based on Predictive Sentiment Analysis of Data," *Soft Computing* 22, no.8 (February 2017): 2731–2752.

19 Urban Institute, *Microsimulation*, www.urban.org/research/data-methods/data-analysis/ quantitative-data-analysis/microsimulation.

20 These include: (1) A Primer on the Dynamic Simulation of Income Model (DYNA-SIM3); (2) The Health Insurance Reform Simulation Model (HIRSM): Methodological Detail and Prototypical Simulation Results; (3) Transfer Income Model, version 3 (TRIM3); and (4) The Urban-Brookings Tax Policy Center Microsimulation Model.

21 Tax Policy Center, The Urban Institute, "Exploring Alternatives to the Tax Cuts and Jobs Act," https://apps.urban.org/features/tax-cuts-and-jobs-act-alternatives/.

22 Brent Thoma et al., "The Impact of Social Media Promotion with Infographics and Podcasts on Research Dissemination and Readership," *Canadian Journal of Emergency Medicine* 20, no.2 (March 2017): 300–306.

23 One being "How do Americans View Afghanistan?" in partnership with the Pew Research Center, and the other being the "Cyber Norms Index" that tracks and compares the most important milestones in the negotiation and development of norms for state behavior in and through cyberspace.

24 Many policy research centers have data explorers and portals; one of the most frequently used is the General Social Survey (GSS) Data Explorer, used by over 400,000 students in class per year. NORC at the University of Chicago, the explorer's creator, claims that the features include the most sophisticated and intuitive interface of any data dissemination tool in current use and robust support through tutorials, FAQs, and a helpdesk. It also includes public and private collaboration spaces that, among other things, allow teachers to use the GSS Data Explorer as a virtual classroom. The portal allows users to search for variables

(with more than 5,000 options), analyze the data, view trends (with their visualization feature), extract data, and save projects.

25 In 2018, NORC at the University of Chicago used data from the US Census Bureau and the 2015 Residential Energy Consumption Survey to illustrate differences in income and housing across the country based on regional and demographic characteristics via virtual reality technology. See Nola Du Toit et al., "Virtual Reality Video: Income and Housing in America," www.norc.org/Research/Projects/Pages/virtual-reality-video-income-and-hou sing-in-america.aspx.

26 In 2016, the Serious Games Initiative at the Woodrow Wilson International Center for Scholars and Brookings Institute launched a game, The Fiscal Ship, to provide an accessible space for both the public and policymakers to learn and appreciate the complex process of putting the budget on a sustainable course. See Wilson Center, "'Fiscal Ship' Game Puts Players in Charge of the Federal Budget," www.wilsoncenter.org/a rticle/fiscal-ship-game-puts-players-charge-the-federal-budget/.

27 Established leaders in the field who are situated within universities include: NORC at the University of Chicago; Center for Education Policy Analysis (CEPA) at Stanford; and the Center for Education Policy Research at Harvard University.

28 One such example of this is the Center for Data Science and Public Policy at the University of Chicago's "Bias and Fairness Audit Toolkit," an open-source bias audit toolkit for machine learning developers, analysts, and policymakers to audit machine learning models for discrimination and bias, and "make informed and equitable decisions around developing and deploying predictive risk-assessment tools." See Aequitas, Center for Data Science and Public Policy at the University of Chicago, "Bias and Fairness Audit Toolkit," aequitas.dssg.io.

29 Jeffrey Levy and Graham MacDonald, "SiteMonitor: A Tool for Responsible Web Scraping," *Data@Urban Blog* (16 April 2019), https://medium.com/@urban_institute/ sitemonitor-a-tool-for-responsible-web-scraping-e759042e296a.

30 Thomas Barta, Markus Kleiner and Tilo Neumann, "Is There a Payoff from Top-Team Diversity?" *McKinsey Quarterly* (April 2012).

31 Lu Hong and Scott E. Page, "Groups of Diverse Problem Solvers Can Outperform Groups of High-Ability Problem Solvers," *Proceedings of the National Academy of Sciences* 101, no.46 (November 2004): 16385–16389.

32 James Surowiecki, "Bringing Tech's Dismal Diversity Numbers out into the Open," *MIT Technology Review* (16 August 2017), www.technologyreview.com/lists/innovator s-under-35/2017/visionary/tracy-chou/.

33 Tracy Chou has also worked at Pinterest and Quora and interned at RocketFuel, Google and Facebook. She is now a co-founder of the non-profit *Project Include*, which works with tech startups on diversity and inclusion.

5

TRANSNATIONAL THINK TANKS AND POLICY NETWORKS IN ACTION

- European Council on Foreign Relations
- International Crisis Group
- Carnegie Endowment for International Peace
- Examples of think tank and policy network impact on global policy

The purpose of this chapter is to provide a select few illustrations of global or transnational think tanks that illuminate the various aspects and details that have been discussed in previous chapters. The selected organizations are the European Council on Foreign Relations (ECFR), the International Crisis Group (ICG), and the Carnegie Endowment for International Peace (CEIP). ECFR, which is primarily a regional think tank, is included in order to demonstrate the growing trend of hybridization, or the blurring previously defined distinctions, as think tanks go global. Therefore, the chapter is divided into sections, with each section pertaining to one of the above organizations.

European Council on Foreign Relations

ECFR, established in 2007, describes itself as a pan-European think tank that "that aims to conduct cutting-edge independent research ... and to provide a safe meeting space for decision-makers, activists and influencers to share ideas."[1] Headquartered in Germany, ECFR is an independent think tank, with a 12-person board overseeing its operations.

ECFR conducts policy-oriented research and policy advocacy. It has offices in seven major cities across Europe; the listed staff includes 21 in London, 17 in Berlin, seven in Paris, five in Madrid, four in Warsaw, three in Sofia, and two in Rome. Members of ECFR and expert networks are not included in staff numbers. ECFR has four programs: Asia & China; Middle East & North Africa; European Power; Wider Europe.

ECFR follows an outlined approach to achieving its goal. It is divided into three distinct strategies—Contagious Ideas, Pan-European Presence, and Community of Leaders. ECFR's approach is aimed to present its findings and ideas across Europe. By connecting research and policymaking, the European Council aims to present its contagious ideas to its four programs. Its offices in seven major cities allow ECFR to be "the only think-tank that has a truly pan-European footprint." The Member Council of leading European political leaders brings expertise to ECFR's findings.

Consisting of heads of government, business leaders, foreign ministers, journalists and other prominent European Officials, the Council is meant to help "Europeanise the national conversations on the EU's foreign policy priorities and dilemmas." ECFR's pan-European Council includes over 330 members who are politicians, decision makers, thinkers, and business people from the European Union's member states and candidate countries. The Council meets once a year at the Annual Council Meeting and is periodically organized and reorganized into geographical and thematic task forces. Accordingly, ECFR works in partnerships with other organizations, but does not make grants to individuals or institutions.

ECFR targets politicians, decision makers, thinkers, and business people from the European Union's member states and candidate countries. Its target audience, to a large extent, comprises of its Member Council. ECFR's policy and advocacy toolbox includes high quality policy reports, private meetings, brainstorms and public debates, advocacy with decision-makers, "friends of ECFR" gatherings in EU capitals, and outreach to strategic media outlets. ECFR runs regular publications, including the annual *European Foreign Policy Scorecard*, which was first published in 2011. The purpose of the report is to give a letter grade to assess "Europe's performance in dealing with the rest of the world." Grading member countries on six issues (Multilateral Issues, Russia, Wider Europe, Middle East & North Africa, United States, Asia & China), the Scorecard is meant to assess whether a European member state is a "leader" or "slacker" in policymaking. Since its inception in 2011, Europe's overall grade on any of the six issues has never been above a B+. Other publications include *China Analysis*, a bi-monthly review, and case studies on human rights. Articles are both published on its website and syndicated in newspapers.

Like most other global think tanks, ECFR has a diverse funding base. KAS, Rockefeller Brothers Fund, UN Foundation, NATO, and Microsoft are all listed as funders. Nearly half of the organization's funding comes from Foundations, a third is from governments, and the remaining portion comes from corporate and individual donors.

ECFR follows different issue priorities in its various global centers. In all offices, ECFR's issue focus is strategic European foreign affairs issues. Berlin, ECFR's largest office, has deep roots in the project "Rethink: Europe." Through regular meetings and roundtable events, the Berlin office fosters a community in which experts, journalists, and government officials can discuss the latest issues. The principal objectives of the Madrid office are "are to disseminate the democratic values of peace, development, solidarity and human rights enshrined in the EU Treaty." The Rome office relies on active engagement with Italian officials and institutions. In Sofia, ECFR particularly studies South Eastern Europe and the Caucasus and the EU's Neighborhood policy. It closely follows developments in the Balkan and Black Sea regions, as well as related EU policies.

The organization's offices are platforms for debate, advocacy, and communications, collecting information as "observation posts" which can be fed into ECFR's research, media, and policy process. ECFR's London office conducts advocacy, policy-oriented research, and administrative functions, acting as the organization's voice within the United Kingdom. The Berlin office hosts regular events and releases regular publications. The Sofia and Warsaw offices consist of advocacy, policy-oriented research, and field research. Rome and Madrid function as advocacy offices, while also hosting public and private events. Paris serves solely as an advocacy office.

ECFR serves as an excellent starting point for the case studies that will follow because it is a prime example of the hybridization that has been occurring at the global level. ECFR is not a truly global think tank like CEIP or the ICG; that will be discussed shortly. Instead, it is primarily a regional think tank but remains reflective of the various types of think tank models, especially the blend of an original research institution with that of an advocacy organization. ECFR, displaying one of the main benefits of a global think tank, brings together a diverse team of researchers and practitioners from all over Europe in order to advance its agenda through the promotion of innovative projects, ideas, and solutions.

Incorporating this multitude of actors and perspectives gives ECFR a pan-European focus that, while regional, is certainly applicable to global think tanks. It also highlights an important point: many of the issues facing states today are global in nature. They are problems that a single state cannot resolve alone. Instead, these issues must be resolved through multilateralism; even though the organization is regionally specific, the fact that ECFR attempts to pursue policy advice and research through a pan-European focus means that it is free from the national restrictions of operating with one particular state framework in mind. In this sense, it is able to prescribe solutions and recommendations that benefit Europe as a whole, and perhaps to a much greater extent, than if it had done so with only, for example, the interests of Germany or France in mind. A framework that incorporates all the various workings and desires of each of the affected actors is far more likely to be successful from a long-term standpoint than one that attempts to resolve a regional or global issue by pushing for a solution that only benefits or alleviates the concerns of an individual state.

Global think tanks can act as information-gatherers, conducting field research that brings hard evidence about the immediacy of policy problems to policymakers in various, particularly Western, countries. This transfer of information can lead to increased awareness and problem solving on various issues, thereby producing more accurate policy advice. ECFR is no different in this respect, despite its regional focus. The hybridization of original research and advocacy has transitioned ECFR into a bridging mechanism between policymakers and experts beyond the political sphere. Its focus on research, debate, advocacy, and communications is a complex blend of interests that can be recognized in every global think tank, regardless of international location.

International Crisis Group

ICG was established in 1995 and is based in Brussels. Its mission and research agendas are premised on the view that the international community has a stake in preventing violent conflict. Subsequently, ICG delves into the sources of friction in hot spots around the world, reports on its findings and proposes ways to head off conflict.

In terms of its overall structure, ICG is an independent, nonprofit organization. The board of trustees consists of 45 individuals from 33 countries, including the President and CEO of ICG, Robert Malley.[2] It has over 110 staff members on five continents who provide field-based analysis, policy prescriptions, and reports that are directed at governments and intergovernmental bodies such as the United Nations, European Union and World Bank.

ICG works toward the prevention and resolution of deadly conflict. Its field-based research is notable for its ability to gather updates on global conflicts, mass violence, and terrorism from global locations that are inaccessible to policymakers in other countries. ICG's analytical output focuses on designing strategies to address global conflict. Therefore, it reports on conflict hot spots and proposes preventative and remedial policy solutions. Mark Schneider, formerly ICG's Washington-based senior vice president, describes the goal of ICG as "to get the unimportant country to decision makers' attention to prevent tragedy," which requires researchers with "expert knowledge of the country and subregion and a feel for the political dynamics there in a way that's hard to do when you're coming in and out."[3]

Research and advocacy are run out of six geographic programs: Africa; Asia; Latin America & the Caribbean; Europe & Central Asia; the Middle East & North Africa; and the United States. Particular issues at the forefront of ICG's work in Africa are to control the threat of violent jihadism and assist in the prevention of political unrest in troubled states. In Asia, ICG is currently focusing on the resolution of conflicts in North Korea and Afghanistan, the reduction of transnational militancy, and studying the disappearance of democratic spaces. The Europe & Central Asia Program is acting on the containment of risk in the "shared neighborhood" between the European Union and Russia, and measures to maintain stability in troubled states. The main goal of the Latin America & Caribbean Program is to reduce the risk of civil war in countries such as Venezuela and Colombia, and to study the issues of migration, corruption, and criminality in the region. In the Middle East & North Africa, ICG is working to reach peace between opposing parties in countries such as Syria, Yemen, and Libya, and is focusing on Iranian peace and commitment to the 2015 nuclear deal. The US Program was recently established to focus on the mitigation of effects on civilians in counterterrorism operations, as well as how to act in international crises.

ICG has a flexible focus that responds to the scope of current global crises. Its sophisticated ability to gather and disseminate information, combined with a focus on high-level advocacy, provides a model for other think tanks that aim to become key players in culling and analyzing information on time-sensitive issues for global policymakers.

ICG's methodology can be described as a three-pronged approach toward appropriate policy proposal. The three major functions of ICG are field research, sharp analysis, and high-level advocacy. In research, its analysts work with all parties of a conflict to propose a solution based on all perspectives. Using its research, ICG publishes commentaries in a timely manner to inform decision making. Through its access to government officials, policymakers, media, and others, ICG is able to "sound the alarm of impending conflict and to open the paths to peace."[4] ICG's advocacy includes agenda setting, in which it brings overlooked conflicts to the attention of policymakers. The primary component of agenda setting is to ring early warning alarm bells. This is achieved primarily in the form of the monthly CrisisWatch bulletin, and in specific "crisis alerts," for example in Ethiopia-Eritrea, Darfur, Somalia, and Pakistan. CrisisWatch is an interactive map on ICG's website in which one can view up-to-date developments, identify trends, and recognize possible opportunities for peace. A newer feature of CrisisWatch includes a personalized selection that one can create to narrow searches in order to focus on one's countries of interest.

ICG is also quite active in contributing, in both process and substance, behind the scenes support and advice to critical peace negotiations. It also offers new strategic thinking on some of the world's most intractable conflicts and crises, challenging or refining prevailing wisdom. Examples include gender equality, the role of Islamism worldwide, the Arab-Israeli conflict, and the way forward in Kosovo, Iraq, and the Western Sahara. One of the more prominent accomplishments of ICG in recent history is its role in the passage of the Iran nuclear deal. In 2003, ICG was alone in its stance for Iran to enrich uranium under strict monitoring. Continuous advocacy pushed the plan into the mainstream, and ICG's 2014 proposal set the stage for the ultimate deal. Iran's foreign minister sent ICG a private message acknowledging the team's contributions. A senior US official wrote, "I am sure you recognize your language in the final text."[5]

ICG produces highly detailed analysis and advice on specific policy issues in scores of conflict or potential conflict situations around the world. This timely analysis and information synthesis assists policymakers in the UN Security Council, regional organizations, donor countries, others with major influence, and the countries at risk themselves, to do better in preventing, managing and resolving conflict, and in rebuilding after it: recent examples include Yemen, Cameroon, Colombia, and Nigeria. ICG provides detailed information unobtainable elsewhere on developments regarding conflict, mass violence, and terrorism of particular utility to policymakers. ICG's handling of the crisis in Cameroon underscores the organization's ability to detect potential crises before they occur. In 2010, ICG published two reports based on interviews with regular Cameroonians on the worsening problems in the region. After these reports were largely ignored, ICG assigned a young postgrad in 2013 to study the country. At this point, ICG concluded that Boko Haram posed a "significant threat" to stability in the Far North. The 2016 report, *Cameroon: Confronting Boko Haram* was a groundbreaking piece which not only outlined the insurgent group's rise, but also the government's handling of the conflict and possible solutions that could be acted upon. Project Director Richard Moncrief states, "We were the first NGO to engage on Boko Haram in Cameroon and we are the only NGO that has consistently produced ideas for a comprehensive approach to stemming the violence in the country's Far North." This proactive research and agenda setting is a model for other advocacy organizations to build credibility and gain a foot in the door to policymaking, as ICG has.[6]

Lastly, ICG actively supports a rules-based, rather than force-based, international order. In particular, ICG supports significantly influencing UN resolutions and institutional structures in relation to the new international norm of the "responsibility to protect." ICG also operates with a number of various modes of dissemination. It is well known for its bulletin CrisisWatch, which is its major publication. CrisisWatch is distributed to all interested parties and provides real-time information on various global conflicts. Individuals are able to subscribe to CrisisWatch in order to receive monthly emails regarding updates to the map. ICG also produces annual reports, field-based analysis, policy prescription, and reports and briefings, which can all be found in the archive on the organization's website.

With regards to international location centers, ICG has a headquarters and eight regional offices. ICG is headquartered in Brussels and has regional offices in Bogota, Dakar, Islamabad, Istanbul, London, Nairobi, New York, and Washington, DC. In addition to these offices, ICG has a presence in at least 20 areas of conflict or potential conflict, including Abuja, Caracas, Gaza City, Hong Kong, Kiev, Mexico City, Mogadishu, and Tunis. This field presence allows ICG to report on 40 conflicts and vulnerable countries, as well as monitor an additional 30.[7]

Global think tanks, ICG among them, act as a bridge between Western institutions and the rest of the world. Although the problem of Western dominance remains, the means of think tanks' global expansion can offer overwhelming opportunities for developing countries to participate in the policy process. Think tanks that expand through the establishment of global centers create hubs of knowledge and research expertise that transfers to the host country, as long as the think tank incorporates local researchers and organizations into its functions. Through exchanges of information and advice, global think tanks can play an important role in training and capacity-building for their members and partners. Information exchange can also go both ways: policy advice and information are transferred from the global think tank to its partners or members in less-advanced economies and data and field information from partners, researchers, and members contribute to the global think tank's central functioning. ICG takes this concept even further by using advocacy means to collect and centralize information in a comprehensible manner and then disseminating that knowledge amongst the policymakers. The result is that policymakers, and perhaps the general public, are fed almost real-time information about an on-going crisis or conflict situation. This not only enables the policymakers or public to be better informed about the global issues that do affect them, but also creates a certain dependency on the global think tank itself. In this sense, policymakers in particular come to rely on the given think tank, in this case ICG, for the knowledge and research expertise regarding conflict areas. So the bridging mechanism that global think tanks can become also has the simultaneous effect of establishing certain dependency ties, which are quite useful in enabling the said organization to gain advantages in the fierce competition for idea management and attention.

By increasing their role as idea managers and idea brokers internationally, think tanks can gain a global reputation that will magnify their ability to have policy influence in each of their international locations *and* in the country of their domestic headquarters. Through its wide array of dissemination methods, ICG has been able to build a reputation as one of the premier global think tanks on crisis situations and conflicts; creating this policy niche has enabled the organization to attract a wide number of policymakers who are interested in determining how a specific conflict will affect their given state.

It should also be briefly noted that ICG, and all the other global think tanks for that matter, simply could not exist without the current communication infrastructure that allows for the real-time transfer of ideas and knowledge. This technology has allowed for increased ease in international collaboration and dissemination of information. Ultimately, global think tanks are highly reliant on the free and unrestricted transfer of information; without it, they would not be able to fulfill many of their agendas or influence the policymaking process as decisively. Without the current and past advancements in communication technology, the advocacy aspect of global think tanks probably would not have evolved much, at least in global terms. Further, ICG has capitalized on the rapid growth of social media to disseminate real-time information. With over 150,000 Twitter followers and over 140,000 Facebook followers, ICG is able to connect with a global community that includes policymakers and journalists. A rebrand in 2016 brought a more modern focus to the organization, including a sleek new logo and an easier to use website that doubled readership of its publications.[8]

Carnegie Endowment for International Peace

Founded in 1910 as a private, nonprofit and nonpartisan organization, CEIP seeks to advance cooperation between nations and to promote international engagement by the United States. It is known as the oldest foreign policy think tanks in the United States and has numerous outreach offices around the world, including in Russia, China, the Middle East, and India. CEIP's research topics range from international trade to global social cooperation. Specifically, CEIP's Project on Trade, Equity and Development "fosters issue-specific, policy-oriented discussion among all voices that have a stake in the role trade policy plays in modern life."[9] In addition, CEIP also established a network of business and global leaders called the

Group of Fifty (G-50). The G-50 seeks to "enhance communication among business leaders at the highest levels, to provide its members with a greater understanding of nascent trends and conditions, and to foster economic and social progress in the Americas."[10] CEIP considers itself a nonpartisan research organization and has been described as "centrist" by Robert Cohen of Newshouse News Service. In 2012, *Prospect Magazine* rated CEIP as "think tank of the year" for its research contributing to foreign policy.

CEIP seeks to "advance peace through analysis and development of fresh policy ideas and direct engagement and collaboration with decision makers in government, business, and civil society." In addition, CEIP works to research, publish, convene, and at times create new institutions and international networks. The relationships between government, business, international organizations, and civil society are all subjects of its research, as they are viewed as integral actors that stimulate global change. CEIP divides its research by issues, regions, and programs. Various issues include trade, nonproliferation, international organizations, US foreign policy, international hot spots and crises, and energy and climate. In addition to its rather diverse topical research, CEIP conducts research on nearly every region on the planet. It pursues scholarly research and policy-oriented research, and promotes dialogue.

As of 2018, CEIP housed ten main research programs with a substantial staff listed: (1) The Asia Program; (2) The Cyber Policy Initiative—which deals with issues related to globalization and houses six additional sub-areas: (a) Democracy, Rule of Law, (b) Middle East, (c) Non-proliferation, (d) South Asia, (e) Trade, Equity and Development, and (f) US Role in the World; (3) The Russia and Eurasian Program; (4) Democracy, Conflict and Governance; (5) Europe; (6) Geoeconomics and Strategies; (7) Middle East; (8) Nuclear Policy; (9) South Asia; (10) Technology and International Affairs.[11] CEIP employs numerous scholars and foreign policy experts, including 43 senior associates; seven visiting scholars and fellows; ten foreign policy editorialists and editors; three communications staffers; and three marketing employees in its Washington office.[12] In Moscow, it had 12 staff, ten staff in China, 14 staff in Beirut (including non-residents), and nine staff in India. These staff members are not necessarily natives to the countries in which their offices are based: "Carnegie is not only staffing its overseas offices largely with scholars native to the regions but also putting greater emphasis on recruiting Washington-based scholars who are fluent in the language of the countries they study."[13] As a result, CEIP often boasts of its very diverse staff, at one point speaking a total of 24 languages.

CEIP seeks to influence the general public, the academic community, international organizations, and members of the business and policymaking communities to promote cooperation among nations. Specific audience targeted also varies by program. The CEIP website includes resources and publications specifically directed toward journalists, policymakers, students, and professors.[14] Each program offers expert opinion in the form of publications, forums, etc. CEIP holds a variety of events related to its research programs. These events include discussions, webcast press conferences, workshops, and conferences. Recent events have included, "One Year After Wuhan: Where Do China and India Stand?," "Democracy Under Assault: How American Foreign Policy Can Rise to the Challenge," and "The MENA Region: From Transition to Transformation." These events are usually geared towards examining and discussing current politically salient issues and events. Scholars and senior associates of CEIP often testify before Congress in the form of congressional hearings. Events are by invitation only.

The endowment's publications include books, policy briefs, Carnegie Papers, op-ed pieces, monographs and other materials. CEIP publishes *Foreign Policy Journal*, a leading magazine on international politics and economics. CEIP policy briefs are disseminated several times a year and address a range of current political and economic topics. Recent briefs have addressed such issues as Chinese power, EU politics, and the possible reunification of North and South Korea. The Carnegie Papers deal with similar topics, are available online, and are published between two and three times per month.[15]

As its name would suggest, the foundation was originally endowed with $10 million by philanthropist Andrew Carnegie. Now a long list of government bodies, foundations, corporations, and people both in and out of the United States are donors.[16] Donors include: The Starr Foundation, The Catherine James Paglia/Robert & Ardis James Foundation, The Ford Foundation, The Tata Education and Development Trust, Boeing Company, The International Development Research Centre, David & Lucile Packard Foundation, and The Rockefeller Foundation. Half of CEIP's revenues that were generated came from its endowment. The G-50 is supported by member fees from individual business associates.[17] As Carnegie has begun to globalize, however, it has also created new methods of funding for its global offices.[18] CEIP does have a policy of separating donors from its research, so that its work remains as politically independent as possible.[19]

As a global think tank, Carnegie has five global centers and an international partner network, the Global Policy Program: "For Carnegie, going global is a major departure from its 97-year-old primary role as a home to US-based scholars studying foreign countries and international relations, with an almost exclusively American board of trustees."[20] These international offices are the Carnegie Moscow Center, Carnegie-Tsinghua Center for Global Policy in Beijing, Carnegie Middle East Center in Beirut, Carnegie Europe in Brussels, and Carnegie India in New Delhi.

Established in 1993, the Carnegie Moscow Center was the first public policy research institution of its size and kind in the region. Carnegie first established its presence in Beijing in 2004, expanding its operations through a joint program with the China Reform Forum (CRF) the following year. In 2010, Carnegie Beijing merged with Tsinghua University to form Carnegie-Tsinghua Center for Global Policy. The Endowment established its regional Middle East office in Beirut in 2006. Carnegie opened its Brussels office in spring 2007, with Carnegie India in New Delhi opening in 2012.

In Moscow, CEIP addresses key issues in domestic and foreign policy, international relations, international security, and the economy. Current Programs are Foreign and Security Policy, Society and Regions, Nonproliferation, The East, Religion, Security, and Society; Russian Domestic Politics and Political Institutions, Economic and Energy Policy. In Moscow, Carnegie conducts academic and policy-oriented research. Its mission is three-fold: to embody and promote the concepts of disinterested social science research and the dissemination of its results in post-Soviet Russia and Eurasia; to provide a free and open forum for the discussion and debate of critical national, regional, and global issues; and to further cooperation and strengthen relations between Russia and the United States by explaining the interests, objectives, and policies of each.[21] However, in recent years, journalists have criticized the Russian government for undermining Carnegie Moscow, limiting its funding as well as letting some of its policy veterans go, in favor of staff more favorable to the Russian government.[22] The Russian government also passed the Foreign Agent Law in 2012 that limited funding to NGOs and publications that are critical of the Russian government. The targeted audience of Carnegie Moscow does generally consist of Russian politicians, media, diplomats, and political and intellectual elites, but its scope has been decreasing since 2013.

In Beijing, CEIP's key issues are globalization and foreign policy. Current joint research activities include: Security, Economics, Redefining Energy Security, Governance and Rule of Law, Environment. A current, multi-year collaboration with the China Foundation for International Strategic Studies on Sino–US crisis management and crisis prevention involves former senior government officials and military officers from both sides. Another project in collaboration with China's Planning Commission (NDRC), the State Development Bank, and the government of Hong Kong focuses on China's system of development finance with an emphasis on infrastructure. In 2007, this office also launched the US-China Climate Cooperation Program. In Beirut and in Beijing, CEIP conducts scholarly and policy-oriented research as well as public policy advocacy. The Beijing office is designed to be the channel of intellectual engagement between China's policy community and their counterparts in the West. Its mission is to advance research on the impact of globalization on foreign policymaking and promote scholarly exchange between the United States and China.[23] After its merger with Tsinghua University in 2010, its focus has shifted to include international economics and trade as well as analyzing security threats in North Korea, South Asia, and Iran. CEIP's Beijing Office generally targets policymakers, senior government officials, and military officers in China, in addition to Chinese think tanks.

In Beirut, CEIP addresses challenges facing political and economic development and reform in the Arab region. Current projects are Turkey/Iran, Islamists, EU Policies, Energy, Polarization, and Security.

In Brussels, CEIP's focus is European foreign policy. It is designed to be a crossroads for the work of all the centers, and conducts liaison and advocacy activities. In accordance with the other international locations, the Brussels office attempts to target foreign policymakers, commentators, and experts.

In New Delhi, CEIP primarily focuses on the internal politics of India, such as economic development and its relations to national security in South Asia. Since it is the newest addition to Carnegie, it serves as an avenue for incoming Indian scholars to make their way into Indian foreign politics and gain experience in policy research.[24]

The various centers are also quite prolific with regards to information dissemination. The Moscow center hosts roundtables, presentations, seminars, and conferences, and publishes articles, books, monographs, reference works, periodicals, interviews, and reports/brochures—up to 30 titles per year in all—in addition to the quarterly Pro et Contra, a series of Working Papers and regular Briefings Papers. Publications appear in Russian, English or both, and are widely distributed in Russia and abroad. The center also hosts discussions/conferences. The other three offices are also engaged in policy analysis and recommendations through the Carnegie Papers, reports, policy outlooks, commentaries, books, articles/op-eds, and brochures. All of the offices also produce conferences, readings, seminars, and debates.

Examples of think tank and policy network impact on global policy

The following section will introduce brief descriptions and case studies of various global think tanks that are particularly successful in utilizing the various opportunities in order to influence global policy. The underlying fact that can be extrapolated from these studies is that there is no absolute, uniform method of going global and achieving success globally. Each of the global think tanks listed in Table 5.1 and those discussed in the text approach and engage each opportunity differently, often reacting and adapting to the specific regional, cultural or societal aspects in their various locations. Just as there are a diverse number of global think tanks, so too there are there numerous means of going global.

Arguably, the best and most powerful opportunity that is available to think tanks and policy networks in order to affect or to influence global policy is to provide important field research and up-to-the-minute information to policymakers on critical issues or on geographically and socioeconomically disparate populations. Subsequently, these organizations should focus on increasing the efficacy of response to time-sensitive policy issues. Furthermore, think tanks and policy networks should tailor or adapt information gathering and research to the needs of disparate populations.

Global think tanks also provide important avenues and entry-points into authoritarian countries. The Brookings Institution, for example, has established global centers in Beijing, Doha, and India, and is especially focused on creating dialogue forums. Brookings has entered into funding or research partnerships with government agencies in these locations, signaling the institution's ability to create relationships with governments in countries where think tanks have little or no independence. Brookings' partnerships abroad help demonstrate to these countries that think tanks can provide high quality advice and act as an important bridge between governments and the public. Brookings' work is of particular importance

TABLE 5.1 Global public policy networks

Organization name	Location of headquarters	Date established
African Liberal Network	United Kingdom	2003
Asian Development Bank Institute	Japan	1973
Aspen Global Leadership Network	United States	1950
Association of Southeast Asian Nations, Institute for of Strategic and International Studies	Indonesia	1981
Atlas Network	United States	1981
BRICS Policy left	Brazil	2010
Brookings Institution	United States	1916
Carnegie Endowment for International Peace	United States	1910
Chatham House	United Kingdom	1920
Conflict Prevention and Peace Forum	United States	2000
Consultative Group on International Agriculture Research	United States	1970
Council for Security Cooperation in the Asia -Pacific	Malaysia	1993
Council of Asian Liberals and Democrats	Philippines	2008
Economic Research Forum for the Arab Countries, Iran and Turkey	Egypt	1993
Euro-Mediterranean Study Commission	Spain	1996
Evian Group	Switzerland	1005
Facultad Latinoamericana de Ciencias Sociales	Costa Rica	1957
Friedrich- Ebert Foundation-Stiftung	Germany	1925
Global Alliance for Improved Nutrition	Switzerland	2002
Global Alliance on for Vaccinesation and Immuniszation	United States	2000
Global Development Network	India	1999
Global Environment Facility	United States	1991
Global Water Partnership	Sweden	1996
Institute for European Environmental Policy	United Kingdom	1980
Institute for International Political Studies	Italy	1934
International Chamber of Commerce	France	1919
International Forum on Globalization	United States	1994
International Policy Network	United Kingdom	2001
International Relations and Security Network	Switzerland	1994
International Strategic Studies Association	United States	1982
International Union for the Conservation of Nature	Switzerland	1948
Konrad- Adenauer Foundation-Stitfung	Germany	1955
Liberal International	United Kingdom	1947
Lisbon Council	Belgium	2003
Network of Arab Liberals	Egypt	2006

Open Society Institutes	United States	1993
Policy Association for an Open Society	Czech Republic	2003
Roll Back Malaria initiative	Switzerland	1988
Stockholm Network	United Kingdom	1997
Think Global Act European, Notre Europe	France	1996
Trans European Policy Studies Association	Belgium	1974
United Nations Global Compact	United States	1989

in that it can create a better environment in which native think tanks can function; the relationships that Brookings and other institutions foster can convince policy-makers of the usefulness and importance of think tanks, thereby facilitating a more widespread acceptance of a functioning civil society governed by authoritarian regimes. These organizations can mobilize and aggregate knowledge and funding resources on global policy issues that span the jurisdiction of national governments. This is critical since there is now a growing number of policy issues that require a global response, but are often sidelined by domestic issues that dominate national policy agendas.

Another such global think tank is the Friedrich Nauman Stiftung Für die Freiheit (the Friedrich Nauman Institute for Freedom), which is based in Germany, and has numerous offices internationally that conduct project work and gather information. The institution is ideologically liberal leaning, and its work provides an important model for a means of bridging the space between democracy and autocracy through the provision of basic services, technical training, education, and policy design advisory. As an independent organization providing essential benefits to the local population through its project work, this global think tank perhaps avoids being labelled as "Western imperialist" that might happen to an international organization or government agency, and achieves great success in its project implementation processes. In this sense, global think tanks can function as a barometer of challenges and prospects of the least developed countries on its way to global prominence.

Carbon emissions and energy security is another area in which global think tanks can become heavily involved and assume a position of importance in affecting global policy. The International Institute for Strategic Studies (IISS) is one such example. IISS is structurally independent and autonomous, a limited company in the United Kingdom and a registered charity. It has global centers in Singapore and the United States. It conducts policy-oriented research and promotes dialogue on peace and security policy through an international member network. Its 2,500 individual members and 450 corporate and institutional members are drawn from more than 100 countries. Members include politicians and diplomats, foreign affairs analysts, international business people, economists, the military, defense commentators, journalists, academics and the informed public, government leaders, business people, and analysts. IISS performs academic research as well as a convening and dialogue-facilitating function in order to promote the provision of solutions to global security problems. IISS is notable for its expansion of its focus on traditional security and defense issues to include new issues of global importance. IISS's Transatlantic Dialogue on Climate Change and Security is a model for the way established networks can utilize their discipline-based membership toward finding solutions to global issues in new discipline areas, such as climate change. Since energy security in particular is a complex process that varies widely from area to area and often requires specific solutions for each region, IISS's structure is at least partially responsible for its success. IISS is a prime example of how influential and successful a think tank can be if it incorporates a multitude of perspectives and knowledge sets.

The process of hybridization that affects think tanks and other institutions is particularly evident in a number of different think tanks that have gone global. In many ways, this hybridization has proven to be particularly useful, especially when considering how foreign policy in general has undergone a globalization process. Two think tanks that are benefiting from the blending of existing think tank models are the Global Environment Facility (GEF) and the World Commission on Dams. The GEF is a hybrid organization, combining a conventional intergovernmental approach with an important network dimension. Established in March 1991 as a pilot program, it became the interim financial mechanism for the UN Framework Convention on Climate Change and the Convention on Biodiversity one and a half years later. It has since established its functional scope by moving from a purely financial mechanism to tri-sectoral networking in order to fund and implement projects in environmental protection.[25] The World Commission on Dams was also an example of a tri-sectoral network that helped overcome a stalemate in a highly conflict-ridden policy arena. The Commission managed to overcome gridlock among development planners, contracting firms, and environmental groups involved in the construction of large dams. Led by Germany and Norway, national governments account for 40 percent of funding for the World Commission on Dams.[26] It operated from April 1997 to 2001 as an advisory commission to the United Nations. These two cases underscore an important point: globalization has created extreme diversity. In order to appropriately react and adapt to this diversity, hybridization becomes especially important in that it can prevent an institution from becoming mired in traditional perspectives and approaches. This line of thinking is perhaps not so surprising: the more diverse an institution is, the better chances it has of successfully tackling problems and issues in which there is no one uniform answer.

Health issues are another area in which global think tanks can become heavily involved, often as a powerful voice of advocacy. The Global Alliance for Vaccines and Immunisation (GAVI) is a health-based global public policy network. It was used as a model for the establishment of other health-related global public policy networks, such as the Global Fund to Fight Against AIDS, Tuberculosis and Malaria, and the Global Alliance for Improved Nutrition (GAIN).[27] Likewise, the

Heritage Foundation is an independent and autonomous foundation that was originally established in 1973 as an educational institute. Its conservative-leaning research agenda includes a focus on healthcare policy. Heritage is an example of a traditional think tank that includes health issues as part of its research and advocacy-based agenda, in contrast to the GAVI model of network establishment for the primary purpose of bringing stakeholders together to address health issues.

Global think tanks can also exert influence over financial architecture and the reformation of international organizations. The Center for Financial Studies is a think tank based in Germany with a global network of researchers and members. As one of the only global think tanks with a focus on financial innovation and financial regulatory policy, it performs a much-needed research and dialogue function in the area of global finance. The Center on International Cooperation is a public policy research institution affiliated with New York University that focuses on enhancing international responses to humanitarian crises and global security threats. The Center specifically targets multilateral organizations and focuses on UN reform in order to improve post-conflict peace-building processes and the functioning of global peacekeeping operations. Conversely, the Friedrich-Ebert-Stiftung (FES) is quasi-governmental but calls itself a private foundation. Its research priorities include globalization process, public sector reform, European Union, democratic development and civic society, social politics in Germany and Europe, international politics, conflict management, and UN reform. The reform focus is only one part of FES's many capabilities. It has over 85 regional offices worldwide and conducts projects with partners in over 100 countries. However, it is the FES's global reach that contributes to the strength of its advocacy activities.

By providing a constructive forum for the exchange of information and negotiations between key stakeholders, think tanks can create a "neutral space."[28] As independent, nonpartisan organizations, think tanks can provide a "neutral space" for public policy discussion by organizing seminars, workshops, and conferences where research findings are presented to the wider community and where key experts discuss current policy issues. For example, the Aspen Institute is an independent, non-partisan institute, that believes the development of good leadership values and open-minded dialogue will lead to better policy decisions. Aspen is governed by a large board of trustees consisting of 79 members. Its mission is to "foster values-based leadership, encouraging individuals to reflect on the ideals and ideas that define a good society, and to provide a neutral and balanced venue for discussing and acting on critical issues." The Aspen Seminar, the main executive seminar promoting choices for a good society is the Institute's main method of providing a "neutral space" for public policy discussion. The promotion of dialogue is obviously important as it can lead to greater policy innovation; it also creates an opportunity for policymakers to intermingle with these institutions, thereby increasing the chances that the civil society sector can become involved in the overall policymaking process.

Furthermore, the Woodrow Wilson International Center for Scholars is an example of a public policy research institution that convenes international scholars and researchers for dialogue and training. Although established within the Smith-sonian Institute, it has its own Board of Trustees, a Wilson Council, and staff that include scholars (interns, public policy scholars, senior scholars, and fellows), librarians, publishers, administrators, and development staff. It remains nonpartisan by refraining from advocacy and advancing a "neutral forum for free and open, serious, and informed scholarship and discussion."[29]

Networks and think tanks have several unique qualities and functions that distinguish themselves from other civil society organizations and entities. Networks have "boundary transcending" qualities that allow them to act as mediators.[30] In this sense, they can articulate policy to the policymakers and the public. Networks can place issues of global importance on the agenda and demand accountability from formal government structures. Global policy networks facilitate the transfer and use of knowledge in the public sphere, preventing a monopoly of information on policy on the part of the government. As discussed earlier, think tanks can do so as well, but the inherent nature of networks, specifically their ability to incorporate an extremely wide array of perspectives, voices, and actors, strongly lends itself to this function. Conversely, a very specialized function that think tanks can perform at the global level is the translation of international governance codes/laws for domestic applicability (World Bank, World Trade Organization, etc.).[31] In other words, these organizations can interpret, analyze, and then adapt the various details of the international codes and laws to fit the specific contexts in which they must operate at the national level or the legal level.

Global think tanks and public policy networks have the capacity to implement policy in distinct areas through contracting, training, and project work. The International Peace Institute (IPI), formerly the International Peace Academy, is an independent institution dedicated to promoting the prevention and settlement of armed conflict between and within states. Established in 1970 and headquartered in New York, it is not a traditional global think tank. However, its reach is global, as IPI conducts technical training and education for military and civilian professionals around the world in peacekeeping techniques, among other research and policy functions. IPI effectively improves the implementation of peacekeeping policy through its training.

Notes

1 European Council on Foreign Relations, *About ECFR*, www.ecfr.eu/about.
2 Crisis Group, *Board of Trustees*, www.crisisgroup.org/who-we-are/board.
3 Julie Kosterlitz, "Going Global," *National Journal* (29 September 2007): 67–68.
4 Crisis Group, *Field Research. Sharp Analysis. High-level Advocacy*, www.crisisgroup.org/how-we-work/methodology.
5 Crisis Group, *History*, www.crisisgroup.org/who-we-are/history.
6 Crisis Group, *A Household Name in Cameroon*, www.crisisgroup.org/africa/central-africa/cameroon/household-name-cameroon.
7 Crisis Group, *Global Operations*, www.crisisgroup.org/how-we-work/operations.
8 Crisis Group, *History*, www.crisisgroup.org/who-we-are/history.

9 John Audley, *Trade, Equity and Development*, https://carnegieendowment.org/files/TED_3.pdf.
10 CEIP, *Carnegie Endowment for International Peace*, www.carnegieendowment.org.
11 CEIP, *Carnegie Endowment for International Peace*, www.carnegieendowment.org.
12 CEIP, *Carnegie Endowment for International Peace*, www.carnegieendowment.org.
13 Julie Kosterlitz, "Going Global," *National Journal* (29 September 2007): 67–68.
14 CEIP, *Carnegie Endowment for International Peace*, www.carnegieendowment.org.
15 CEIP, *Carnegie Endowment for International Peace*, www.carnegieendowment.org.
16 Carnegie Endowment for International Peace, *Funding*, https://carnegieendowment.org/about/development/funders.
17 Ibid.
18 Julie Kosterlitz, "Going Global," *National Journal* (29 September 2007): 67–68.
19 Carnegie Endowment for International Peace, *Funding Policy Statement*, https://carnegieendowment.org/about/development/funding.
20 Julie Kosterlitz, "Going Global," *National Journal* 29 September (2007): 67–68.
21 Carnegie Moscow Center, *About*, https://carnegie.ru/en/about/4484.htm.
22 James Kirchick, "How a U.S. Think Tank Fell for Putin," *The Daily Beast* (27 July 2015).
23 CEIP, *Carnegie Beijing Program*, https://carnegieendowment.org/about/pdfs/beijing.pdf.
24 Carnegie India, *About*, https://carnegieindia.org.
25 Jan Martin Witte, Wolfgang H. Reinicke and Thorsten Benner, "Beyond Multi-lateralism: Global Public Policy Networks," *International Politics and Society* (January 2000): 9.
26 Wolfgang H. Reinicke, "The Other World Wide Web: Global Public Policy Networks," *Foreign Policy* 117 (2000): 44–57.
27 Diane Stone, "Transfer agents and global networks in the 'transnationalization' of policy," *Journal of European Public Policy* (June 2004): 545–566.
28 David M. Malone and Heiko Nitzschke, "Think Tanks and the United Nations," *Magazine for Development and Cooperation* (January 2004).
29 Wilson Center, *About the Woodrow Wilson Center*, www.wilsoncenter.org.
30 Diane Stone, *Knowledge Networks and Global Policy* (Coventry, UK: University of Warwick Press, 2003), 1–32.
31 Diane Stone, Asian Development Bank Institute Symposium 2005, *Think Tanks and Policy Advice in Countries in Transition, How to Strengthen Policy-Oriented Research and Training in Viet Nam*, www.adb.org/sites/default/files/publication/156673/adbi-dp36.pdf.

6

CHALLENGES AND OPPORTUNITIES FOR GLOBAL THINK TANKS AND POLICY NETWORKS

- Past, current, and future challenges
- Defining a mission
- Tracking impact
- New forms of communication
- Effect of disinformation
- Effect of artificial intelligence and emerging technologies
- Global challenges for transnational think tanks
- Global challenges for global structurally-independent policy networks
- The rise of populism/nationalism
- Unique opportunities for global think tanks
- Opportunities for structurally-independent public policy networks
- Implications for global public policy

The purpose of this chapter is to examine the various challenges and opportunities that surround global or transnational think tanks and policy networks. As has been discussed previously, think tanks have been and will continue to be increasingly crucial in helping policymakers to manage the flood of information, disinformation and deep fakes, and continually rapid changes in societal function stemming from advances in artificial intelligence and big data. These organizations will also be highly influential concerning policy issues on a global scale. However, they, just like any other institutions, suffer from inherent flaws, and face certain challenges that potentially affect how they operate and how successful they are in achieving their goals of influencing the policymaking process. Therefore, the intention of this chapter is to illuminate some of the issues that these transnational entities face as well as the means and methods by which they can avoid them and fully utilize any opportunities to improve their ability to influence policymakers and the policymaking process.

Past, current, and future challenges

Although both global think tanks and global policy networks have the potential to be effective agents for social change, they are faced with a series of internal and external challenges. Think tanks and global policy networks are plagued by inadequate funding and the need for sponsorship.[1] These organizations find it extremely difficult to raise funds for independent policy research, and donors often find it difficult to continue to sponsor an operation that does not produce immediate, quantifiable results. Attracting donors who do not have an immediate or direct interest in a project also proves difficult.[2] Even if funding is secured, these think tanks face the additional challenges of finding a niche in the "global marketplace of ideas" and translating the ability to gather information or consult on policy into the ability to affect or implement policy change. Once these institutions have distilled valuable ideas from the plethora of available information available, they must work to get government actors and those in positions of official authority to utilize these ideas and produce results. Creating objectives and defining an agenda can be a potential complication for both think tanks and policy networks; protraction and a subsequent loss of focus are potential issues that inevitably arise due to the considerable start-up costs and the time required to produce and promote viable and visible results.[3]

Defining a mission

Global think tanks in particular face distinctive challenges apart from funding and policy change issues. They must overcome the substantial hurdle of finding a balance between communication competencies and research competencies. There is a particularly acute lack of resources in developing nations and a failing to adequately focus on research could undermine think tank missions in such countries. Furthermore, although committing significant resources to research is important, it is also important that these institutions work to increase their visibility. Without a certain amount of legitimacy, credibility and influence are lost.

Policy networks face additional, unique challenges because they function in the absence of an established bureaucracy and a rigid hierarchy. Among these challenges are a lack of consensus due to poor communication, a poorly developed organizational structure and leadership, difficulties recruiting and retaining members, and questionable legitimacy.[4] In terms of modes of operation, policy networks often lack the intellectual and scholarly resources that many global think tanks have. Instead, they work to influence policy by attracting media attention, political patronage, and government support and resources. Furthermore, consistent commitment—especially investment in strengthening management capacity and sustained monitoring from all participating members within a network—is critical to remaining effective.

Policy networks' evolutionary nature, as well as their flexible structure, creates a further sense of malleability and fluidity, allowing for the entry of new players and the exit of old ones as issues and agendas change with time.[5] Networks can be organized as "open assemblies,"[6] where admission for prospective membership is quite easy to obtain, or as networks that admit members according to given criteria. Both policy networks and think tanks have significant independence and autonomy from government influence and are free to pursue their own agendas and dictate their own policy goals. However, policy networks can also arise in a different temporal context than global think tanks, taking the form of temporary "issue networks" in order to influence a very specific policy issue. While think tanks are concerned with bringing knowledge to bear on public policymaking, policy networks are organized to mobilize stakeholders on a specific policy issue in an effort to influence the policy process and achieve policy results that are in the interest of its stakeholders. These results however, in addition to the network as a whole, are highly contingent on the continued existence of trust amongst the network members, the level of transparency and equitable power symmetries amongst the network members.[7] Since a defining aspect of a policy network is its adaptability and open structure, establishing and maintaining high levels of sustainable trust as new links are added and old ones are removed can be difficult. Power asymmetries are yet another critical issue confronting policy networks, especially those that are unable to gain access to financial or other resources and are thus disadvantaged within the partnership process. Moreover, the volatility of policy networks necessitates careful and constant management and much attention in order to maintain and promote their effectiveness. Policy networks tend to be fluid by nature because they are often defined by the policy issue around which they coalesce. So, unless the issue is an enduring one, the network tends to dissipate after the policy objective is achieved.

Tracking impact

Perhaps the most difficult challenges faced by both global think tanks and policy networks are producing results and measuring their impact in the public sphere.[8] Although think tanks and policy networks certainly have political and social influence, they operate externally from existing power structures. As a result, their impact is difficult to infer. As noted in Chapter 1, the recent cluster of think tanks' anniversaries have driven think tanks to search for markers of their own individual impact. However, because policy networks and think tanks that have expanded their global functions are still in the primary phase of their development, it is very hard to measure their effectiveness and judge their influence, or lack thereof, in the policymaking process.

Drawing on case studies, the literature offers theories on certain actions that can increase effectiveness despite varied organizational structures and aims.[9] Particular organizations are often chosen as case studies for their effectiveness at one specific task, such as communication, funding or managing international expansion. They serve as an example of a success story that offers insight into how to manage the variety of obstacles that global think tanks and policy networks face. These case studies suggest that the challenges of wider participation, global communication, better utilization of resources and funding, increased transparency, and strengthened relationships with both government actors as well as private actors, must be addressed in order to facilitate direct policy impact.

As the process of globalization continues, think tanks and policy networks of all types will have to adapt in order to deal with emerging challenges and to capitalize on the opportunities presented to them.[10] Compiled research on the impact of think tanks provides the foundation for the analysis of such challenges and opportunities facing global think tanks.[11] Despite their influence, global think tanks often do not fully escape the limitations and flaws that affect other types of think tanks or institutions. Beyond even the traditional challenges for typical think tanks, transnational think tanks face an additional and entirely different set of obstacles as well. These challenges are particularly important in that they potentially affect how these organizations operate and how successful they are in achieving their goals of influencing the policymaking process.

Evidence from this research illuminates the following examples of obstacles to think tank impact, distilled from the responses from a primary survey of think tanks globally: lack of institutional support, lack of access to information, lack of public funding, lack of technology, and lack of relationships with government officials. Funding was by far the most frequently identified challenge: 120 think tanks, or 75 percent of the responding total, listed a lack of funding as a serious hindrance. Regional wealth has not been shown to be strongly correlated with lack of funding. For example, Latin America had the lowest rate (60 percent) of think tanks listing funding as a major problem, which provides an interesting contrast.[12] Recruiting and retaining qualified staff was also determined to be a major problem for think tanks worldwide and was specifically identified as such by 33 percent of respondents. Many institutions listed issues related to determining the fundamental direction of their future research efforts as a major problem. Think tanks in Eastern Europe (27 percent) and Latin America (47 percent) were more likely to cite challenges related to the future direction of their research than the global average.[13] This may suggest a rapidly changing policy space within those two regions which has left think tanks anxious to ensure their continued relevance by staking out progressive research agendas. Lastly, 20 think tanks reported facing the challenge of maintaining or improving output quality. While not addressing the challenges and opportunities facing global think tanks and structurally-independent public policy institutions in particular, these conclusions provide an indicator as to where global institutions might face roadblocks to impacting global public policy. Global think tanks and policy networks face similar obstacles, especially the funding challenge.

Less-cited challenges included government attitudes, attaining private sector influence, maintaining neutrality, institutional competition, and transparency of government. We expect many of these challenges to come to the forefront during this latest phase of think tank expansion and networking, when the private sector begins to play a greater role in policymaking. Lack of funding requires alliances with non-neutral parties, and competition between think tanks for funding becomes increasingly fierce. We also conclude that the challenges and opportunities facing structurally-independent public policy networks may overlap with those facing global think tanks, but may not necessarily be the same.

New forms of communication

As technology progressed, it became inevitable that think tanks had to move with the times in order to reach a broader audience. One of the recent criticisms about think tanks is that they had deviated away from their main purpose: forming a bridge between the public interest and government.[14] Rather, they now serve a specific agenda, often focusing research on one specific area as a means of obtaining funding from interested parties. As a result, some members of the general public have become disillusioned with the prospect of think tanks as the solution for government accountability. With the advancement and prevalence of social media, however, this is starting to change, as think tanks are finding different ways of engaging the public through the use of new forms of communication.

While the term "social media" is often used as an umbrella term for online platforms such as Facebook, Twitter, Instagram, etc., it is important to note the influence of other outlets such as blogs and newspaper op-eds. According to the Brookings Institution's senior communications advisor, David Jackson, the use of regular blogs has proved effective in reaching out to a larger audience. He noted, "Our most successful examples of communications are generally with more traditional means—individualizing the research findings for segmented audiences, showing them both the problems and the assets of their region, what you have to do to build on to make it a successful place."[15] Individualized blogs, he asserted, are most successful because they cater to a specific group of people who are interested in the topic and therefore can contribute more to finding policy solutions. Jackson recognized that it should not only be policymakers and governments that think tanks reach out to, but also to other experts and the public to gauge their opinions as to what works best. For other global policy networks, such as the GDN, blogs and visual graphics are frequently used to distribute recent news and attract attention to various research publications, and it seems to be paying off.

As for other social media platforms, their impact and effects on public outreach are mixed at best. Many think tanks do not have a strong social media presence, making it harder to gain public attention. However, a notable exception is the Heritage Foundation, an ideological think tank based in Washington, DC. Since the election of Donald Trump in 2016, it has experienced a massive increase in web traffic and accessibility to American conservatives.[16] In a 2019 *Forbes* magazine report, the Heritage Foundation ranked as the "best" in social media presence among think tanks.[17] It boasts 2,062,000 Facebook likes, 640,000 Twitter followers, and 40,600 Instagram followers, beating out the Brookings Institution and Chatham House in web traffic and monthly website visits. At this rate, it far outpaces other think tanks in social media outreach, and is a prime example of using internet resources to reach out to a targeted audience. Through its online posts and articles, Heritage has been successful in garnering a popular following to promote conservative ideology around the United States. Since then, the Heritage Foundation has been a guide for the Trump administration to disseminate policy ideas and proposals.

While most think tanks are slow to adapt to these new technologies, most of the evidence indicates that making use of online resources is an excellent method to expand the outreach and credibility of think tanks. In a society where most information is distributed online, think tanks around the world would do well to quickly and purposefully adapt to this new dynamic in order to remain relevant in political and democratic discourse.[18]

Effect of disinformation

The emergence of new forms of communication has given rise to two distinct consequences in relation to the impact of the dissemination of news which global think tanks must now grapple with. Beneficial to the spread of information, social media has provided an avenue for many to disseminate and consume information without the constraint of borders (or publication by a newspaper).[19] On the other hand, the ease with which an individual or organization can publish "false news" has increased dramatically.[20] Such an increase in fake news, and the leveling of the information infrastructure, has resulted in an increase in distrust of think tanks and the stories they produce.

Although the intentional spread of false or sensationalized news stories is not a new problem, the rise of social media has allowed any source to amass a following and circulate these types of stories. The intimacy of sites such as Twitter and Facebook allows sources to communicate directly with civilians, bypassing the old safeguard of traditional news organizations. As such, one emerging and crucial role of think tanks is to identify how disinformation sources have become so effective, in addition to determining ways to utilize digital media to prevent the spread of disinformation. For example, the Atlantic Council, a Washington, DC-based think tank, focused on one fake story to determine how it ended up on Fox News. In 2014, a satirist published a fake letter posing as an American sailor aboard a ship that had just been attacked through electronic warfare from a Russian ship. This letter was posted on a Russian parody site. To drive traffic toward the site, the letter was posted on Facebook, which, through sharing of the post, made it accessible to a universal audience. Three years after the Facebook post, a Russian state-controlled Rossiya-1 broadcast shared this story, citing the Facebook post as its source. To feign legitimacy, the Russian broadcast fabricated a statement by Frank Gorenc, the former commander of the US Air Force in Europe. After publication by a major Russian news source, the British tabloid, *The Sun*, picked up the story with an even more sensationalized headline. Finally, Fox News picked up the story, spreading it among its strongly conservative audience.[21] From a satirical website in 2014 to one of the largest news distributors in the United States, this piece of false news travelled through social media to reach the homes of millions of Americans. With a rise in the capabilities of the creation and the dissemination of fake news, think tanks have an impetus to fight against dissemination so that their work, and other facts, may be trusted.

One way that think tanks can fight false news is to publish their own findings in a similar, easily digestible way. News spread on social media, both false and true, comes in the form of easy to understand, such as quick reports. The utilization of YouTube videos, Twitter and Instagram posts allows findings from think tank research to have the same universal scope as disinformation stories. Think tanks must enter the 21st century of news reporting if they wish to remain relevant in the world of quick and simplified information consumption. Nevertheless, because social media profiles can be created by any person or organization at any time, fully eliminating false news is nearly impossible.

Effect of artificial intelligence and emerging technologies

As was extrapolated upon in Chapter 4, the advent of AI has been hailed as the Fourth Industrial Revolution. Think tanks have the potential to incorporate these emerging technologies, such as machine learning, big data processing and the internet of things into the political sphere. These technologies are proliferating and growing in importance, and think tanks need to increase their focus on this field to stay relevant in policy. With aspects such as machine learning, robotics, data collection, and use of algorithms, technology is crossing into many areas of civil society. Therefore, in contexts such as the economy, international relations, and national tech strategies, think tanks are conducting research about emerging tech and its implications on policy.

Specifically, many think tanks are researching cybersecurity and the developing threats associated with technology. The vast majority of technology research in the economic setting is dedicated to the current and future states of labor markets. Some think tanks have attempted to act as the go-between for the private tech companies developing the technology, and the policymakers who want to understand and regulate the digital sphere. Other organizations examine AI from a security perspective, viewing AI as an "arms race" literally and figuratively, as automated weapons become more prevalent, and as different countries vie for the title of "farthest along" in their development and implementation of these technologies. Think tanks explore emerging technology and its relevance to policy in the hope of informing policymakers, researchers, and the general public. Policy and tech institutions also collaborate to produce work on emerging technology and policy. Therefore, as technology continues to develop, think tanks are using it as a growing focus for policy research.

On the whole, think tanks have been slow to engage with another crucial opportunity with emerging technologies: how to use it. Few traditional think tanks have incorporated machine learning technology into their research processes. Given the immense potential these algorithms possess to process data to draw new conclusions, more think tanks should incorporate these technologies to maximize their research potential. As an example, AI could help to reduce errors that often come with sampling in research by using more comprehensive data. Think tanks that can develop research techniques that take advantage of AI are likely to become leaders in the field. Think tanks that work directly with large data sets, complex sample surveys, and statistical modeling have a lot to gain from pursuing greater data science capabilities. Advancements in natural language processing, application programming interfaces, and machine learning have made record-keeping, data management, and data analysis cheaper and easier than ever before. These advancements also lead to greater accessibility for researchers, policymakers, and the public alike. Data visualizations and organized data sets will continue to make think tanks' work more relevant. Private companies such as Google and Microsoft have been leaders in emerging technology research due to their ability to innovate the technologies themselves. However, these companies implement their innovations as much as they research it. As the issue of emerging technologies grows in prominence, global think tanks should be looking to improve their own research capabilities to keep up with the changing field.

Global challenges for transnational think tanks

By their very nature, global or transnational think tanks face truly global challenges in their quest to influence and affect the various policymaking processes. While their global presence may enable them to deal more efficiently and effectively with certain obstacles with which more traditional think tanks struggle, being global also brings with it a host of additional considerations and challenges.

First and foremost amongst these challenges is the highly increased competition for funding. This competition is further exacerbated by the fact that said funding is often available in less-than-desired amounts. In many cases, these organizations must compete for a decreasing amount of funding. This inverse relationship creates an interesting dilemma for any think tank: in order to fulfill their mission of improving public policy, think tanks must operate in two distinct but overlapping markets. These markets are, of course, funding and policy advice. Money is the most reliable "carrier of interests," and it is important to ensure that adequate funding creates significant incentives for think tanks and networks to carry out the following functions globally: communicate knowledge (informative function), advocate values (normative function), and lobby for interests (affective function).[22]

The exact sources of think tank funding can be quite diverse, and the global expansion of think tanks has only increased the overall complexity of the funding issue. Project-based funding is, and will likely remain, critical for global think tanks. However, it remains imperative that these institutions continue to seek out and secure a consistent inflow of funds for the administrative staff, rent, communication, and other aspects that inevitably consume a good deal of financial capital. The costs associated with establishing and operating a global think tank present a major challenge for think tanks that have gone global. In addition, transnational think tanks involve complex legal, management and staffing issues. Unfortunately, these global operational centers are not subject to uniform regulation, because each country has a unique set funding, labor, and legal requirements.

Since foreign funding is an essential element of a global think tank's overall financial resource pool, it is perhaps wholly unsurprising to find that there is often intense competition for it. Funding and financial independence are an incredibly complex set of issues, as they often directly affect a think tank's credibility as well as their ability to operate in difficult and occasionally hostile environments, such as those found under authoritarian regimes. Ascertaining the potential for private and public international donors may also be problematic if there is a significant shortage of overall financial resources for the country in which a think tank is considering expanding its operations. The absence or limited supply of financial support hinders a global think tank's ability to have the resources necessary to substitute for and diversify domestic funding. The funding issue is further complicated by the fact that many host countries often view think tanks that are supported entirely by foreign donors as "outside agitators."

Therefore, competition increases among think tanks for already-scarce domestic funding sources, and, in some cases, leads to the inability to function without foreign support. Additional considerations, such as sudden changes in funder interests, are present as well. These shifts in funder interests are serious risks to sustainable funding for think tank operations. In many countries, there is a continuing risk of a return to authoritarian governments that will not tolerate independent voices that might criticize the regime. Even for think tanks, challenging politically insecure governments in countries with weak democratic traditions and institutions remains a risky business.

Questions regarding organization independence inevitably arise when considering the important role that funders assume within think tank operations. As competition for funding of global expansion increases, think tanks must constantly search for new ways and methods to finance the establishment of global centers. Think tanks with strained funding may find it preferable, or even necessary, to create a partnership with another institution in establishing a global operational center in a given country. For example, a think tank can align with a university in order to establish a public policy research center in that country. While this diversification of expansion funding facilitates global expansion, it also raises concerns about lack of independence. As think tanks are forced to look to universities, other organizations, and even governments for start-up and overhead funding, policy objectivity and purity of agenda can be compromised to reflect the interests of the funding partner. These concerns therefore give rise to calls for increased transparency amongst think tanks, particularly those with global operational centers. This transparency, for the aforementioned reasons, is especially important within the context of total funding or start-up funding: a high level of transparency assists in alleviating concerns that funders have compromised an individual think tank's objectivity or agenda. The more transparency that is made available regarding start-up or establishment funding in foreign locations, the more confidence can be placed in the relevance, accuracy, and objectivity of policy analysis emanating from these global operational centers of global think tanks.

Beyond questions or concerns of funder interests having an unhealthy and negative impact on a think tank's policy objectivity and agenda, managing Western influence is a considerable challenge to any global think tank. The internationally prominent institutes tend to be Western organizations, or at least based in Organisation for Economic Co-operation and Development (OECD) countries. This is partly due to the longer history of the think tank in Western political systems.[23] Global think tanks in developing parts of the world such as Asia, Africa, and Latin America often lack the necessary infrastructure, tax laws, and philanthropic traditions to support public policy research, so these organizations turn toward established Western institutions for funding and support. Not only does this increase competition for funding, as noted in the previous point, but also creates a strong bias toward Western sources in the global composition of funding. This poses a possible challenge for translating and transforming knowledge, values and interests to other political cultures.

A related risk is what can be referred to as the "tyranny of best practices." As the funding of policy advice, policy ideas and practices all become further internationalized, think tanks can argue for incorporating distinctive national or regional contexts and perspectives in dealing with policy problems, such as restructuring financial industries or pension systems. However, these organizations may find that such approaches attract little sympathy or interest from international funders and international transnational agencies like the IMF.

Lastly, the entrance of Western-based global think tanks into developing countries may reduce or inhibit the growth and proliferation of that country's own fragile think tank sector. If an international agency or a Western government is sponsoring a study of how to restructure a developing country's pension system, for example, it may prefer to hire a think tank or consulting firm from its home base rather than from the country being studied. The former are likely to be seen as more familiar and as having a longer record of accomplishment and more substantive expertise than an institution indigenous to the society being studied, even though an indigenous institution would most likely have greater expertise regarding the country being studied. This development, in turn, creates a vicious cycle. The country's indigenous think tanks encounter great difficulty in establishing themselves and creating working relationships with these international agencies, which then ensures that non-indigenous institutions work in a region that may have been better served by an indigenous organization that was inherently familiar with its home country.

As a by-product of globalization, the market of ideas has expanded exponentially. This phenomenon can be referred to as the competition for ideas management. With an increasing variety of actors, from power international organizations to tiny one-man operations—all able to promote their individual ideas across state borders—it has become increasingly difficult to effectively process and analyze the sea of information and ideas that is spreading from every corner of the world. Unfortunately, it is simply not possible to consider and analyze every idea, concept or piece of information completely and thoroughly. With this in mind, think tanks are not the sole producers of forward-looking ideas, as universities, businesses, and management-consulting firms also perform policy thinking.[24] These types of firms may have an already-established global reach and reputation. Global think tanks are constantly challenged to assess the work and mode of operation of these competitors or partner institutions, and maintain their own policy-setting niche in order to communicate knowledge and values globally. Additionally, relationship building is a key element of continuing to be relevant in the competition for idea management. A steadfast challenge for any global think tank is the dual task of managing and maintaining the relationships that it currently has, in addition to cultivating and creating new ones in the areas in which it expands. This may be problematic, since other firms and organizations that are already established and entrenched may have secured solid control over the important relationships and partnerships in that area.

While a think tank's physical expansion may be driven by a particular policy agenda or a demand from policymakers for specific location-based information, a global think tank still faces a myriad of challenges in defining its global expansion strategy. The decision to enter a new international location potentially creates a drain on resources, a lack of credibility in the new area, a potential inability to gather the information needed or a failure to influence public policy. Global think tanks also must be aware of how the locations in which they establish physical centers impact and, ultimately, define their "niche" as global think tanks. Defining a strategy for global think tank expansion, therefore, becomes imperative for continued success at the global level.

A critical element of this strategy initiative involves learning new civil society norms and traditions. Global think tanks are still exploring a new, unmapped frontier in which they must familiarize themselves with a new civil society and policymaking structure in the countries or regions of their global expansion. In new international locations, think tanks may face completely different structures of policymaking, policy-influence, and civil society actors. Operating in foreign countries often means dealing with a state-controlled or constrained media, underdeveloped political parties, taxes, and a hostile government. Without a global political system and global political parties, think tanks will always face the challenge of re-learning policy-influence techniques from the ground up each time they enter a new international location, and these techniques may be incongruous with previous techniques or ideals.

Global challenges for global structurally-independent policy networks

One of the most pressing challenges for any policy network is perfecting its organizational structure. Policy networks can be structured as flat, loose or rigid organizations with a distinct central leadership and advisory body. In all three cases, it is essential that network founders establish the correct network dynamics from the start by establishing an appropriate organizational and membership structure. Getting the process right while getting the product out remains an important yet challenging objective for networks as they get the network up and running. Extensive consultation and discussion among members give legitimacy to the newly founded network and is advantageous, especially in the start-up phase. However, too much reliance on member input can risk delay in network establishment.

Given these considerations, maintaining effective network dynamics can be problematic. The problem of network organization transforms into a problem of network leadership after the start-up phase, as networks must continue to balance comprehensive member contribution with a need for effectiveness and efficiency. This a tremendous challenge, because for most members the benefits of membership in a network must always be greater than the transaction costs associated with their participating in the network. The big challenge for networks is to share power among members and to encourage members to "lead from behind" after the common, shared vision has provided the spark for a new network. Overall, maintaining "structured informality" by keeping relationships flexible while keeping an organizational structure to maintain the original vision and purpose of the network is the most challenging mission for a policy network's leadership.[25] The network must maintain its relevance as an actor itself in order to maximize the effectiveness of its members individually and to encourage collective and group-based agendas, research, and action within the network. Networks gain power and maintain relevance by creating a body that functions as more than the sum of its parts. However, this is often easier said than done, as members routinely face internal agenda issues that distract them from the network's goals.

Therefore, balancing funding and participation remains critical for continued success and relevance. Ensuring adequate funding is a required and particularly complex task for network managers. Networks can gain funding from members but, in doing so, risk placing too much funding pressure on the organization itself. If organizations do not feel that the funding contribution is worth the policy impact or knowledge resource return, the network will dissipate. If a network chooses not to place funding pressure on members, instead preferring to engage as many members as possible by creating a loose and open association, the network also risks the possibility that members feel less enfranchised and less motivated to contribute to the network's functioning. When the network's aim is dialogue, this consequence is less problematic; when the network's aim is true policy impact or implementation, a lack of member participation is debilitating. The nature of networks poses a danger of appearing informal and inefficient; the consultation process for defining objectives and agenda may create an image of the network as a mere "talking shop."[26] Thus, it is important to pay attention to the manner in which funding is obtained in order to maintain the network's credibility and sustainability.

As always, funding constitutes a major and consistent issue for any organization; in the case of policy networks, obtaining outside funding presents a particularly pressing challenge. Unless the network is a pet project created by an international organization or a spin off from an established think tank, policy networks face possibly even greater challenges than think tanks in securing overhead funding from third parties. A network can make a better case for project-based funding because it is earmarked for a specific project, but even then, donors are skeptical. If a donor looks for impact, it is extremely hard for a network to demonstrate impact beyond a specific member contribution to a policy debate or the intangible benefits of membership in a policy network, e.g. information sharing, coalition building, and strategy development.

Yet another challenge is that there are strong political barriers to networks across countries. In certain areas controlled by authoritarian regimes, we expect that increased networking with institutions in said areas could be seen as a threat to the country's regime. Pressure placed by these regimes on domestic institutions could hinder the development of networks in these countries, which would prove to be an insurmountable obstacle to that which is crucial to creating truly global policy analysis networks.

The rise of populism/nationalism

Populist movements in the past decade have not been kind to think tanks. Recent surges of nationalism and populism around the world have profoundly shaped public perceptions of think tanks, often undermining their credibility. As mentioned earlier, think tanks and other non-governmental organizations are often associated with establishment-types of government and traditional politics. As such, they are not seen as drivers of change or reform among populists, but simply as institutions that maintain the status quo and the power of those in charge. As populism becomes a more powerful political force in the 21st century, it is imperative that think tanks are aware of populist influence so that they may remain resilient in the face of massive scrutiny.

Despite populism's appeal on both the left and the right, think tanks on all parts of the political spectrum remain wary of concentrated power. A joint report by the Center of American Progress and the American Enterprise Institute, two American conservative think tanks, concluded that "extreme populists who pose a threat to democracy focus on the system being irredeemable. Their 'burn it down' sentiments tap into popular frustration and can drive their opponents into a race to the bottom that usually fails."[27] For other nations recently experiencing populist governments such as Brazil and Hungary, prospects are similarly bleak. Since 2008, the number of think tanks, particularly advocacy think tanks, have tripled in Brazil in response to public outcry of government corruption and unaccountability.[28] However, these think tanks are still figuring out how they can play a role in Brazil's civil society. According to Tatiana Teixeira de Silva, think tanks are still viewed pessimistically in Brazil regarding their effectiveness in government.[29] In Hungary, while many think tanks were established in the area following the Cold War, their impact on government and public policy has been waning as authoritarian as well as populist regimes gained traction.[30] Think tanks and other research that are not seen as promoting Hungarian interests are either forced to relocate elsewhere or to face cuts in funding.[31] Meanwhile, think tanks have been created and used by those in power to carry out and disseminate their policy initiatives, rendering think tanks as little more than advocates to defend a particular ideology.

Unique opportunities for global think tanks

Despite the numerous challenges that global think tanks face, they are also rewarded with a plethora of opportunities that would not necessarily be available to a more traditional, regional think tank. The various opportunities that global think tanks can utilize are discussed in this section.

One of the more dynamic of the aforementioned opportunities is the increased potential for project funding. Global think tanks that carry out international project work receive mostly project-based funding or consultant fees, which can come from donors in the headquarters country, recipient-country donors or even from other interested third-country parties. This funding is motivated by a particular interest or project goal and thus can be easier to acquire, just as agenda-based funding for domestic think tanks is also easier to acquire. When donors perceive a tangible result from their donation, repeated and perhaps even consistent funding is much more likely. Thus, international project work widens the possible base of interested parties who will fund think tanks' projects and agendas, allowing these organizations to diversify their funding base and potentially gain a more stable position in the fierce competition for global funding. Particularly active donors are political parties with ideologically-motivated agendas. These funds are not widely accessible to every think tank, as, in order to receive such financial resources, the perspectives and goals of both the think tank and the funder must match, thereby reducing the overall number of think tanks that would be eligible to receive such funding. Subsequently, these funding opportunities are not always readily available and could potentially have a negative impact on the think tank, as funder-driven interests might override the actual objectives or findings of the institution. Foreign funding enables think tanks to motivate transnational policy transfer, but applying for these funds can involve complex bureaucratic procedures. These procedures not only may be complex, but also may require a lengthy amount of time to complete, thereby delaying the arrival of necessary funds for research. In this vein, then, think tanks may have to postpone or possibly even abandon their research programs due to inefficient bureaucratic processes.

As previously noted, funding can constitute a major problem for any global think tank, but it can also serve as a positive factor as well. A think tank responds to the problem of funding competition by sharpening its core product of original, long-term ideas, which can help to ensure its survival in the long-term.[32] In this sense, these think tanks are able to disseminate truly innovative ideas and policy recommendations because the intense competition for funding weeds out the inefficient or ineffective solutions and thus encourages these organizations to focus on their unique programs and fully develop them. Unfortunately, this trend does have the negative side effect of potentially encouraging think tanks to focus on what works rather than fully exploring radical ideas or solutions. This problem is an example of what was described earlier as the "tyranny of what works" or the simple act of not challenging the status quo. In other words, the nature of the environment encourages these organizations to be more conservative, fearful that a radical venture might prove too risky and thus too costly to pursue. Nevertheless, this problem does have a dual benefit in that it might also stimulate think tanks in fully developing and thoroughly examining every innovative idea rather than pushing forward one that is subject to limitations or serious flaws.

Moreover, global expansion of think tanks may also possibly allow for an increase in the precision of policy decisions. Global think tanks can act as information-gatherers, conducting field research that brings hard evidence about the immediacy of policy problems in developing countries to policymakers in Western countries. This transfer of information can lead to increased awareness and problem solving on specific developing-country issues on the part of Western organizations. When Western organizations are provided with a more accurate grounding in facts about the on-the-ground situation, they, in turn, can produce more accurate policy advice. This is particularly relevant when considering that a lot of information presented to policymakers is typically framed within a biased perspective. For example, US policymakers will generally interpret and receive information that is presented through a US national security perspective, which may obscure or overlook many of the fundamental problems or issues that are regionally inherent or culturally-specific within a given crisis area. This is simply a consequence of national politics and is not exclusive to the United States. However, global think tanks offer the possibility of collecting information and analyzing it with a non-country bias, thereby enabling the think tanks to extract the pertinent details that a policymaker operating with a national security perspective might have missed or misinterpreted.

An inherent element of going global is the ability to build and strengthen developing-country research capacity. Global think tanks act as a bridge between Western institutions and the rest of the world. Although the previously discussed problem of Western dominance remains, the means of think tanks' global expansion can offer overwhelming opportunities for developing countries to participate in the policy process. Traditional think tanks have been actively engaged in exporting their models to other countries. The Urban Institute, the Heritage Foundation, the FPRI, and the Hudson Institute have previously promoted their approach to policy analysis to groups in Eastern Europe and the former Soviet Union. These models are often reinterpreted in the target nations and are then modified to fit the regional and cultural requirements that foster the process of hybridization. Thus, this blending or blurring of lines is occurring not only within Western institutions but also amongst developing countries. Developing nations may take the newly hybridized, traditional models and then adapt them to fit within the regional, cultural or societal context in which these organizations will operate. Global think tanks, then, can serve as excellent stimuli to jump-starting civil society sectors, as well as a thriving think tank environments, in these areas. A stable civil society, in turn, may perhaps lead to further democratization and the greater establishment of liberal institutions that would assist these states in fully transitioning into fully-fledged and functioning democracies.

Transnational think tanks that expand through the establishment of global centers abroad create hubs that transfer knowledge and research expertise to the host country as long as the think tank incorporates local researchers and organizations into its functions. Both the Urban Institute and the Heritage Foundation, for example, have established overseas affiliates as a form of global physical establishment. Furthermore, think tanks that expand through the establishment of international networks of researchers or members also bring capability to the developing world. Programs such as the Woodrow Wilson International Center for Scholars and the German Marshall Fund (GMF) provide opportunities for the staff of think tanks and universities in the developing and transitional economies to come to the West. These visiting scholars are then able to mingle with peers there so that they can gain access to both specific policy ideas and ideas about how to make their institutions function more effectively. Not surprisingly, this further facilitates the process of hybridization, as these researchers return home with knowledge of the best features or aspects of the more traditional Western models and thus are able to incorporate those details into their own institutions.

The information age has greatly expanded the scope and impact of collaboration between institutions and scholars. Exchanges are taking place every day as technological advances allow think tank staff to communicate and operate more effectively across international borders. Through exchanges of information and advice, global think tanks can play an important role in training and capacity building for their members and partners. Information exchange can also go both ways. Policy advice and information is transferred from the global think tank to its partners or members in less-advanced economies, and data and field information from partners, researchers, and members contribute to the global think tank's functioning.

For example, GMF in the United States is an independent, nonpartisan American public policy and grant-making institution that promotes greater cooperation and understanding between North America and Europe. GMF is notable for its function as a beneficiary to other public policy research institutions and development projects across the world. The funding-function model of think tank global expansion can be a formidable force in increasing both the visibility and reputation of the funder as well as the capacity and policy-analysis contributions of the funded organizations (especially in developing countries) and their surrounding civil society. GMF has proven to be particularly successful in facilitating the growth of the civil society sector in a number of different developing countries, and these successes have been mutually beneficial. GMF is widely known and influential, and the various recipients of its funds have been able to establish themselves, thereby creating voices for institutions that are intricately familiar with and invested in the various issues in the area. This familiarity, in turn, produces information that is much more accurate and perhaps even policy advice that is at least somewhat freer from the bias of foreign organizations that often clouds or distorts analysis.

There is also the potential for Southern-led expansion. In the developing world, it is still expected that think tanks will gain a greater footing and increased local support, and, at the same time, simultaneously begin to develop regional networks and movements spearheaded by organizations based outside the United States or Europe. Although they face challenges, these Southern-led initiatives maintain certain advantages over US or European-led efforts in terms of effective policy change and regional development, and they provide a counterbalance and source of expertise for Washington and Brussels. Several decades ago, this Southern-led expansion probably would not have been possible due to the lack of existing civil society foundations and liberal institutions. More importantly, real-time communication was simply not available on a widespread and affordable level. Now that the internet and other means of communication have enabled even the smallest organization to broadcast its ideas across borders and to garner an audience, these Southern institutions can now promote their innovations to a much broader area than that to which they were previously confined. This possibility allows the organizations to explore positions and ideas that might fully contrast with the US or European institutions, effectively creating an important element of the Southern-led expansion: the promotion of radical or innovative ideas that are wholly different from those of European or US think tanks.

Additional opportunities also include increasing legitimacy and policy power. By increasing their role as international idea managers and idea brokers internationally, think tanks can gain a global reputation that will expand their ability to influence policy in each of their international locations *and* in their domestic headquarter country. Achieving a perception of global expertise is quite lucrative because it greatly appeals to policymakers when they are seeking policy advice on an issue area that is beyond their own realm of familiarity or knowledge. For example, a US policymaker seeking to understand regional conflict in Eastern Europe might seek out a global think tank that has established locations in that area and has built a reputation of expertise in that region. Likewise, policymakers in that region might also appeal to that particular think tank in order to gain a better understanding of certain US policies or decisions. This duality allows the think tank to occupy positions of importance in both worlds; the more the organization fosters its image as an international idea manager and broker, the more likely it will be solicited by various entities involved in policymaking.

Lastly, global think tanks can further the internationalization of education and learning in developing countries. This powerful capability has strong long-term implications and ramifications. As the world becomes increasingly interconnected, many of the most pressing issues are best approached by groups of scholars and researchers with expertise from diverse backgrounds. Greater levels of education and learning assist in cementing and further developing civil society and other democratic processes.

Opportunities for structurally-independent public policy networks

Flexibility is a key component of any structurally independent policy network, and this flexibility appeals to diverse actors. Policy networks' flexibility means that their organizational structure can include diverse actors from different disciplines and sectors. The major strength of networks is therefore diversity, not uniformity; a network loses much of its comparative advantage to a conventional hierarchy when it institutionalizes and degenerates into just another bureaucratic institution.[33]

Different analyses can create effective pragmatic solutions. Different policy analyses offered by network members can create creative, effective solutions to global policy problems that require input from geographically varied organizations with different functions and orientations. Possessing a varied and diverse range of actors can often lead to innovative ideas; the more unique perspectives that are incorporated, the more likely that the subsequent idea or proposal will incorporate important regional, cultural or societal components that would enable it to be successful where other, more uniform and stoically Western, ideas may fail. Incorporating a wide array of voices and actors enables for the accumulation of unique knowledge sets, thereby building a greater foundational knowledge base from which to construct unique and innovative recommendations or solutions.

By their very nature, these policy networks can be helpful for immediate issues. In today's world, where nearly everything occurs in real-time and therefore often requires a near-immediate response, the ability of policy networks to disseminate information and ideas in a timely manner is highly valuable. Policy networks can act as "issue networks" that can facilitate idea sharing across a multiplicity of non-state actors, international organizations, and states with an interest in a specific, pressing policy issue. Networks' comparative advantage to think tanks in terms of time-to-establishment makes them especially unique structures for the effective production of policy analysis on a specific pressing agenda point. Networks thus have a greater possibility to gain recognition when government and international organizations are too slow to solve immediate issues.[34]

Aggregating funding for global policy is a particularly important aspect of supporting global think tanks. Just as centralizing a diverse number of perspectives and knowledge sets allows for the creation of a more developed and intricate knowledge base, incorporating many different actors also increases the overall range and array of resources that the network can utilize to further its agenda. The establishment of connections between institutions, civil society, and government in international locales could eventually help ensure the aggregation of financial resources to solve those problems that sit on the global agenda.[35] In a version of the public goods problem, one actor alone might not have the capacity or desire to fund research on a global policy problem. However, actors united into a network may be able to agglomerate their funding sources and expertise effectively enough to address such an issue.

Implications for global public policy

What do these challenges and opportunities facing global think tanks and structurally-independent public policy networks mean for the creation of truly global public policy? Global public policy essentially means public policy that incorporates opinions and analysis from actors across multiple geographical and functional orientations, draws on evidence from the locations in which policy is implemented, and provides solutions that are appropriate for the society and political structure of distinct and disparate locations.[36] The policy problems that must absolutely be addressed in this global way include global warming and carbon emissions concerns, natural disasters recovery, health crisis responses, response to global terrorist units and threats, the organization of financial policy and regulatory architecture, and, now, the growing challenge of disinformation permeating democracies abroad. These problems and issues are simply so large and complex—so global in scale—that one state simply cannot hope to resolve them by itself. This is further complicated by the fact that these issues often have unique and specific effects on individual areas and regions. This often means that regionally-tailored solutions are the ones with the highest possibility of succeeding, rather than generalized and uniform policy solutions that attempt to lump everything together. Thus, ideas and perspectives that are intricately familiar with the various processes and unique aspects of each particular area and region must be incorporated into potential solutions for these global issues. Naturally, this is a challenge that no institution, entity or state could possibly resolve alone.

Notes

1 James G. McGann, "Think Tanks and Global Policy Networks," in *International Organization and Global Governance*, ed. Thomas G. Weiss and Rorden Wilkinson (Abingdon, Oxon: Routledge 2018): 400.
2 Diana Stone, "Knowledge Networks and Global Policy," paper presented at the Central and Eastern European International Studies Association and International Studies Association joint conference, Budapest, Hungary (28 June 2003). For funding opportunities, see Julie Kosterlitz, "Going Global," *National Journal* (29 September 2007): 67–68; and Thorsten Benner, Wolfgang H. Reinicke and Jan Martin Witte, "Global Public Policy Networks: Lessons Learned and Challenges Ahead," *Brookings Review* 21 (2003): 18–21.
3 Raymond J Struyk, "Management of Transnational Think Tank Networks," *International Journal of Politics, Culture, and Society* 15, no.4 (2002): 625–638.
4 For an excellent analysis of legitimacy and funding challenges for policy networks, see ibid. For discussion about establishing leadership and legitimacy, see Stella Z. Theodoulou, *Policy and Politics in Six Nations: A Comparative Perspective on Policy Making* (Upper Saddle River, NJ: Prentice Hall, 2001); and Vanesa Weyrauch, "Weaving Global Networks: Handbook for Policy Influence," CSGR Working Paper no. 219/07 (February 2007).
5 Charlotte Streck, "The Role of Global Public Policy Networks in Supporting Institutions: Implications for Trade and Sustainable Development," *Institute for International and European Environmental Policy* (23 June 2009).
6 Raymond J. Struyk, "Management of Transnational Think Tank Networks," *International Journal of Politics, Culture, and Society* 15, no.4 (2002): 625–638, 627.
7 Charlotte Streck, "The Role of Global Public Policy Networks in Supporting Institutions: Implications for Trade and Sustainable Development," *Institute for International and European Environmental Policy* (23 June 2009).
8 James G. McGann, "Think Tanks and Global Policy Networks," in *International Organization and Global Governance*, ed. Thomas G. Weiss and Rorden Wilkinson (Abingdon, Oxon: Routledge 2018): 404.
9 James G. McGann, "Global Go-To Think Tank Ratings," *University of Pennsylvania* (2010).

10 Jan Scholte, "Civil Society and NGOs," in *International Organization and Global Governance* ed. Thomas G. Weiss and Rorden Wilkinson (Abingdon, Oxon: Routledge 2018), 363.
11 James G. McGann, "Global Trends in Think Tank Impact," *Think Tanks and Civil Societies Program, Foreign Policy Research Institute* (2008).
12 James G. McGann, "Think Tanks and Civil Societies 2006 Survey," *University of Pennsylvania* (2006).
13 Juliette Ebele and Stephen Boucher, *Think Tanks in Central Europe* (Budapest, Hungary: Freedom House Europe 2006).
14 Diane Stone, "Recycling Bins, Garbage Cans, or Think Tanks? Three Myths about Policy Analysis Institutes," *Public Administration* 85, no.2 (June 2007): 259–278.
15 Barbara Ray, "How Think Tanks Are Using Social Media," *Hired Pen*. N.d. www.hiredpeninc.com/blog/how-think-tanks-are-using-social-media/.
16 Jonathan Mahler, "How One Conservative Think Tank is Stocking Trump's Government," *New York Times* (20 June 2018).
17 Alejandro Chafuen, "The 2019 Ranking of Free-Market Think Tanks Measured by Social Media Impact," *Forbes* (10 April 2019).
18 Nick Anstead and Andrew Chadwick, "A primary definer online: the construction and propagation of a think tank's authority on social media," *Media, Culture, and Society* 40, no.2 (May 2017): 246–266.
19 For more, see James G. McGann, *2018 Global Go To Think Tank Index Report*, Think Tanks and Civil Societies Program, Lauder Institute, University of Pennsylvania, https://repository.upenn.edu/think_tanks/16.
20 While there are slight variations to what the true definition of false news is, it is, as the European Commission Communication on Tackling Online Disinformation states, "Verifiably false or misleading information that is created, presented and disseminated for economic gain or to intentionally deceive the public, and in any event to cause public harm." Bertin Martens et al., "The Digital Transformation of News Media and the Rise of Disinformation and Fake News," *Digital Economy Working Paper 2018–2, Joint Research Centre, European Commission* (April 2018): 4–56.
21 Neil Macfarquhar and Andrew Rossback, "How Russian Propaganda Spread From a Parody Website to Fox News," *The New York Times* (7 June 2017).
22 Jiri Schneider, "Globalization and think-tanks; Security policy networks," SAREM International Seminar, Istanbul (30 May 2003): 5–6.
23 Diana Stone, "The New Networks of Knowledge: Think Tanks and the Transnationalization of Governance," *The Social Science Research Council* (September 2008): 7.
24 Francesco Grillo, "Think Tanks in the Global Marketplace of Ideas," *openDemocracy* (5 September 2001).
25 Stella Z. Theodoulou, *Policy and Politics in Six Nations: A Comparative Perspective on Policy Making* (Upper Saddle River, NJ: Prentice Hall, 2001). For further discussion about establishing leadership and legitimacy, see James McGann, "Networking Strategy, Lessons Learned and Challenges Ahead."
26 Raymond J. Struyk, "Management of Transnational Think Tank Networks," *International Journal of Politics, Culture, and Society* 15, no.4 (2002): 625–638.
27 Dalibor Rohac, Liz Kennedy and Vikram Singh, "Drivers of Authoritarian Populism in the United States," *Center for American Progress* (10 May 2018).
28 Ciara Long, "Brazil's Think Tank Boom" *The Brazilian Report* (12 December 2017).
29 Tatiana Teixeria da Silva, "Think tanks brasileros: entre o passado e o futuro," *Policy Analysis in Brazil the State of the Art* (Bristol: Policy Press, 2012).
30 Aron Buzogány and Mihai Varga, "The ideational foundation of the illiberal backlash in Central and Eastern Europe: The Case of Hungary," *Review of International Political Economic* 25, no.6 (2018): 814.
31 Zoltan Simon, "Orban's Science Crackdown Brings Hungarian Academics to Streets," *Bloomberg* (23 April 2019).
32 Charlotte Streck, "Global Public Policy Networks, International Organizations and International Environmental Governance," *The Road to Earth Summit 2002* (New York: 2001).

33 Jan Martin Witte, Wolfgang H. Reinicke and Thorsten Benner, "Beyond Multi-lateralism: Global Public Policy Networks," *International Politics and Society* (2000): 4.
34 Diane Stone, "Transfer agents and global networks in the 'transnationalization' of policy," *Journal of European Public Policy* (June 2004): 559.
35 For further analysis of funding opportunities, see Julie Kosterlitz, "Going Global," *National Journal* (29 September 2007): 67–68; and Thorsten Benner, Wolfgang H. Reinicke and Jan Martin Witte, "Global Public Policy Networks: Lessons Learned and Challenges Ahead," *Brookings Review* 21 (2003): 18–21.
36 Thomas G. Weiss and Rorden Wilkinson, "From International Organization to Global Governance," in *International Organization and Global Governance*, ed. Thomas G. Weiss and Rorden Wilkinson (Abingdon, Oxon: Routledge 2018): 9.

7

CONCLUSION

As global think tanks and other transnational organizations continue to influence and affect the entire policy-making process, one must look to the future of global public policy. Subsequently, two questions emerge in regard to this future context: How can global think tanks and policy networks continue to improve their impact and overall reach? Second, how can policymakers increase the utility of global think tanks and policy networks and address their key obstacles? As highlighted in this second edition and discussed in Chapter 6, emerging technologies and AI are a critical avenue for increased impact. However, measuring and controlling for impact in a broader sense are incredibly difficult to do; there are no established standards or measurements by which to do so. Nevertheless, certain recommendations can be offered, and there remain particular means of improving think tanks' impact, which can act as a foundation. Independence, policy-orientation, and strategic agendas for research create *capacity* for think tank impact, in addition to the stability of research-focused think tank budgets; financial resources are the most commonly selected factor affecting performance worldwide. Lastly, it appears that think tanks see policy-oriented products, rather than long-term scholarly work, as a better tool for creating impact.

There are a number of options and opportunities available to policymakers in order to increase the utility of global think tanks and policy networks for global public policy, in addition to addressing key obstacles to their effectiveness. These potential solutions vary, but they generally include addressing: (1) the global lack of funding; and (2) the relative lack of policy research institutions in developing countries. Policymakers can also be quite important in encouraging the formation of networks that incorporate or include actors from developing countries, as well as multi-sectoral integration and flexibility in global think tank networks.

In regard to addressing the global lack of funding or, at the very least, the massive funding discrepancies in various areas of the world compared to others, international organizations and government development agencies are particularly effective in creating think tank development funding programs. Consistent support from policymakers to do so should, at least partially, alleviate many of the issues that global think tanks, and those that are considering going global, face. In particular, widely dispersed think tank development funding programs may allow for increased diversity overall, thereby lessening the reliance of think tanks on Western institutions or organizations. Furthermore, policymakers can also encourage the transfer of philanthropic work from private foundations and multilateral organizations to the think tanks and networks with the most global impact. By identifying the influential and effective global think tanks and using their political clout and public position to promote these institutions within the greater public sphere, donations and contributions that may have previously been reserved only for certain organizations might start trickling down to think tanks and policy networks.

A second option for policymakers is to address the relative lack of policy research institutions in developing countries. In this sense, policymakers can use existing institutions to immediately address the lack of resources and expertise, which is essentially the encouragement of expansion *to* underrepresented regions. Encouraging global think tanks and policy networks' public education activities and community relations activities in developing countries is certainly another possible opportunity. Doing so provides much-needed policy information to these populations; this can often be accomplished through partner networks or physical expansion. Additionally, policymakers can also encourage the expansion and establishment of networks and physical centers in key fragile countries. Doing so may serve as a strong boost to the establishment and growth of a functioning civil society within the respective state, which might possibly assist in the overall transition from a potentially failed or fragile country to a more stable and secure one.

Moreover, policymakers can provide a framework for knowledge transfer to and from developing countries, which is essentially interaction *with* underrepresented regions. They can encourage the formation of international dialogue platforms, particularly *among* developing country actors. Doing so brings advice from the practitioners who have experienced similar policy challenges. Politicians are often essential in cultivating the necessary cultural framework for organic future think tank growth (expansion *from* underrepresented regions). They also play pivotal roles in encouraging the ideology of the importance of civil society and liberal democracy for increased welfare, poverty alleviation, and growth. Furthermore, they can encourage programs that incentivize a reversal of "brain drain" to developed countries. Lastly, policymakers can assist in stimulating the formation of non-Western institutions and assist developing countries in developing their own models, thereby assuaging the fear that think tanks are "importing agendas" or are "echoes of colonialism."

Shifting away from a specific focus on the contributions that policymakers can have on improving think tank impact and influence, it is important to further encourage the formation of networks that incorporate actors from developing countries. This is a particularly crucial point because as fragile civil societies develop, these networks can help foment and solidify the strength of institutions in these societies by transferring knowledge and technical expertise. Creating and preserving multi-sectoral integration and flexibility in global think tank networks and structurally-independent policy network structures not only ensures continued relevance on a global scale, but also allows such networks to avoid the lag times that often complicate reaction and adaptation times in response to emerging issues. Witte and Reinicke argue that the private sector's integration with a "tri-sectoral network" of states, international organizations, and civil society actors increases public policy's responsiveness to a changing environment.[1] Streck includes the private sector in her definition of tri-sectoral, asserting that global public policy networks are "ideally tri-sectoral networks characterized by collaboration between governments, representatives of civil society and of the for-profit private sector."[2] In this sense, "multi-sectoral" is perhaps a more appropriate term to describe the global public policy networks that invite collaboration among governments, civil society organizations, think tanks, academic institutions, and corporations. Multi-sectoral networks that include the private sector are a recent innovation that is necessary to raise awareness of private sector innovations among policymakers and translate concerns from the private sector to government. The subprime and credit crisis beginning in 2007 is a prime example of the detriment of a lack of communication and aligned incentives between the private sector and policymakers, which led to a lack of appropriate financial regulatory policy.

Encouraging effective network management is especially relevant given the global scale of these organizations and networks. By encouraging effective network management, think tanks can reduce resources drained by ineffective networks. Network management is the challenge at the forefront of the issues facing network development; network management is a crucial means of improving impact. International organizations can play a role in establishing fora and training courses for network management and encouraging interdisciplinary research. Maintaining an effective and efficient network management not only reduces the already considerable strain on financial resources, but also increases the reaction and response time in relation to new developments or emerging issues. As with almost anything else, solid network management greatly improves think tank efficiency; the more resources at its disposal that do not need to be siphoned off to deal with problems such as network inefficiency, the more funds and other assets can be directed at fulfilling the organization's agenda.

An additional component of increasing think tank and policy network impact and influence is the importance of international organizations. Specifically, international organizations should develop comprehensive strategies for partnerships with global think tanks and policy networks. As global public policy, which has traditionally been the domain of international organizations, begins to involve and incorporate more actors on a worldwide scale, international organizations need to incorporate and embrace these actors rather than create a competition or tension for policy influence. This is a particularly important observation; the rapid proliferation and expansion of globalization in its various forms has created a considerable amount of misinformation, miscommunication, and distrust among and between organizations. As such, cooperation will prove to be mutually beneficial for both parties by establishing and encouraging stable working relationships built upon trust and confidence. Whereas competition will only exacerbate the existing issues and further fragment the global landscape, a fusion of Intergovernmental Organizations and think tanks will greatly expand and strengthen the overall policy environment. International organizations and other civil-society organizations can play a much-needed role in tracking and evaluating the proliferation of think tanks and policy networks in order to create trust among actors.

The encouragement of ownership of impact analysis should also be promoted; established methods or standards of evaluating impact on the part of the institution is not only beneficial, but also necessary for improving global policy impact. The task of think tank and network evaluation must be done independently, but improvements in overall effectiveness can be accomplished by also encouraging systematic impact analysis on the part of institutions themselves. Therefore, institutions must be encouraged to create a standardized internal procedure for measuring and evaluating effectiveness, perhaps incorporating some of the aforementioned metrics into a systemic internal analysis procedure. Metrics for evaluating the effectiveness of global policy networks will also have to be developed.

In the cyber-age, the *caveat emptor* principle is more appropriate than ever before for those seeking information. Attempts to reduce uncertainty can be successful by taking the following steps. First, there must be established monitoring of government registration restrictions on civil society organizations or attempts to infiltrate networks through "phantom" think tanks. Phantom think tanks are entities set up by governments with the sole purpose of keeping tabs on the civil society sector and perhaps even undermining it, while masquerading under the false pretense of being independent and autonomous. In reality, these organizations are entirely government funded and run. Nevertheless, these phantom think tanks, when recognized as such, can still contribute positively to global public policy by evaluating other think tanks and analyzing their impact.

In this vein, it is important to conduct continued analysis, especially of developing-country dynamics and of opportunities for global impact. In the past several years, increased emphasis has been placed on South-South collaborations (e.g. between India, Brazil, and South Africa) in academic and policy circles. This represents a distinct shift away from Washington-led development models that dominated following World War II. Analysis of why think tanks do or do not proliferate in developing countries, and why South-South networks of think tanks and NGOs do or do not form, provides a lens or barometer through which challenges to South-South collaboration and locally-led development efforts might be studied and better understood. Such understanding has clear and relevant implications for policy, especially considering that global public policy and the opportunities for impact are still in developing stages.

With these aspects and details in mind, one should consider what is in store for the future. Ultimately, global think tanks and policy networks will be crucial in helping policymakers manage the "Four Mores" on a global scale: more issues, more actors, more competition, and more conflict. The advancements in technology and communication have given rise to the need for real-time reactions to emergent issues. These problems, coupled with the sea of information available, has created a vast need for timely and accurate policy advice that is able to shift through the overwhelming amount of information and produce effective solutions or recommendations. The world has simply become too complex; its problems are too complicated and diverse for policymakers to do so on their own. Think tanks, and other organizations, can fill these gaps. To do this, they need to master the "Three Rs": rigor, relevance, and reliability.

International organizations, academic institutions, and private organizations need to work together to increase funding, transparency, and flexibility of global think tanks and policy networks and incentivize expansion in developing countries— through academic research on the think tank phenomena, the design of monitoring programs, and fiscal support and incentive programs—in order to ensure better outcomes in the future. With the proper foundational base and support, global or transnational think tanks can better fulfill their various agendas and purposes with the ultimate goal of expanding global public policy impact.

The economist George Stiglitz commented that think tanks must "scan globally and act locally" if they are to be effective in today's policy environment.[3] Accordingly, policymakers, researchers, and professionals need to examine and draw on this net of more numerous public policy research institutions, internationally-established think tanks, and growing international networks in order to better coordinate global policy ideas and work toward global development.

Due to their global presence and their ability to incorporate or embody a truly international perspective, global think tanks and policy networks will be increasingly critical in assisting policymakers in resolving issues such as the climate crisis. Global policy networks and think tanks are best suited for responding to such situations, which potentially require massive fundamental reforms to the existing architecture or even complete overhauls, since these institutions, at least theoretically, are not regionally constrained. Here, again, is an opportunity for the incorporation of emerging technologies. Furthermore, global think tanks are less limited by funding or budget concerns than non-global think tanks are, and as such can devote more resources to crafting and influencing policies and solutions from a global perspective.

Notes

1 Jan Martin Witte, Wolfgang H. Reinicke and Thorsten Benner, "Beyond Multi-lateralism: Global Public Policy Networks," *International Politics and Society* (2000).
2 Charlotte Streck, "Global Public Policy Networks, International Organizations and International Environmental Governance," *The Road to Earth Summit 2002* (New York: 2001).
3 Quoted in James G. McGann, "The Global Go-To Think Tanks," *Think Tanks and Civil Societies Program, Foreign Policy Research Institute* (Philadelphia, Pennsylvania: 2009).

SELECTED BIBLIOGRAPHY

Mahmood Ahmad and Muhammad Ayub Jan, "Diversity of information sources: An evaluation of global think tanks knowledge construct," *Research Evaluation* 28, no.3 (May
2019): 273–278. In their analysis of a total of 17,801 references, Mahmood Ahmad
(Allama Iqbal Open University, Islamabad, Pakistan) and Muhammad Ayub Jan (Department of Political Science, University of Peshawar, Pakistan) found that newspapers and
reports were the preferred sources of information for global think tanks' reports, instead of
research or conference papers. They also found that the diversity level of think tanks'
sources decreased with an increase in the number of reports produced, and the diversity
level of sources increased with a higher page count. They conclude that many global
think tanks are more inclined towards producing material in a timely manner that is
readily available and accessible.

Thorsten Benner, Wolfgang H. Reinicke and Jan Martin Witte, "Global Public Policy
Networks: Lessons Learned and Challenges Ahead," *Brookings Review* 21 (2003): 18–21.
This article featured in the *Brookings Review* emphasizes the importance of states, international organizations, NGOs, and businesses responding together to the pressures of globalization. The authors list the different types of global public policy networks as
examples of the workings of the different sectors' interdependent approaches to global
problems. The article also includes three tasks that are central for the networks to live up
to their potentials.

Carnegie Endowment for International Peace, "Global Policy Program" (August 2001): 1–6.
This paper illustrates how globalization is pushing to the fore a new policy agenda,
changing the identity of policy actors, and transforming the processes of international
relations. It focuses on the Global Policy Program, which developed under the leadership
of the Carnegie Endowment's President Jessica Matthews.

Julius Court and Enrique Mendizabal (Overseas Development Institute), "Networks and
Policy Influence in International Development," *Euforic Newsletter* (May 2005): 1–5. This
article analyzes networks by first defining the term, then looking at why networks matter,
and how networks can help in linking information to policy processes. It concludes with
ten keys to success that can help maximize policy influence.

Bob Deacon, "Global Social Governance Reform," Globalism and Social Policy Program, Policy Brief No. 1 (January 2003): 1–8. This policy brief addresses the prospects for improved social governance at the global level. The message is that while there are on the international policy agenda a number of desirable institutional reforms that should be implemented globally and while the struggle to shift global policy from its neo-liberal character to something more socially responsible constitutes much international effort, to improve the world's management of global social issues is centered upon networks, partnerships, and projects.

EastWest Institute, "Event Report: Global Leadership Consortium" (July 2008). This is an event report of the Global Leadership Consortium held by the EastWest Institute on 14–17 July 2008. The Institute convened a worldwide think tank network to address the timely question of "Can the major global policy think-tanks of the world focused think together about the challenges facing humanity?"

"Going global," *The Economist* (17 January 2008). This article published by *The Economist* discusses the Corporate Social Responsibilities (CSRs), driven by globalization in recent years, used in different countries. The focus is on the BRIC—Brazil, Russia, India, and China—countries as a one-size-fits-all approach to corporate responsibility is not working for global companies with differences in priorities. The idea of corporate citizenships, and the influence of CSRs on public policy and corporate behavior in order to establish a socially responsible market are explained. The article also emphasizes the importance of openness of markets, which is usually taken for granted.

Francesco Grillo, "Think Tanks in the Global Marketplace of Ideas," openDemocracy (5 September 2001): 1–3. This article states that think tanks must adapt to a change of scale. The author of the article—a director of a think tank in Italy and one of the promoters of the European Think Tanks Forum—recognizes a set of problems. He argues that think tanks are on the verge of a transnational new frontier in need of scaling up the thinking and action level to a global one.

Juliana Cristina Rosa Hauck, "What are 'Think Tanks'? Revisiting the Dilemma of the Definition," *Brazilian Political Science Review* 11, no.2 (July 2017). Juliana Cristina Rosa Hauck, from Universidade Federal de Minas Gerais, Brazil, has sought to reduce non-specificities in the concept of a think tank.

Peter Hayes, "The Role of Think Tanks in Defining Security Issues and Agendas," Global Collaborative Essay, *Northeast Asia Peace and Security Network* 21 (October 2004): 1–11. Essay produced by a think tank, Nautilus Institute Executive Director Peter Hayes introduces the idea of Transnational Think Nets (TTNs) in comparison to Traditional Think Tanks (TTTs). Hayes provides structured classification system, delineates roles, summarizes key debates, and provides two case studies on US security and foreign policy impact for TTTs. The article concludes with a brief history of the emergence of TTNs and makes the case for further attention to this phenomenon.

Julie Kosterlitz, "Going Global," *National Journal* (29 September 2007): 67–68. This article emphasizes the need for think tanks to go global, especially in the vital but under-represented regions. Kosterlitz especially explores the cases of think tanks based on Washington going global, such as the Carnegie Endowment for International Peace, the Brookings Institution, and the International Crisis Group. Not only the significance of going global, but also problems and challenges associated with it are raised and discussed.

Aisha Labi, "Columbia U. Opens First 2 International Research Centers," *The Chronicle of Higher Education* (20 March 2009), www.chronicle.com/article/Columbia-U-Opens-First-2/47124. The article explains the significance of the network building of six to eight research centers in capitals around the world by Columbia University; as the world becomes more interconnected, many of the most pressing issues nowadays are best approached by groups of scholars and researchers bringing their expertise from diverse backgrounds. Columbia University opened its first two international research centers in Beijing, China and in Amman, Jordan, to engage in serious research, and to work with local institutions and their own students and faculty.

Jing Linbo, "Global Think Tanks and the AMI Index Evaluation System," *China Economist* 11, no.4 (July/August 2016): 104–125. Jing Linbo, from the Chinese Evaluation Center for Humanities and Social Sciences, focuses mostly on the posturing of Chinese think tanks, concluding that there is a lack of staff mobility and exchange between think tanks and government departments in China as compared to the United States.

David M. Malone and Heiko Nitzschke, "Think Tanks and the United Nations," *Magazine for Development and Cooperation* (January 2004). Malone and Nitzscke, from an independent think tank, International Peace Academy, explain how the UN system benefits from the cooperation with think tanks in this article. Bridging the academia-policy gap, providing timely analysis and policy advice, and access to a global network of experts are discussed. In addition, necessity of providing a neutral forum for discussion only policy issues is emphasized. The authors argue that despite the differences in organizational forms, the group of think tanks works with the UN system with similar goals today as both friends and critics.

James G. McGann, "Global Go-To Think Tanks," IRP, University of Pennsylvania, 2009. This is the first comprehensive, global assessment of the leading thinks in the world. It discusses major trends in global public policy and policy advice.

James G. McGann, "Think Tank Impact Assessment Study; Initial Global Trend Report" (August 2008). The Think Tanks and Civil Societies Program developed and tested an 18-page survey instrument that was then used to collect data on the role and impact of think tanks on public policy worldwide. The survey focuses on a few key areas of a think tank's operations and performance: (1) the development and allocation of resources (financial, institutional, and human); (2) the outputs produced by think tanks; (3) the utilization of think tank research and related activities by policymakers and civil society actors; and (4) the impact of think tanks activities on the policymaking process and the public.

James G. McGann, "Think Tank Index," *Foreign Policy* (January/February 2009). Provides a summary of the Think Tank Index which is a ranking of the world's top think tanks, based on a global survey of hundreds of scholars and experts.

James G. McGann, "Think Tank Networks and Transnational Security Threats," Foreign Policy Research Institute (March 2004). This paper first examines the rise, benefits, and dilemmas of networks, then evaluates the effectiveness of current networks in addressing states' security threats. It goes on to assess and integrate the evaluations into a set of best practices that will contribute to the improvement of the operation of security networks.

Kenneth Prewitt, *Winning the Policy Wars* (London, UK: Global Public Policy Network, London School of Economics). This book prescribes ways of effectively making global public policy. The author explores how to win the policy wars without giving up on the science and evidence that goes into effective policymaking.

Wolfgang H. Reinicke, "The Other World Wide Web: Global Public Policy Networks," *Foreign Policy* 117 (2000): 44–57. The article looks at how public policy networks, the alliances of governments, and international organizations and corporations are improving the principles and methods of global governance. It also explains problems that inhibit formal policymaking institutions from formulating effective policy, and sources of support for global public policy networks.

Priscilla Roberts, "A century of international affairs think tanks in historical perspective," *International Journal* 70, no.4 (June 2015): 535–555. Priscilla Roberts, from the University of Hong Kong, has surveyed the patterns of linkages between foreign policy think tanks and a broader Anglo-American, imperial, and internationalist network and relationship, discussing the recent proliferation and frequent globalization of foreign policy think tanks.

Alejandra Salas-Porras and Georgina Murray, eds. *Think Tanks and Global Politics: Key Spaces in the Structure of Power* (New York, NY: Palgrave Macmillan, 2017). In a book edited by Alejandra Salas-Porras and Georgina Murray, scholars examine topics such as the rise and decline of the business roundtable, neoliberal think tank networks in Latin America and Europe and think tanks as key spaces in the structure of power in global politics.

Jiri Schneider, "Globalization and think-tanks; Security policy networks," SAREM International Seminar, Istanbul, Turkey (30 May 2003). This paper presented at the SAREM International Seminar attempts to explain the effects of globalization on security research and analysis. In the first part, globalization's security and economic aspects are observed from a perspective of different forms of governance. In the second part, think tanks' ability to deal with challenges of globalization is presented. Lastly, the author suggests that think tanks can play a significant role as critical connectors of the global security policy network by communicating among security experts and allowing them to exchange views.

Diana Stone, "Knowledge Networks and Global Policy," the Central and Eastern European International Studies Association and International Studies Association Joint Conference, Budapest, Hungary (28 June 2003): 1–32. This paper outlines the notion of "knowledge network" or KNET and distinguishes it from related network types of "transnational advocacy coalition" and "global public policy network." The primary mission of a KNET is knowledge creation and dissemination, unlike the other network types that are directly political and policy oriented.

Diana Stone, "The New Networks of Knowledge: Think Tanks and the Transnationalization of Governance," The Social Science Research Council (September 2008): 1–9. Think tanks do not operate in a vacuum, but are nested in a web of relationships. The impact and influence possibilities are magnified through network interactions. Therefore, networks often illustrate the most feasible organizational mode through which transnational activity can be secured. Stone emphasizes realistic problems of becoming a truly "global" think tank, given the domestic roots of most think tanks.

Charlotte Streck, "Global Public Policy Networks, International Organizations and International Environmental Governance," The Road to Earth Summit 2002, New York, USA (20 April 2001). This article is the reflection of the author's work with Wolfgang Reinicke and his team in the "Global Public Policy Network Project" led by Wolfgang Reinicke and Francis Deng. Streck argues that strong environmental governance structures, built on a set of networks, coordinated by international organizations can bridge the participatory, the operational, and the institutional gaps. As examples, Streck explains the modern network structures and workings of the WCD and the CEF. Both examples demonstrate the importance of flexibility and open and transparent process to bring different actors and stakeholders together.

Thomas Teichler, "Think Tanks as an Epistemic Community: The Case of European Armaments Cooperation," The International Studies Association 48th Annual Convention, Chicago, USA (28 February 2007). In this essay, Teichler takes four think tanks in three European countries as case studies to examine their discussion concerning the creation of the European Armaments Agency in the period from 2003 to 2005. He argues that they can certainly be considered as an epistemic community even though they do not agree entirely with regard to consensual knowledge. He suggests a refinement of the notion of consensual knowledge, which will account more appropriately for the character of the knowledge examined in the empirical case, but also point to another understanding of how epistemic communities become involved in the political process.

Stella Z. Theodoulou, *Policy and Politics in Six Nations: A Comparative Perspective on Policy Making* (Upper Saddle River, NJ: Prentice Hall, 2001). This book explores the comparative study of public policy through case studies, statistical studies, and focused comparisons.

Vanesa Weyrauch, "Weaving Global Networks: Handbook for Policy Influence," CSGR, Working Paper no. 219/07 (February 2007). This working paper presents an in-depth analysis of the organization, leadership structure, policy aim, and reach of policy networks. It presents four case studies of successful policy networks and provides tools for other policy networks facing the same issues. There is an extensive discussion of the challenges networks are faced with, and how these challenges can be met.

Jan Martin Witte, Wolfgang H. Reinicke and Thorsten Benner, "Beyond Multilateralism: Global Public Policy Networks," *International Politics and Society* (February 2000). This article looks beyond multilateralism and instead looks to global public policy networks as an answer to global problems. It especially focuses on tri-sectoral networks, which bring together government, civil society, and the private sector.

INDEX

Taylor & Francis Group
an **informa** business

Taylor & Francis eBooks

www.taylorfrancis.com

A single destination for eBooks from Taylor & Francis
with increased functionality and an improved user
experience to meet the needs of our customers.

90,000+ eBooks of award-winning academic content in
Humanities, Social Science, Science, Technology, Engineering,
and Medical written by a global network of editors and authors.

TAYLOR & FRANCIS EBOOKS OFFERS:

A streamlined
experience for
our library
customers

A single point
of discovery
for all of our
eBook content

Improved
search and
discovery of
content at both
book and
chapter level

REQUEST A FREE TRIAL
support@taylorfrancis.com

Routledge
Taylor & Francis Group

CRC Press
Taylor & Francis Group

For Product Safety Concerns and Information please contact our EU
representative GPSR@taylorandfrancis.com
Taylor & Francis Verlag GmbH, Kaufingerstraße 24, 80331 München, Germany

www.ingramcontent.com/pod-product-compliance
Lightning Source LLC
Chambersburg PA
CBHW070342270326
41926CB00017B/3941

9 780367 278557